Economics
and
Antitrust Policy

Economics
and
Antitrust Policy

Edited by
Robert J. Larner
and
James W. Meehan, Jr.

QUORUM BOOKS
New York • Westport, Connecticut • London

Library of Congress Cataloging-in-Publication Data

Economics and antitrust policy / edited by Robert J. Larner and James
W. Meehan, Jr.
    p.   cm.
   "In memory of H. Michael Mann"—Prelim. p.
   Bibliography: p.
   Includes index.
   ISBN 0–89930–386–2 (lib. bdg. : alk. paper)
   1. Antitrust law—United States. 2. Antitrust law—Economic
aspects—United States. 3. Mann, H. Michael (Harold Michael). 1934–
   I. Larner, Robert J. II. Meehan, James W. III. Mann, H.
Michael (Harold Michael), 1934–
KF1652.E26 1989
343.73′072–dc19
[347.30372]   88–18515

British Library Cataloguing in Publication Data is available.

Library of Congress Catalog Card Number: 88–18515
ISBN: 0–89930–386–2

First published in 1989 by Quorum Books

Greenwood Press, Inc.
88 Post Road West, Westport, Connecticut 06881

Printed in the United States of America

The paper used in this book complies with the
Permanent Paper Standard issued by the National
Information Standards Organization (Z39.48–1984).

10 9 8 7 6 5 4 3 2 1

In Memory of H. Michael Mann

Contents

Figures and Tables

Economics
and
Antitrust Policy

Introduction

Robert J. Larner and James W. Meehan, Jr.

Antitrust policy in the United States has changed dramatically since 1960. During the populist era of the late 1960s and early 1970s, antitrust policy and law focused on the effects of business conduct on market structure, especially on concentration and barriers to entry. Any business activity that threatened to increase market concentration or to raise barriers to entry into the market was presumed to be anticompetitive and was subject to attack. The fact that the conduct under scrutiny had the potential to improve efficiency or consumer welfare was often ignored or in some cases even cited as evidence in support of anticompetitive purpose or effect.[1] By the end of the 1970s, the courts and the antitrust enforcement agencies began to shift their emphasis from the structural effects of business conduct and pay more attention to the effects of the conduct on economic efficiency and consumer welfare. This shift accelerated during the years of the Reagan administration and has become its formal antitrust policy. Currently, with the exception of price-fixing, business activity is generally presumed to be efficiency enhancing, and is subject to challenge by the federal enforcement agencies only where there are clear indications that the anticompetitive effect of the conduct is sufficiently great to offset its positive effect on efficiency.

This dramatic change in emphasis has had an enormous impact on both the volume and substance of antitrust activity. The major monopolization cases brought during the 1960s and 1970s—most notably the ones against IBM and AT&T—were dismissed or settled, and no monopolization cases of this scale have been brought under the Reagan administration. Challenges to conglomerate mergers have also disappeared, and challenges to vertical mergers and vertical restraints by the federal enforcement agencies are rare. With the revision of the Department of Justice's *Merger Guidelines* in 1982 and 1984, fewer horizontal mergers are also being challenged.

Today, business is free to engage in a wide variety of conduct that was considered unlawful just 15 or 20 years ago. The impact of the recent developments in antitrust enforcement on social welfare is still an open question, however. While many economists believe that the policies pursued in the populist era gave too little weight to economic efficiency, a growing number argue that the Reagan administration has ignored the strategic aspects and anticompetitive effects of some forms of business conduct.

It was, of course, a marked shift in the political climate, reflected in the election of Ronald Reagan as president in 1980 and 1984, that caused these changes in antitrust policy to be made. But changes in the thinking and research output of economists contributed significantly to the intellectual underpinnings for the shift in antitrust policy and provided an important impetus to the policy changes of the 1980s.

The purpose of the articles in this volume is to explain and evaluate the changes in policy that have taken place in the past two decades and also to assess the areas of disagreement that still remain among economists and legal scholars.

The first part of this introduction highlights the recent changes in antitrust policy and law and discusses the role that economics has played in effecting these changes. The second part summarizes the contributions made by the chapters in this volume.

CHANGES IN ANTITRUST POLICY

The intellectual foundation for the structural approach to antitrust policy is contained in the structure-conduct-performance paradigm. The paradigm states that market power (that is, the ability to restrict output and raise price) is determined by a few key elements of market structure, in particular, market share, concentration, and barriers to entry.[2] Since a large number of empirical studies by economists found evidence that supported the link between market power and market structure, the implications for antitrust policy seemed obvious.[3] Mergers that increase concentration or foreclose competition should be prevented. Business conduct that is either predatory or exclusionary also should be prevented because it can increase concentration or raise barriers to entry.[4] In addition, dominant firms in industries that remain concentrated over a long period of time, with little or no threat of entry, should be forced to divest assets sufficient to restore competition.

Both the federal antitrust enforcement agencies and the Supreme Court adopted this line of reasoning. Horizontal mergers were treated with particular hostility because they reduced the number of actual competitors and increased concentration. Almost all horizontal mergers, even those involving relatively minor increases in market shares, were found unlawful on the grounds that they might contribute to a trend that would eventually create a concentrated market.[5] Vertical and conglomerate mergers were treated more leniently than horizontal mergers, but they were also viewed with suspicion. Vertical mergers were illegal if competitors were foreclosed from a relatively small part of the market controlled by the merging partners under the theory that foreclosure can lead to an increase in concentration and raise barriers to entry in one or both of the vertically related markets.[6] Conglomerate mergers were unlawful if they eliminated potential entrants from highly concentrated markets or if they raised barriers to entry into highly concentrated markets.[7]

A broad range of business conduct was considered illegal on the theory that the conduct may have some (direct or indirect) effect on market structure. Vertical price-fixing and territorial restraints were held to be per se illegal because they reduced intrabrand competition among retailers, even though there may have been a substantial amount of interbrand competition within the market. Exclusive dealing contracts and tie-in arrangements were also held per se illegal because they foreclosed competitors from part of the market, even if the percentage of the market foreclosed was relatively small.

The government also sought to restructure a handful of highly concentrated industries. Monopolization cases were filed against IBM, Xerox, and AT&T, and a shared monopoly (or oligopoly) case was filed against the three leading manufacturers of breakfast cereal and later against the major oil companies. In each of these cases the government charged the defendants with acquiring and maintaining their monopoly (or oligopoly) by the use of conduct that restricted their rivals from competing (that is, the conduct increased or maintained concentration) or excluded potential competitors (that is, raised barriers to entry). And in each of the cases the government requested some form of structural relief: Had the government prevailed, the defendants would have been required to divest a substantial part of their assets, as well as to terminate the conduct that allegedly raised barriers to entry.

At about the same time that the antitrust activity of the structuralist era was reaching its zenith, economists and legal scholars from the Chicago school initiated a frontal assault on the structure-conduct-performance paradigm. One line of attack focused on the empirical studies that supported the structure-conduct-performance paradigm. In the most telling criticism of these studies, Harold Demsetz argued that the positive correlation between concentration and profit rates found in these studies is more consistent with an efficiency explanation than it is with the market power hypothesis expounded by proponents of the structure-conduct-performance paradigm.[8] Demsetz's interpretation of the evidence suggests that industries become more concentrated as the efficient firms grow and become more profitable and the inefficient firms shrink and become less profitable. The higher profit rates of the efficient firms are not monopoly profits but simply economic rents or rewards for being efficient. In another line of attack, the students of Aaron Director argued that much of the conduct that the courts found to be predatory and exclusionary rarely, if ever, reduces competition and in most instances actually enhances economic efficiency and increases competition.[9]

In 1977 the Supreme Court moved efficiency considerations to center stage when it ruled in the *Sylvania* decision that the efficiency effects of nonprice vertical restraints must be considered in evaluating their effects on competition.[10] Since that decision, the Court has extended its consideration of efficiency to other types of firm conduct such as tie-ins, exclusive dealing arrangements, mergers, and even some aspects of vertical and horizontal price-fixing. Perhaps the most dramatic change in policy has taken place at the federal enforcement agencies during the Reagan administration—economic analysis is now the dominant, if not sole, criterion used in evaluating policy action. Business practices that are viewed as efficiency enhancing, such as vertical restraints, tie-ins, customer restrictions, and distribution requirements, are hardly ever challenged, which is also the case with vertical and conglomerate mergers. Horizontal mergers are only challenged when they would join substantial rivals in concentrated industries with significant barriers to entry, and even then the merger may be allowed if the merging partners can demonstrate that significant economies are a likely outcome of the merger. In addition, most of the monopoly and oligopoly cases that were filed in the late 1960s and early 1970s have been either dropped or decided in favor of the defendants; only the AT&T matter was settled with any structural relief. The only cases pursued with undiminished vigor involve horizontal price-fixing.

Since there has been no systematic study of the impact of current antitrust policy on societal welfare, we don't know for sure whether the shift in emphasis from market structure to economic efficiency has improved economic welfare or diminished it. Many, if not most, economists would concur that the restraints placed on mergers between direct competitors during the populist era were overly restrictive and prevented some horizontal mergers that had the potential to improve efficiency. Mergers were instead diverted to the conglomerate kind and a number of these mergers turned out to be inefficient.[11] In addition, there appears to be a generally held view that a good deal of the vertical or customer restraint cases brought by the government during the populist era did more to protect competitors than competition and as a result probably had a detrimental effect on social welfare. However, a number of respected economists and legal scholars contend that current antitrust policy fails to challenge a significant amount of business activity that is anticompetitive.

Whether the future will see a return to a tougher antitrust policy depends upon the political environment that exists during the next decade. If the past is any indication, however, a new intellectual foundation will have to be constructed to support the change in policy, and economics will play a central role in formulating that foundation. At the present time the seeds of change are being planted by a new school of industrial organization economists, who are using the tools of modern microeconomic theory to demonstrate that some types of business conduct can be used as strategic tools to reduce competition.[12] Because much more analysis and research remain to be done, it is too early to predict the effect that these new developments will have on antitrust policy. Empirical tests will have to be devised to demonstrate that strategic behavior is more than a theoretical curiosity. In addition, the theories will have to be made operational, so that the courts can have some easily identifiable criteria they can use to determine when firm conduct is likely to be anticompetitive and when it is likely to be efficiency enhancing.

While no one can foresee the scope and content of future changes in antitrust, such changes that are made are likely to be based upon recent and future developments in economic theory and research. Understanding how economics has contributed to changes in antitrust policy and law in the recent past can provide lawyers and businessmen with some insight about the possible future impacts of economic learning on antitrust policy and law. Such is the hope of the authors of this volume.

OVERVIEW OF THE VOLUME

In the opening essay, Kenneth G. Elzinga, professor of economics at the University of Virginia, examines a fundamental issue in antitrust economics—how to identify monopoly. He evaluates each of four traditional indicators used by economists to unmask monopoly and points out the limitations of market share, accounting profits or rates of return, the relationship between price and marginal cost captured in the Lerner Index, and firm conduct as measures of monopoly. Noting a growing consensus among economists that the essence of monopoly power is the ability to restrict output, he finds that there is no single index that will unfailingly diagnose monopoly.

Charles A. Holt, professor of economics at the University of Virginia, and David T. Scheffman, a former director of the Bureau of Economics at the Federal Trade Commission, discuss strategic business behavior and its implications for antitrust. They develop a conceptual framework for the analysis of strategic behavior, defined as actions that shape the future behavior of the "strategist" or its rivals, and use this framework to critique the business strategy literature and its antitrust implications. Holt and Scheffman find that although this literature has advanced the understanding of how firms compete, discerning the circumstances in which consumers do not gain from such competition is still a formidable task since the strategic literature indicates that many types of strategic conduct can produce gross benefits for consumers even when the firm has market power.

F. M. Scherer, the Joseph Wharton Professor of Political Economy at Swarthmore College, considers merger policy in the 1970s and 1980s. He delineates the analytical framework developed by the "structuralist" school of economists that, together with the strong mandate articulated by Congress in the Celler-Kefauver Act of 1950 and tough antimerger precedents issued by the Supreme Court, provided the driving force behind the aggressive enforcement policy of the 1970s (and the 1960s also). With the ascendency of the "Chicago" school of economics and the Reagan administration's appointments to key antitrust enforcement positions, the number of challenges issued per year by the two federal enforcement agencies dropped to half of the average level of the previous two decades, despite all-time peak levels of merger activity. The debate among economists and the conflict in values continue regarding whether current merger policy, in seeking to avoid challenges to benign or efficiency-enhancing mergers, pays too high a price by not blocking mergers with price-raising effects.

Two papers focus on the changing legal treatment of vertical relationships. Lawrence J. White, professor of economics at New York University, traces the evolution in economists' analysis of vertical relationships from the early monopoly explanations and "inhospitality tradition" to the efficiency explanations developed by the Chicago school and the more recent counterrevolution that has identified areas of continuing antitrust concern. He concludes that the revolution in antitrust analysis of vertical relationships over the past three decades has pushed policy in a sensible direction and that a continuing dialectic process between the "revolutionists" and "counterrevolutionists" is likely to yield a better understanding of and a better policy toward vertical relationships.

Robert J. Larner, an economist and vice president of Charles River

Associates, considers the asymmetry in the legal standards applied to price and nonprice vertical restraints. Evaluating recent economic learning on vertical restraints, he develops a case for replacing the per se treatment of resale price maintenance with the same rule-of-reason standard used for nonprice vertical restraints. His case rests on the proposition that, in motivation and effects, vertical price restraints are more akin to nonprice vertical restraints than to horizontal restraints.

Two essays by attorneys consider some of the impacts economics has had—and should have—on the development of antitrust law and policy.

Donald I. Baker, a partner in the law firm of Sutherland, Asbill & Brennan and a former assistant attorney general for antitrust at the U.S. Department of Justice, addresses future politics as a factor in antitrust analysis. He points out that markets rarely exist in a political vacuum and that government intervention with respect to foreign exchange rates, import restrictions, or deregulation can have important consequences for long-run market performance. He concludes that antitrust analysis ought to take into account the economic consequences of reasonably foreseeable political action. For example, the antitrust enforcement agencies and courts, in evaluating a merger between two major domestic competitors in an industry with import competition, ought to discount the current market shares of importers if some form of import restriction is likely to occur.

Timothy J. Waters, a partner in the law firm of McDermott, Will & Emery and a former assistant to the chairman of the Federal Trade Commission, examines the issue of whether the nation's antitrust statutes, as refined and shaped through case law, have kept pace with new developments in economic learning in the field of industrial organization or whether they require amendment, such as proposed by the Reagan administration. He finds that the existing statutes have accommodated changing economic theories and goals, as well as contemporary business concerns. Moreover, the rule of law, which has developed and continues to develop through thousands of court decisions, has fundamentally served the nation well. The history of judicial decisions in antitrust demonstrates that the antitrust laws are sufficiently broad to evaluate legal challenges to business conduct in the context of changing economic theories and political climates.

The last essay, by James W. Meehan, Jr., professor of economics at Colby College, and Robert J. Larner, provides an overview of the development of the economic thinking and research related to the issues discussed in the other chapters in this volume. Meehan and Larner evaluate the structure-conduct-performance paradigm of the structuralist school and its influence on antitrust policy and law. After also examining the alternative methods of antitrust analysis developed by the Chicago school, the "transaction cost" approach, and the literature of the "new industrial organization," they assess the contribution of the structuralist school to economists' understanding of markets and to antitrust policy. They also critically evaluate what economists have learned about antitrust issues in the last three decades, as well as the changes in antitrust policy during the last decade.

The editors are grateful to the authors of the chapters in this volume for their enthusiasm, support, and cooperation from the outset of the project. In addition, James A. Dalton contributed insights and comments on an earlier draft of the chapter titled "In Memory of H. Michael Mann." Finally, the production staff of Charles River Associates did its usual sterling job in typing the manuscript. Special thanks go to wordprocessors Beverly Hegdal, Tim Hughes, Kim Pederson, and Betty Stenhouse.

NOTES

1. See, for example, *Brown Shoe Co.* v. *United States*, 370 U.S. 294 (1962) and *F.T.C* v. *Procter & Gamble Co.*, 386 U.S. 568 (1967).

2. The complete paradigm states that market structure determines market conduct (that is, the pricing and other product policies of the firm), and market conduct determines market performance (that is, the allocative and productive efficiency of the market). Since conduct is just a link between market structure and performance in this paradigm, the implication is that market performance is directly determined by market structure.

3. Most of these studies found a positive correlation between various measures of market structure (that is, market share, concentration, and barriers to entry) and accounting profit rates, which were used as a measure of allocative inefficiency.

4. This policy implication is based on a slightly different version of paradigm that argues that conduct that is predatory or exclusionary can have a feedback effect on market structure by increasing concentration or raising barriers to entry.

5. See, for example, *Brown Shoe Co.* v. *United States*, 370 U.S. 294 (1962) and *United States* v. *Von's Grocery Co.*, 384 U.S. 270 (1966).

6. In the Brown Shoe case, the merger between Brown Shoe Co. and G. R. Kinney Co. had the potential to foreclose less than 4 percent of the retail shoe market to rival shoe manufacturers. In a study of vertical merger enforcement policy, Alan A. Fisher and Richard Sciacca found that in 60 percent of the 62 government vertical merger cases for which they had data the amount of foreclosure was less than 10 percent. See Alan A. Fisher and Richard Sciacca, "An Economic Analysis of Vertical Merger Enforcement Policy," *Research in Law and Economics* 6 (1984): 1–133, at p. 69.

7. See, for example, *F.T.C.* v. *Procter & Gamble Co.*, 386 U.S. 568 (1967).

8. Harold Demsetz, "Two Systems of Belief about Monopoly," in *Industrial Concentration: The New Learning*, ed. Harvey J. Goldschmid, H. Michael Mann, and J. Fred Weston (Boston: Little, Brown and Co., 1974), 164–184.

9. The most cogent explanation of these arguments can be found in Robert H. Bork, *The Antitrust Paradox* (New York: Basic Books, 1978).

10. *Continental T.V. Inc. et al.* v. *GTE Sylvania Inc.*, 433 U.S. 36 (1977).

11. In a comprehensive study of mergers that took place during the conglomerate merger wave of the 1960s, David Ravenscraft and F. M. Scherer found that, on balance, conglomerate mergers were not very successful. They found that the performance of the unprofitable divisions improved when they were sold to firms that were in the same industry or to firms in vertically related industries. See David J. Ravenscraft and F. M. Scherer, *Mergers, Sell-Offs, and Economic Efficiency* (Washington, D.C.: Brookings Institution, 1987).

12. See, for example, Thomas G. Krattenmaker and Steven C. Salop, "Antitrust Analysis and Anticompetitive Exclusion: Raising Rivals' Costs to Achieve Power over Price," *Yale Law Journal* 96 (November 1986): 209–295, and Richard Schmalensee, "Antitrust and the New Industrial Economics," *American Economic Review* 72 (May 1982): 24–28.

Unmasking Monopoly: Four Types of Economic Evidence

Kenneth G. Elzinga

In graduate school, my teacher in welfare economics was Abba P. Lerner, a prominent contributor to the neoclassical concept of marginal analysis. My mentor in antitrust was Walter Adams, a prominent industrial organization economist of structuralist persuasion. Neither one of them liked monopolies. Both tried to teach me how to identify them.

Professor Adams said one could recognize a monopoly by its share of the market. He warned us against trying to discern market power from measures of firm performance. Professor Lerner said no, one recognized a monopoly by the difference between the price it charged and its marginal cost or what has come to be called the Lerner Index. He warned us against trying to discern monopoly from structural measures like market share.

It was a privilege to study under both of these men. But as graduate students, we wondered: Which of our professors was right?

Most of us came to realize that long before our own graduate education had begun there was concern and debate about the character of monopoly power. This predated economics as a social science, and when economics was being birthed as a social science, the same concern was present.[1] The virtues of competition relative to monopoly, after all, provided much of the fodder for Adam Smith's *The Wealth of Nations*.

It was not until later in the history of economic thought that particular interest was expressed in the identification and measurement of monopoly power. This interest was provoked by two unrelated events that took place in 1890: the publication of Alfred Marshall's *Principles of Economics* and the passage of the Sherman Antitrust Act. Marshall's *Principles* widely dispersed among economists a set of theoretical tools for studying competition and monopoly. Its influence was intellectual. The Sherman Act generated a practical need to make decisions as to what was monopolizing and what was not. The two events joined to place the issue on the economists' research agenda.

In *The Masquerade of Monopoly*, Frank A. Fetter described the identification of monopoly as a task in unmasking.[2] His prominent book portrayed the business monopolist as an economic Aristide whose clever disguise deludes even customers and government officials into thinking such a firm is benign in its tactics and beneficent in its behavior. About 50 years after Fetter wrote about removing the disguise of monopoly, Franklin M. Fisher wrote about "diagnosing monopoly."[3] The terms have changed, but the fundamental issue being explored has not.

The scholarly literature on identifying monopoly and its consequences is enormous and evolving. Some of the disguises that Fetter and others thought they had unmasked, for example, some forms of basing-point pricing, have been reinterpreted in recent years as being forms of competition, not a masquerade for its opposite.[4] While the amount of research has been sizable, progress in distinguishing market processes under competition versus monopoly has not been galloping, and specialists on the topic have not always been in agreement.

THE STRUCTURE-CONDUCT-PERFORMANCE PARADIGM

As the postscript to this volume by Robert J. Larner and James W. Meehan shows, beginning with his doctoral dissertation and throughout most of his scholarly publications, as well as in his government service, H. Michael Mann made contributions to this ongoing inquiry of distinguishing competition from monopoly.[5] Like many industrial organization economists of his generation, Professor Mann wore comfortably, at least until late in his career, the structure-conduct-performance paradigm. Indeed he was an important contributor to that paradigm. His article "Seller Concentration, Barriers to Entry, and Rates of Return in Thirty Industries, 1950–1960" is an oft-cited examination of two structural variables and their relationship with a performance measure Mann identified as related to monopoly power.[6]

The structure-conduct-performance paradigm affords many angles from which the phenomenon of monopoly and competition might be glimpsed, if not studied. Some who work within this paradigm have emphasized one link in that "chain" as being more valuable than the others.

Structuralists focus on the first link. They view industry behavior mechanistically and posit a cause-and-effect relationship between market structure and the resolution of economic forces. For example, a structuralist might conclude that a dominant firm will generate a price-output combination in which price will be higher and output lower than if the firm operated in an atomistically structured market.

Those whose focus is on conduct examine the behavior of firms. Unpersuaded of a consistent link between a market's structure and its performance, they counsel instead the detailed study of what a commerce professor might call the "marketing mix" of firms suspected of having monopoly positions. Research on practices involving pricing and distribution is to be informed by the tools of economic analysis. One of Professor Mann's mentors, Alfred E. Kahn, combined with Joel B. Dirlam (one of my teachers) to write an important book describing this approach to diagnosing monopoly.[7]

A focus on the last element of the structure-conduct-performance triad entails measuring and assessing the track record of a firm or industry. The track record may be with regard to such variables as profits, innovation, growth, or others thought to reflect or represent the fruits of competitive market behavior. The inquiry is not directed at the structural characteristics of a market nor upon the strategies of firms, but rather on developing measures of desirable performance and applying them with regard to particular markets.

The study of antitrust policy and its enforcement provided impetus for the popularity of the structure-conduct-performance paradigm. The bipolar models of perfect competition and monopoly, while conceptually of enormous use in economic analysis, have been inadequate for policy purposes in the antitrust arena. If a policy against monopoly was to be pursued, it was not especially useful to rely upon a model, such as that of perfect competition, in which all price-searching firms are by definition monopolists. If competition was to be the desideratum of antitrust policy, it was not very useful to characterize only that element of the economy populated by price-taking firms as being in compliance with the policy. The structure-conduct-performance framework was sufficiently elastic to allow research on antitrust policy to be done within its boundaries that had a modest theoretical character.

Most economists today do not focus singlemindedly on only one element of industrial organization's trinity. H. Michael Mann's work illustrates this. While considering himself to be a structuralist, he remained interested in the empirical evidence that attempted to link performance and structure in a predictable and causative relationship. Without this linkage, he would have argued, a structuralist position was neither tenable nor relevant. For many economists, a virtue of using the entire structure-conduct-performance paradigm is that it provides a framework for studying an industry. Researching an industry or a firm's place in an industry generally has come to imply a detailed examination of variables that fall within this tripartite organization.

This chapter concerns four elements of the structure-conduct-performance paradigm that have had varying degrees of influence on antitrust policy. One is associated with structure, one with conduct, and two with performance. Each has been suggested as a means of unmasking monopoly.

In the following section, I discuss the fall from grace of a particular structure variable. Then follows an assessment of two performance variables associated with identifying monopoly. The final section discusses aspects of the conduct approach and its utility in identifying and measuring monopoly power. The discussion in each instance is selective, which the chapter's context requires. Book-length elaborations would be necessary to unpack fully any one of these topics.[8]

THE FALL OF A STRUCTURE MEASURE

George J. Stigler once generalized that "an industry which does not have a competitive structure will not have competitive behavior."[9] This proposition became the foundation for much of the thinking among industrial organization economists with regard to industries dominated by a single firm and industries where a handful of firms were thought to collude tacitly or overtly. This position—the market share doctrine—focused on individual firm market share and high market concentration as the critical variables in identifying monopoly. It is a position that has waned in influence.

Part of the market share doctrine's diminishing influence is due to statistical research that questions the relationship between an industry's structure and its performance, particularly its profits. The literature itself is voluminous and was the meat and potatoes of industrial organization for several years; it will not be summarized here.

Suffice it to say there is now, even among the unconverted and skeptics, an openness to the proposition that some dominant firms are dominant because they are more efficient; they make, in common parlance, a better mousetrap. What persuaded many economists that this was a possible if not a probable situation was evidence that small firms in concentrated industries were less profitable than large ones.[10] If dominant firms or oligopoly leaders raised prices in umbrellalike fashion above competitive levels, cost-efficient smaller firms should prosper as much as the industry leaders. Often the small firms appear not to, suggesting that the larger, dominant firms have lower costs; this, not monopoly power, explains their higher rates of return.

Further weakening the concern about horizontal dominance has been the recognition that a high market share has little or no monopoly consequence if fringe firms can expand output or barriers to new entry are low. This recognition is not new. Economists associated with the structuralist wing of industrial organization generally have conceded that high concentration or even horizontal dominance are not problematic if barriers to entry are trivial.[11] Indeed, Joe S. Bain's seminal work on entry barriers was, its author said at the outset, provoked by the complaint that too much energy has been expended by economists on the topic of competition among existing firms and not enough was known about the actual importance of "new competition."[12]

A great deal has been done in response to Bain's complaint. The bottom line of this response has been that entry conditions either are or have become more relaxed than had been the conventional wisdom. Industries that once had been characterized as virtually impenetrable have been entered (albeit frequently in the form of foreign competition). A professor who drives to the university in an automobile manufactured in the Far East, who passes en route a farm equipment dealer whose inventory of tractors is from the Far East, and who at work composes a paper using a typewriter imported from the Far East is made to pause in rereading the industries that Bain once listed as having "very high entry barriers."[13]

Furthermore, new competition is understood to come about in fashions that were not imagined or understood earlier. The truck rental market, for example, is ostensibly highly concentrated, particularly for one-way rentals. The industry leaders are Jartran, Ryder, and U-Haul. There has been essentially no new entry into the industry for some time. By an artless application of the market share doctrine, U-Haul could be classified as a dominant firm. Moreover, it would be costly to replicate a national fleet of trucks complete with dealer locations in hundreds of cities. By these two structural conditions, the market might be construed as a candidate for antitrust concern.

However, the enormous increase in the number of individuals who own trucks and vans has resulted in de facto entry into the market, particularly the market for local moves. Almost anyone moving from one apartment to another, particularly within a hundred mile radius, has access to a noncommercial vehicle capable of accomplishing such a move. Even if the three industry leaders were to collude, and localized one-way rental firms could be ignored as fringe firms incapable of supply expansion, the pricing power of such a cartel would be limited by non-commercial supply over which Jartran, Ryder, and U-Haul have no control. The three could not have thwarted this competition through lock-step collusive behavior.

At this juncture, the influence of contestability theory merits citation as well.[14] It is too simplistic to characterize contestability theory as teaching that concentration does not matter so long as entry barriers are low. But that captures a portion of it. A notable contribution of the contestability literature is its setting out with some precision the conditions under which high market share might be ignored as an indication of monopoly power.

Additional undermining of the market share doctrine has come in the form of industry studies, some related to antitrust cases, others not, concluding that firms in concentrated industries, even those with increasing concentration, have exhibited sharp rivalry between the industry leaders. Finally, the lessening influence of theories that equated oligopolistic interdependence with monopoly has reduced further the import of the market share doctrine.[15] Duopolists and oligopolists are no longer presumed to read each other's minds with such precision as to attain the price-output combination of a single firm monopolist who is protected by high entry barriers.

The major role that horizontal firm dominance plays today in antitrust is through the influence on Herfindahl indices used in antimerger enforcement. Under the Department of Justice *Merger Guidelines*, high concentration is a filter that, along with other indicia, enables decisions to be made on merger challenges. The chapter by F. M. Scherer in this volume evaluates this issue and others in the antitrust-merger arena.[16]

In monopoly cases many economists now would maintain that there should be no antitrust concern even though a leading firm had, say, 80 percent of a market if, because of low barriers to entry, a dozen firms could expand output or enter the market at the slightest rise in price. This conclusion might be reached by two different avenues. In the first, the 80 percent market share, high as it seems, is rendered impotent by the low barriers to entry. In the second, the existence of the low entry barriers dictates a broadening of the relevant market's definition to incorporate the supply side substitutes; a recalculation of the leading firm's share may produce such a low concentration figure that even under the market share doctrine the firm is inferred to have no market power. From both an analytical and a public policy standpoint, the matter is six of one, half-dozen of the other.

Since a firm with a high market share can not safely be defined as one with market power, economists have restrained their enthusiasm for the measure. As a result, market share is not the index it used to be. Alone it may mislead in the unmasking or diagnosing of monopoly.

THE DECLINE OF THE PROFIT INDEX

The association between monopoly and high profits is an altogether common one. The expression "rich as Rockefeller" has its roots in the notion that monopolies make money—and in the case of the oil trust, much money indeed.

To unmask monopoly by studying business profits has theoretical appeal: Every teacher of microeconomics has drawn diagrams that show the appearance of economic profits as a competitive industry is transformed into a monopoly. In addition, to diagnose monopoly from evidence on high rates of return has intuitive appeal: If monopolies are firms that restrict output in an attempt to increase profits, successful monopolists might be expected to be firms with high profits.

The scholarly use of profits as an index of monopoly power has its modern roots in the writings of Joe S. Bain.[17] The work of Bain influenced a generation of industrial organization economists to use accounting rates of return as a proxy for market power. But ever since the publication of his well-known article, there has been a flow of research taking issue with the use of profits as an index of monopoly. The nexus Bain and later others found between profits and the structural conditions of concentration and barriers to entry was attacked from two angles.

The major critique held that there was, in fact, no statistical or no causal relationship between profits and the structural variable of concentration. The rear guard attack contended that even if there were a relationship, it had no economic meaning or policy consequence in that profit rates, at least the ones normally being used and studied, were not reliable indicators of monopoly power. Important contributors to this latter position have been Yale Brozen and George J. Benston.[18]

The most prominent recent contribution in this vein has been that of Franklin M. Fisher and John J. McGowan.[19] They show that even if adjustments could be made to accounting data that would remedy the shortcomings economists associate with such numbers, firm-specific rates of return still would be inadequate indicators of monopoly profits. The Fisher-McGowan argument is complementary to the critique of Brozen, Benston, and others but differs fundamentally from it. Fisher and McGowan base their case upon the differences over time in which a firm receives income and incurs costs. In other words, firms with the same economic rates of return will have different accounting rates of return depending upon their growth rates, the life of their assets, and their depreciation methods. On the basis of this intertemporal analysis, they conclude that "there is no way in which one can look at accounting rates of return and infer anything about relative economic profitability or, a fortiori, about the presence or absence of monopoly profits. The economic rate of return is difficult—perhaps impossible—to compute for entire firms."[20]

There are two topics on which the literature attacking the antitrust use of accounting rates of return is silent. The first is that the economist most closely linked with the use of accounting data to unmask monopoly expressed strong reservations about its use. This is one untold story. The second untold story is how close the institution of antitrust once came to adopting accounting rates of return as a primary device for unmasking monopoly.

Bain's Restraint

Joe S. Bain never contended that rates of return could serve as strong evidence of monopoly power. He believed that industrial markets were best studied through what he called "qualitative analysis" and that to study rates of return was a "supplement."[21] His research on the profit rate as a measure of monopoly power was provoked in part because of a "tendency on the part of the theoretically unsophisticated to identify large profits with monopoly profits and small profits with competition."[22] While his work had the effect of provoking future studies using accounting data in an effort to locate market power, paradoxically Bain was attempting to "state the very considerable limitations upon this hypothesis." His language at one point, if it did not predate, could be side to echo that of Fisher and McGowan:

It is now possible to state briefly the relationship between the accounting profit rate and the existence of monopoly power. The unadjusted accounting rate of profit, as computed by the usual methods from balance sheets and income statements, is prima facie an absolutely unreliable indicator of the presence or absence either of monopoly power or of excess profits in the sense defined. The relationship between price and accounting average cost tells nothing about the degree of monopoly power, and little about the extent of excess profit.[23]

Bain did contend that a "persistent deviation [from competitive equilibrium] over a period of years" was "an indication of a failure of the competitive mechanism to force an approximation to equilibrium."[24] In this regard, his position was very close to Frank H. Knight's remark that monopoly profits were simply those that were "too large" and "lasted too long."[25] It was Bain's followers who were less restrained in their use of the index.[26]

The FTC's Enthusiasm

In the Federal Trade Commission's complaint filed against the Borden company, the commission endorsed two propositions about accounting rates of return. The first was that an average rate of return figure based on accounting data from a representative sample of firms could serve as a proxy for the competitive equilibrium rate. The second was that this average rate of return figure could be used as a "competitive benchmark" from which the monopoly power of individual firms could be inferred. The inference of market power was to be drawn (at least absent evidence to the contrary) when a firm's profits regularly exceeded the benchmark by a given amount. The case in which these propositions were adopted involved a subsidiary of Borden that made reconstituted lemon juice and sold it under the brand name Rea-Lemon.[27] The commission held that Borden consistently earned a rate of return on sales from its reconstituted lemon juice division that was above the average rate of return earned by all manufacturing corporations and by all firms engaged primarily in food manufacturing. Both of these averages were considered proxies for the competitive profit level.[28]

Shortly thereafter the Federal Trade Commission brought a parallel action against the General Foods Corporation in which accounting rates of return also figured prominently as evidence of market power.[29] In this instance, the rate of return for General Foods' Maxwell House division was compared to a broad-based accounting average (the proxy for the competitive rate of return). The fact that the respondent's profits on the sale of its regular ground coffee were in excess of this benchmark was argued to be evidence of market power. In the context of this volume, it is worth noting that H. Michael Mann was the economist exponent for the Federal Trade Commission in both of these cases.[30] During this era, the commission was not the sole antitrust agency using rates of return in this general fashion. At the Department of Justice's Antitrust Division (pre–William Baxter), accounting profits were an important component of the government's case against IBM.

In the General Foods litigation, Professor Mann relied upon the *Quarterly Financial Reports* (QFR) all-manufacturing average and the QFR average for food and kindred products as indicators of what profit rates should be under competitive conditions. The QFR database contains a varied mix of firms, large and small, prosperous and bankrupt, filing audited and estimated figures, all averaged on an unweighted basis. QFR data on rates of return, either on a broad all-manufacturing basis or by two-digit SIC (Standard Industrial Classification) sector, generally have been used by economists for macroeconomic purposes. The use of QFR data in the lemon juice and coffee cases represented a novel microeconomic application that, by an unspecified rendition of the law of large numbers, was to produce an estimate of the economist's normal rate of return.

In both the coffee and lemon juice cases, the FTC flirted with the adoption of a 1.5 factor for excessive profits. Monopoly profits were to be judged as those that exceeded 150 percent of the QFR-derived benchmark for a seven-year average. The all manufacturing average for the QFR during the period 1971–1977 was 11.04 percent; for food and kindred products, the average was 11.49 percent. Firms with sustained rates of return averaging 16.56 to 17.24 percent or more, therefore, would be found to possess and to be exercising market power.

During its trial, Borden submitted evidence contending that the profits of its ReaLemon division approximated only one and one-half times the QFR benchmarks and were more modest than the representations of the FTC. While not relying on higher than average profits as the sole indicator of Borden's monopoly position in reconstituted lemon juice, the commission concluded from even these more modest figures that "this persistent high profitability is further evidence of Borden's monopoly power."[31]

Standard deviation data for the QFR are publicly unavailable so the subset of firms that would be categorized as monopolies because of their disproportionately high rates of return cannot be measured. Nor was it ever made blindingly clear in either of these cases what the justification was for 1.5 as the factor of excessiveness.

Theoretically, if applied over a long enough time period, the FTC's benchmark approach would seem to avoid attributing monopoly power to situations where the "excessive" rate is due to short-term increases in demand. But there is no way in which the 1.5 excessiveness factor can distinguish between profits attributable to monopoly power and those that are the result of superior economic performance. Even if accounting rates of return were correlated with economic rates of return, this problem remains.

In addition, a high rate of return, even assuming it to be an economic rate of return and even assuming it is not due to superior efficiency, cannot necessarily be attributed to monopoly power. If ten wildcatters drill for oil and nine strike out instead of striking oil, the rate of return earned by the one successful driller provides no information for diagnosing the presence of monopoly rents for that firm. The risk-adjusted rate of return on invested funds for the entire set of wildcatters could be modest (or normal) even if the rate of return on invested funds for the fortunate driller was substantial.

Moreover, as the General Foods litigation showed, the benchmark approach can lead to bizarre results. The flagship of General Foods' coffee division is its Maxwell House brand, once the nation's leading seller. The pricing and promotion of this brand provoked the FTC lawsuit. A much smaller brand marketed by the Maxwell House division is Yuban. By the application of the excessiveness factor, Yuban had monopoly power in seven of the Maxwell House division's sales districts. Its after tax return on invested funds in some areas exceeded 40 percent for the 1971–1977 period. By way of comparison, the QFR benchmark for all manufacturing was approximately 12 percent. Yet

Yuban's market share was as little as 0.3 percent in these areas and never exceeded 4 percent.[32]

The malleable character of accounting data in antitrust is exemplified in the coffee case as well. The FTC's accounting expert, Professor John Deardon of Harvard University, estimated Maxwell House's profitability on a sales district basis, this taxonomy being dictated by the FTC's thesis that sales districts were relevant geographic markets. The breakdown entailed a sizable reworking of the respondent's profit data in that company's records normally were not disaggregated below the national level. When the General Foods' accounting records were reworked according to sales district by its own financial expert for the case, Donald Klein (the company's director of financial planning and control), very different rates of return were generated.

For example, in the two "markets" (that is, sales districts) of Boston and New York, Professor Deardon estimated General Foods' appropriate rate of return to be 25.5 percent and 18.6 percent, respectively; Mr. Klein put the figures at 15.7 percent and 10.4 percent for the same "markets" in the same time frame.[33] The former expert accountant worked with data for the regular Maxwell House brand of ground coffee alone; the latter expert accountant included the other less prominent brands of the firm's ground coffee along with the flagship brand of regular Maxwell House. Each handled or estimated differently the allocation of fixed assets, certain cash investment items, types of accounts payable, corporate tax rates paid by the respondent, the inclusion of interest and accounts receivable in the rate of return denominator, the allocation of military costs, the inclusion of can plant savings, and profits from coffee's byproduct of caffeine. The difference in rates of return proposed by the two accountants became even greater when Klein amortized the advertising expenditures of General Foods to reflect their investment character.[34]

The FTC's Restraint

Notwithstanding its position in *Borden* and the theories put forth by the FTC staff and its experts in *General Foods*, the commission has largely abandoned if not totally jettisoned accounting rates of return as an index of market power. The evidence is less explicit, but a similar position seems to be held at the Department of Justice.

The abandonment began with the opinion of the administrative law judge in *General Foods*, which took a skeptical posture with regard to this index. Judge Lewis F. Parker was unpersuaded that the arbitrary breakdowns of accounting data necessary to make the numbers fit relevant markets made sense, at least in the coffee case. Conceptually his concern paralleled that discussed at length by Benston and others in their critique of the FTC's Line-of-Business Program.[35] Judge Parker expressed wariness of QFR data as a benchmark and he argued that even if one accepted high accounting profits as (in some sense) real numbers, the benchmark approach does not preclude the possibility that the numbers reflect something other than market power.[36]

In the full commission opinion in *General Foods*, Chairman James C. Miller went even farther. He concluded that any correlation between the profits and sales share of the Maxwell House division was due "in large part from respondent's superior efficiency in advertising, promoting and maintaining the quality of that brand in those areas."[37] Miller rejected implicitly the concept of accounting rates of return as valid indicators of monopoly and in the process bypassed the earlier teaching by the commission in the *Borden* case on this subject.

Parts of Virginia are horse country. People there say that any horse running the track by itself looks fast. To see how genuinely talented an animal is, it needs to be paced. Accounting records are not very good pacers. High rates of return can be misleading; so can low rates of return. J. R. Hicks, one of the first Nobel laureates in economics, held that the best of monopoly profits is a quiet life. This would imply that low profits are evidence of monopoly, not high.

The limited use that might be made of profit measures for unmasking monopoly in the future probably will come more through the use of stock market data than numbers generated by accountants.[38] Among economists, ranking not too far below the dogma that demand curves slope downward and to the right, is faith that stock markets are very efficient markets. There are several implications of this. One is that the economic profits of a firm should be reflected in its combined dividend rate and stock appreciation regardless of what the accountant does with the numbers.

If a firm gains a significant monopoly position, its new status should be reflected by a change in the stock market's valuation of the enterprise. The share price of a firm should represent the value of expected profits in a way that is unbiased by many factors—such as nonrecurring events or changes in accounting conventions—that may influence current accounting profits. The use of this measure might skirt some of the difficulties found in utilizing accounting rates of return. An efficient capital market will not be as fooled by the fact that some company's book values are cockeyed or that the accountant is showing no profits this year because of an accelerated depreciation schedule. The use of stock market data is not without its own pitfalls. The stock market reflects many variables about a firm besides its expected monopoly rents.

In an example of this approach, Thomas F. Hogarty authored a study on cross subsidization of retail gasoline operations by large, vertically integrated oil companies.[39] There has long been the allegation that the majors subsidize their company-owned and operated retail outlets who compete with independent retailers of petroleum products. The predation allegedly enables the majors with many retail outlets to raise prices later.

A study like this could be a time-intensive exercise in futility using only accounting records. One approach Hogarty took was to compare the profitability of those oil companies that had the greatest increase in the number of company-owned retail outlets with those that had the smallest. Presumably if this were a workable predatory strategy, those with the largest increases in profits would be those who relied the most on company-owned stations. As a measure of profits, Hogarty took the total return to stockholders (capital gains plus dividends) for the time period under consideration. This allowed him to make cross-section comparisons without getting into the question of whether the firms were using comparable accounting conventions during the time period and trying to compensate for them if the companies did not. Approaches such as this probably will be offered as superior replacements for the use of historical accounting records. If so the change will be a remarkable one.

It was not very long ago that the Federal Trade Commission embarked on a major, costly program to gather profit data on a line-of-business basis to guide antitrust enforcement policy. That project has been abandoned. It was only a few years ago that the commission had adopted and its staff was using accounting data to contrast how a respondent's rate of return compared with an all-manufacturing average or the average of the two-digit SIC code in which respondent could be classified. The purpose was to diagnose cases of monopoly. This approach has been abandoned. As of now, stock in the use of accounting data for unmasking monopoly has dropped considerably.

The opinion of Judge Parker and Commissioner Miller in the *General Foods* litigation parallels somewhat that of economists today: At best, rate of return data may be used for insight, but such data cannot be used either solo or woodenly to draw conclusions about the existence or extent of monopoly.

Monopoly and Price, Not Profits

Due to the difficulty in working with accounting data, some economists have stopped using profit rates entirely. For them, the focus has shifted to another economic variable. Leonard W. Weiss, for example, has argued that monopoly power, or at least the consequences of high market concentration, can be predicted by an analysis of price data, not profits.[40]

Weiss argues that most oligopoly theories predict a restriction of output and a corresponding rise in price. He therefore has searched for empirical evidence supporting a positive relationship between price and market concentration. In the case of certain industries, such as cement, Weiss has found statistically significant correlations between these variables. An analysis of broader sectors, such as all consumer goods, has provided a less clear relationship.

To support his contention that concentration can predict price, Weiss looked at price-concentration correlations in several markets. These included auctions, cement, and airlines. The auction markets, which included tax-exempt bonds, offshore oil tracts, and national forest timber, showed the clearest relationship between concentration and price.[41] In each case, the number of bidders seemed to affect the level of the winning bid, with a positive relationship between the number of bidders and the price paid. This effect was due to the elevated maximum order statistic, or the increased probability of having a bidder who places a high value on the object present.

This raises the question of whether the number of bidders in an auction market can serve as a proxy for monopolistic behavior in industry. The effect of an increased maximum order statistic has no clear parallel in normal marketing behavior. Moreover, as Kessel argued, the relationship between price and the number of buyers in such markets is likely due to imperfections in the information markets, as explained by Stigler's theory.[42] This explanation, if accurate, limits the usefulness of such studies in identifying monopolies. Another implication of Kessel's work is that only a few bidders yields a competitive result. He found that the price of bonds rises sharply with the number of bidders. Only eight bidders are needed to approximate perfect competition. With less than six bidders, the underwriter's costs rise exponentially as the number of bidders falls.[43]

Weiss's work with auctions does imply that concentration ratios (as a proxy for the number of competing firms) will be an important consideration where suppliers bid for a contract. However, most markets do not function through explicit bids or offers. Moreover, auction markets generally involve concentration on the buyer's side. Monopolies, not monopsonies, have been the primary concern of antitrust policymakers.

On the producer side of the market, Weiss has analyzed price-concentration data for the cement and airline industries. He concluded that concentration in the former industry has a significant positive impact on price in five of the six years studied. With airlines, Weiss found that a combination of concentration and entry can account for as much as 39 percent of the minimum unrestricted daytime fare charged. However, when all unrestricted daytime fares are averaged, the same regressions account for less than 10 percent of the price differentials. Weiss also has evaluated the price-concentration relationship for broad types of goods. Regressions utilizing costs, production levels, and concentration ratios yielded a small positive effect on price for consumer goods. No significant effect was noted on producer goods.

The price-concentration nexus represents an intriguing attempt to skirt the murkiness of accounting data on profits. In many markets, however, the task of gathering data on actual transaction prices itself is problematic. The terms of a transaction can be difficult to ascertain and often difficult to monetize as well. Moreover, it is unclear whether additional research on the price-concentration relationship will assist in recognizing specific instances of market power. Heightened input costs may increase concentration and increase prices, without the presence of market power. Absent detailed knowledge of an industry, it is not evident whether a given price increase is due to increased concentration or other economic forces.

THE LERNER INDEX

The most pristine theoretical measure of monopoly is the Lerner Index. This measure of a monopoly's power is based on the special property of a price that equals marginal cost. Abba P. Lerner is the economist most responsible for explaining this special property. Paul A. Samuelson reported that it was Lerner's article on the measurement of monopoly power that explained to him precisely what this particular characteristic was.[44] Samuelson wrote: "Today this may seem simple, but I can testify that no one at Chicago or Harvard [where Samuelson was educated] could tell me in 1935 exactly why $P = MC$ was a good thing."[45] Abba Lerner did.

Lerner's Index is $(P - MC)/P$ where P is a product's price and MC its marginal cost.[46] Lerner argued that this ratio portrayed "the degree of monopoly power in force." A perfect competitor, the seller with no market power and for whom $P = MC$, generated a Lerner Index of zero.

Empirical applications of the Lerner Index are few. The earliest (at least that I can locate) was by John T. Dunlop in the year 1939.[47] Within the veil of antitrust, the index has had only a minor role and was usually confined to textbooks until it was given a prominent role in the analysis of market power put forth by William M. Landes and Richard A. Posner.[48] The Landes-Posner article generated more publicity for the measure.[49] It may prove useful to summarize the ability of the index to unmask monopoly for antitrust purposes.

A characteristic of the Lerner measure that would be uncongenial to the head of the Antitrust Division or the Federal Trade Commission is that there is no Q in the equation. That is, the index takes no account of the amount of commerce or the size of a market.[50] As a result efficiency gains from removing market power may be greater in a large market with a modest Lerner Index than a tiny one with a greater index. This is no doubt one reason Landes and Posner do not adopt the Lerner Index as it stands but instead turn to a dead-weight loss measure by which they endeavor to account for the size of a market. This is only one of several drawbacks the index has.

One measurement problem occurs when using the Lerner Index in its alternate form. The index is the reciprocal of a firm's elasticity of demand (except when the firm is the whole industry, as in the case of a pure monopoly, when it becomes the reciprocal of the market elasticity of demand). This means that the Lerner Index would be positive for two firms, both of whom are the sole sellers in their respective markets. But if demand elasticity differs between the two markets, the index will be higher for the pure monopolist in the market with the lower elasticity of demand. Thus, differences in the magnitude of the Lerner Index do not indicate differences in the degree of monopoly, where "degree" pertains to control of the market.

In antitrust cases, even a so-called dominant firm rarely is found to control an entire industry. Firms with 100 percent market shares are rare. So are 60 percent shareholders. Most antitrust actions are waged in oligopolistic market structures. In such a market, a firm's demand curve is not well specified. The output it will sell at various prices depends upon its expectations regarding rivals' reactions to its output changes. This complicates firm-specific elasticity measurements of market power. Charles A. Holt has modeled some of the consequences of using Lerner's approach to assessing monopoly in markets characterized by oligopolistic interdependence.[51]

When the index is estimated directly from Lerner's formula, other measurement problems surface. The Lerner Index requires that price be plugged into the equation. In the case of most firms, what is P is not apparent. By way of example, there is no "price" that Anheuser-Busch charges for its beer. The firm has a list of prices encompassing a variety of container sizes and package types for several brands of beer, not all of which will be offered for sale to its many wholesale customers. Moreover, on a geographic cross section, the price for any one product segment, such as cases of 12-ounce cans of Budweiser Light, may vary between sales territories at a point in time and will change over time. The "price" for many manufactured products sold by a company will be affected by volume discounts, merchandising allowances, periodic and selective rebates, coupons, credit terms, delivery charges, and clandestine discounts. The result is a complex array of prices about which the Lerner Index provides no selection criteria.

The Lerner Index also requires a knowledge of marginal cost. Lerner, the consummate theorist, believed that rational managers and business owners would know their marginal costs. They do not, nor can the figure be calculated readily for many enterprise settings. The complexities of marginal cost estimation were considered so great by the authors of the Areeda-Turner test for predation that they substituted average variable cost as a proxy for marginal cost.

Use of the Lerner Index in antitrust enforcement or litigation has been rare. When used, it can produce strange and misleading results. In a recent private antitrust case between rival floral delivery services, Professor Jerry A. Hausman submitted an expert economist's affidavit in which he contended that one of the defendant floral delivery services possessed "a substantial amount of market power."[52] He reached this conclusion relying heavily upon a Lerner Index calculation.

The defendant floral clearinghouse, Florists' Transworld Delivery Association (FTD), is a nonprofit membership association. It charges a 6 percent commission to those retail floral establishments who are its members. Of this 6 percent service charge, .75 percent was estimated as being the direct costs required to process a transaction. The remainder was used by FTD for other purposes such as the network advertising of its floral arrangements. Hausman used the .75 percent figure as the measure of FTD's marginal cost. Under the Lerner formula of $(P - MC)/P$, the problem then could be set up as Lerner Index = $(6 - .75)/6 = .875$. Since the Lerner Index can at most be 1.0, Hausman's affidavit concludes that a "Lerner Index so close to its theoretical maximum of 1.0 makes the existence of market power indisputable."[53]

The possibilities of this application of the Lerner Index are intriguing. Consider an antitrust action against a local movie theater. With a ticket price of $4.00, and a marginal cost (assuming there is an empty seat) approaching zero, the Lerner Index approaches its maximum of one. A commercial airline whose marginal cost of serving an additional passenger consists of the added cost of fuel, ticketing and baggage processing, and beverage service would generate a Lerner Index that even for short flights would be high. By this approach educational institutions and railroads could be shown to exhibit sizable degrees of monopoly power.

Far from unmasking monopoly, high Lerner Indices can mask competition. In the floral wire service case, low barriers to entry alone should restrain market power. Notwithstanding the "substantial amount of market power" allegedly displayed via the Lerner Index, successful entry into the industry had taken place with only a $500 capital expenditure.

Joe S. Bain had little enthusiasm for the Lerner Index as a device for unmasking monopoly. He argued that gathering the measure's requisite data would be "next to impossible."[54] In their assessment, however, Landes and Posner claim that the Lerner Index is "a precise economic definition of market power." Both characterizations of the index are on point. Precise it may be as a definition, practical it is not as a yardstick.

The scholarly literature stemming from the Lerner article has been sizable. For example, Robert Dorfman and Peter O. Steiner used the index to show the relationship between the marginal value product of advertising and a firm's demand elasticity;[55] Roger Sherman and Robert D. Tollison derived from the index a measure of fixed costs within an industry;[56] David R. Kamerschen used Lerner's Index to estimate market demand elasticity.[57] And a number of authors have used the framework of the Lerner Index in attempts to measure not the market power of a firm but the extent of market power in an industry.

None of these contributions has a direct bearing on measuring the market power of a particular or potential antitrust defendant. As mentioned earlier, it was the Landes-Posner article and its commentary that endeavored to weave the Lerner Index further into the theoretical fabric of antitrust enforcement. But it remains at best a loose end. Rarely has the Lerner Index been used. And this probably is just as well.

CONDUCT MEASURES OF MONOPOLY

In 1949, Edward S. Mason published a famous article in the *Harvard Law Review* titled "The Current Status of the Monopoly Problem in the United States."[58] The article is interesting reading some 35 years later because it shows how antitrust scholars at that time devoted their attention *either* to measures of structure *or* performance in assessing the existence of monopoly. The Adams-Lerner disagreement mentioned at the outset of this paper was one example of that division. The paradigm is structure-conduct-performance. But the first and third links of the chain, like the first child in a family and the third, received most of the attention.

Since Mason's article, research into the task of unmasking monopoly has revealed that some of the unmasking techniques are unreliable. While the structural concept of entry barriers remains important to the analysis of monopoly power, its companion structural variable, firm market share, turns out to be less useful than once generally thought. Among performance variables, conventional measures based on profit rates and theoretical indices such as the Lerner Index have deficiencies. Given the shaky character of these measures, some economists are developing new approaches to scrutinizing monopoly power. I call these the "New Conduct" methodologies. It is not my purpose to catalog or discuss them. Part of that task is performed elsewhere in this volume by David T. Scheffman and Charles A. Holt.[59] In this section I shall offer several observations on this approach.

The problem with studying business conduct to diagnose monopoly is that the field is so large. Firms price, advertise, engage in research, litigate, add and subtract capacity, and much more. The virtue of using economics to study conduct is that it provides a road map to the inquiry.

In antitrust studies, second only to research on collusive conduct, has been the analysis of predatory conduct. Within this particular set of business behavior the most common element has been the study of predatory pricing. Here the unmasking of monopoly occurs when a firm has been shown to have priced predaciously. No one would admit to having read all that has been written on the topic of predatory pricing. Beginning with John S. McGee's classic article on the subject to the outpouring stimulated by the Areeda-Turner contribution, the literature has been enormous. The studies on the subject almost can be summarized as a dispute between those who believe price predation is rare, the way a one-cent 1856 black-on-magenta British Guinea stamp is rare, or rare the way a unicorn is rare.

As price predation came to be considered exceptional, scholarly attention has turned to raising rivals' costs as a variation on the predation theme. Since lowering prices hurt both the predator as well as its business prey, a strategy that asymmetrically raised rivals' costs might prove a rational way to accomplish the same monopolizing goal. Within the government enforcement agencies (especially at the Federal Trade Commission), non–price predation is a topic that is more than academic.

It has long been understood that using the government to raise a rival's costs was a tempting and potentially successful monopolizing tactic. In most instances, the tactic is rather easily observed and at least qualitatively measured. What the "new conduct" approach seeks to identify, however, is the use of conventional business techniques to raise a rival's costs so as to deter its entry or promote its exit. The root question is: Are there avenues, short of persuading the government to put lead in rivals' saddlebags, by which a firm can raise its competitors' costs relative to its own?

The seminal contribution in this field of study is A. Michael Spence's "Entry, Capacity, Investment and Oligopolistic Pricing."[60] This paper generated other research that modeled strategies involving capacity additions, research and development expenditures, and advertising budgets (as well as price) that were designed either to deter entry, raise the costs of rival firms, or both. Some of the models incorporate strategies involving multiple instruments.

As examples of the monopolizing strategies being modeled, a dominant firm observes a new entrant making a move into its market. The new entrant is uncertain about the demand for its product. It estimates it will need to spend $5 million to inform customers of the product in order to gain a share in the market enabling profitable operations. Unbeknownst to the entrant, the dominant firm significantly increases its own advertising. As a result, the new entrant does not gain the market share it had expected, but may (erroneously) attribute the reason to consumer dislike of its product. The entrant withdraws from the market. Or a large company strategically bargains with the union for a high wage rate that will be the benchmark for the industry. This handicaps smaller firms that are more labor intensive in their operations. The wage increase becomes a form of input predation, burdening small firms more than large.

The alleged advantage of input predation is this: the *price* predator, because it sold more, lost more money than the prey. This was no fun for the predator. The input predator is one who raises the entrant's costs more than its own.

As the paper by Scheffman and Holt in this volume shows more fully, there is a subset of the non–price predation literature that entails much more than formal modeling. Its intended audience embraces those concerned with antitrust enforcement policy as well as academic economists. The literature attempts to incorporate non–price strategic behavior into the antitrust corpus of exclusionary conduct. Three articles by Steven C. Salop, in one instance writing with David T. Scheffman and in another with Thomas G. Krattenmaker, have been influential.[61] In particular, the Krattenmaker-Salop paper endeavors to integrate the theory of raising rivals' costs into the case law of antitrust.

The effort is impressive and merits close attention. But as an unambiguous method of unmasking monopoly or distinguishing between firms with and without market power, the approach is marred in a fashion that will make the new conduct approach difficult to use as a measure of monopoly in antitrust litigation.

If a firm invents a new drug for reducing high blood pressure and sweeps the field, monopoly power is its reward for the invention—at least for a season. During this time, the firm's pricing power will be constrained at a minimum by the availability of earlier drugs for high blood pressure. If the firm then commits itself to spend $10 million for additional R & D expenditures on high blood pressure drugs, can anyone ever show what portion of that expenditure is socially optimal and what portion is being used strategically to raise rivals' costs by an even greater amount? In the case of a dominant firm, faced with a new entrant, can its advertising budget be limited to a court-determined optimum on the grounds that greater amounts will frustrate an entrant's ability to obtain a clear reading on the location of the "true" demand curve for its product? Given the vagaries of antitrust's history, one must be wary of responding negatively to such questions. But as attorneys are prone to say (almost) to raise such questions is to answer them.

Building excess capacity to deter new entrants is one of the favorite variables in the models of New Conduct scholars. This is a prepositioning strategy, an investment in low-cost reactive output to enhance one's price-war credibility. The modeling is elegant and provocative. It also can badly misread industrial experience about capacity decisions.

Currently a major brewing company has mothballed an 8-million barrel brewery in the Midwest that it recently built but never opened. By the time the plant was completed, the expected increase in the demand for the company's beer had not appeared. As a consequence of the region's excess capacity, it probably would be foolhardy to put a new brewery in the Midwest at this point. Technically, entry is forestalled. But no one at the firm holding this unused capacity considers the construction of the plant to represent a clever and enterprising strategy. It is a strategy whose "benefits" the company would gladly wish upon any of its rivals.

In short, it will prove difficult to take business practices such as R & D, advertising, or capacity expenditures and for antitrust enforcement purposes distinguish when they are carried out suboptimally to burden a rival or new entrant from when they are incurred optimally (or innocently?) with the consequence of enhancing consumer welfare. Empirically the task will be formidable if not intractable. Conceptually it is also murky in that *all* R & D, advertising, and capacity expenditures in oligopolistic markets can be construed as attempts to raise rivals' costs. Even forms of cutting prices, at many firms, are viewed by management as increases in their merchandising costs and promotional efforts; in deciding the amount of these "costs" to be incurred, managements commonly consider the "cost" that will be incurred by rivals who respond to such an increase in marketing efforts. Preemption is, in many instances, merely a strong word for rivalry.

Tactics to preempt a field can have good as well as bad consequences for consumers. Business behavior that places rivals at a disadvantage in competing with parity product, service, and cost offerings is not necessarily an undesirable masquerade of monopoly. If a new rival or prospective rival finds it difficult to compete with an existing firm because of the latter's first-mover advantages, it may be socially wasteful to adopt antitrust measures enabling the former firms nonetheless to put scarce resources into the industry. Viewing (or modeling) com-

petition only as parity confrontation overlooks welfare-enhancing behavior that occurs when new or prospective rivals are forced to adopt
"new ways of attacking the market."[62]

With the weakening of structure and performance measures in the
structure-conduct-performance chain, it is inevitable that conduct receives more attention. And it deserves to. One reason conduct used to
receive such low grades in antitrust was the propensity of some attorneys to take the language of business executives and give it economic
content. Thus, the militaristic memo of a regional sales manager to
sales personnel in the field was put forth as evidence of predation when
it was nothing of the sort.

Conduct can regain the high ground when one considers not so much
language but the actual behavior of firms in their institutional setting.
This involves much effort of course. The work of John A. Stuckey and
that of Franklin M. Fisher, John J. McGowan, and Joen E. Greenwood
are cited only as illustrations of the detailed, nuts and bolts factual
inquiry needed to assess a firm or group of firms' ability to restrict a
market's total output and thereby raise price.[63] These studies and ones
like them, written with the attention to detail that marked Fetter's
The Masquerade of Monopoly, portray how conduct can be used to assess
the extent of monopoly power.

CONCLUSION

Monopolistic restriction of output may take many forms: restriction
on the output of potential entrants, restriction of output by cooperating
rivals, restrictions on the output (or viability) of existing rivals. What
makes the identification and prevention of such output restrictions a
difficult exercise is that their consequences ultimately are manifested
in the long run by reductions in national income. National income is
reduced as resources flow from monopolized markets to those satisfying
less urgently sought ends. The loss in national income caused by output
restriction in a particular industry is not directly recognizable from
national income statistics. This provokes the search for more observable and reliable indicators of output restriction.

The contemporary literature on competition and monopoly reveals
a growing concensus that the essence of monopoly power is output
restriction. This view is being adopted in the antitrust courts as well.
In *Ball Memorial Hospital, Inc.* v. *Mutual Hospital Insurance, Inc.*, the
influence of the economic approach to market power is profoundly evident. Market power is defined as the "ability to cut back the market's
output and so raise price."[64] If a firm lacks this ability, it lacks market
power, regardless of its share of the market and rate of return.

F. M. Scherer once wrote of the difficulty an antitrust enforcement agency had in finding a "good" monopolization case. His explanation complements the market power definition put forth in *Ball Memorial*. By a good monopolization case, Scherer meant one where:

1. Monopoly power is present and has been demonstrably exercised.
2. The possession or retention of that power is due to something more than superior products, service, or business acumen.
3. Remedies can be defined that will benefit the consumer.[65]

Without these elements, antitrust cases will be misdiagnosed, misguided, or both.

In the most famous portion of his first letter to the church at Corinth, the Apostle Paul wrote of faith, hope, and charity: "And now abideth faith, hope, charity, these three; but the greatest of these is charity." In antitrust economics there now abideth structure, conduct, performance, these three; but the greatest of these is ... well, frankly, there are problems with all three. E. H. Chamberlin compared monopoly to health. There are a few quantitative indicators of salubrity: body temperature, blood pressure, to some extent body weight. There is, however, no single index of good health. The parallel holds for the diagnosis of monopoly as well.

NOTES

The author is indebted to William Breit, Mark P. Henriques, Thomas F. Hogarty, Charles A. Holt, Robert J. Larner, Kenneth A. Letzler, James W. Meehan, Jr., and David E. Mills for their comments.

1. For a history, see Vernon M. Mund, *Monopoly* (Princeton, N.J.: Princeton University Press, 1933).

2. Frank A. Fetter, *The Masquerade of Monopoly* (New York: Harcourt, Brace, 1931; New York: Augustus M. Kelley, 1971).

3. Franklin M. Fisher, "Diagnosing Monopoly," *Quarterly Review of Economics & Business* 19 (Summer 1979): 7–33.

4. See David D. Haddock, "Basing-Point Pricing: Competitive vs. Collusive Theories," *American Economic Review* 72 (June 1982): 289–319.

5. Robert J. Larner and James W. Meehan, Jr. "Postscript: In Memory of H. Michael Mann" (herein) 209–210.

6. H. Michael Mann, "Seller Concentration, Barriers to Entry, and Rates of Return in Thirty Industries, 1950–1960." *Review of Economics and Statistics* 48 (August 1966): 296–307.

7. Alfred E. Kahn and Joel B. Dirlam, *Fair Competition: The Law and Economics of Antitrust Policy* (Ithaca, N.Y.: Cornell University Press, 1954).

8. There are other approaches regarding the unmasking of monopoly such as experimental economics and rent seeking, that are not addressed in this chapter.

9. "The Case against Big Business," *Fortune* (May 1952): 123, 167.

10. See Harold Demsetz, "Two Systems of Belief about Monopoly," in *Industrial Concentration: The New Learning,* ed. Harvey J. Goldschmid, H. Michael Mann, and J. Fred Weston (Boston: Little Brown, 1974), 164–184, especially 177–181. See also his earlier article, "Industry Structure, Market Rivalry, and Public Policy," *Journal of Law & Economics* 16 (April 1973): 1–9.

11. For example, in his article on seller concentration and entry barriers referenced in note 6, H. Michael Mann hedged on the proposition that market dominance would always yield supracompetitive profits. He emphasized the word *may.* However, when discussing situations of low entry barriers, structuralists in the tradition of Joe S. Bain and Edward S. Mason generally describe how oligopolists *choose* a low price to discourage entrants. Mann mentioned that if entry were relatively easy, "oligopolists may set a price close to the competitive level." The choice of words is notable. In the structuralist tradition, even in situations of easily entered industries, rarely is there reference to sellers having no pricing discretion because the market has set a price close to the competitive level.

12. Joe E. Bain, *Barriers to New Competition* (Cambridge: Harvard University Press, 1956), see especially, 1.

13. This gives new life to the expression, "the tariff is the mother of the trust." Sans foreign competition, it is an open question whether such manufacturing industries as steel, automobiles, tractors, and liquor would evidence the competitive vigor they now do.

14. See generally William J. Baumol, John C. Panzar, and Robert D. Willig, *Contestable Markets and the Theory of Industry Structure* (New York: Harcourt Brace Javanovich, 1982). For a summary, see William J. Baumol, "Contestable Markets: An Uprising in the Theory of Industry Structure," *American Economic Review* 72 (March 1982): 1–15. An important critique of the theory and its implications can be found in William G. Shepherd, " 'Contestability' vs. Competition," *American Economic Review* 74 (September 1984): 572–587. Another evaluation of the theory of contestable markets can be found in A. Michael Spence, "Contestable Markets and the Theory of Industry Structure: A Review Article," *Journal of Economic Literature* 21 (September 1983): 981–990.

15. Kenneth G. Elzinga, "New Developments on the Cartel Front," *The Antitrust Bulletin,* 19 (Spring 1984): 3–26.

16. F. M. Scherer, "Merger Policy in the 1970s and 1980s" (Chapter 3 herein).

17. Joe S. Bain, "The Profit Rate as a Measure of Monopoly Power," *Quarterly Journal of Economics* 55 (February 1941): 271–293. My own baptism to the profits issue came not through Bain but under the tutelage of John Blair, the irrepressible chief economist for the Senate antitrust and monopoly subcommittee under Senators Kefauver and Hart. As a junior economist working under Blair, I gathered data on accounting profits for large firms. No matter what I found, he seemed pleased. If the profits were large, this showed market power. If the profits were modest, this demonstrated the inefficiency of big business. At a young age, I became leery of the measure.

18. See Yale Brozen, "Bain's Concentration and Rates of Return Revisited,"

Journal of Law & Economics 14 (October 1971): 351–369 and more generally his "Significance of Profit Data for Antitrust Policy," in J. Fred Weston and Sam Peltzman, eds. *Public Policy toward Mergers* (Pacific Palisades, Calif.: Goodyear, 1979), 110–127; George J. Benston, "Accounting Numbers and Economic Values," *The Antitrust Bulletin* 27 (Spring 1982): 161–215.

19. Franklin M. Fisher and John J. McGowan, "On the Misuse of Accounting Rates of Return to Infer Monopoly Profits," *American Economic Review* 73 (March 1983): 82–97 and the subsequent response in *American Economic Review* 74 (June 1984): 492–517.

20. Ibid., 90.

21. Bain, "The Profit Rate as a Measure of Monopoly Power," 272.

22. Ibid.

23. Ibid., 291.

24. Ibid., 288.

25. Frank H. Knight, "An Appraisal of Economic Change, Discussion," *American Economic Review* (Proceedings) 44 (May 1954): 65.

26. The article titled "Seller Concentration, Barriers to Entry, and Rates of Return In Thirty Industries, 1950–1960," by H. Michael Mann is representative of this. It references (at p. 300) the proposition that "rates of return may be inadequate indicators of price-cost margins" as a problem needing further research.

27. *In the matter of Borden, Inc.* The Commission's opinion is at 92 F.T.C. 669 (1978).

28. Ibid., 791–792.

29. *In the matter of General Foods Corporation*, 103 F.T.C. 204 (1984).

30. It is also worth noting that the author served as the economic expert for the respondent. Professor Mann's testimony entailed more than a comparison of respondent's accounting profits and his competitive benchmark. In the General Foods litigation for example, evidencing his structuralist roots, Professor Mann also testified about the relationship between the respondent's market share and its price and profit. See the testimony of H. Michael Mann, *In the matter of General Foods Corporation*, transcript pages 3597–3599. See also Complaint Counsel Exhibits 1104, 1106, 1110, and 1112. The transcript and all exhibits are on file at the Federal Trade Commission.

31. *In the Matter of Borden, Inc.*, 792, citing *U.S.* v. *General Electric Co.*, 82 F. Supp. 753, 894–895 (1949).

32. See *In the Matter of General Foods Corporation*, Respondent Exhibit 1268.

33. Compare Complaint Counsel Exhibit 1115-C with Respondent Exhibit 1171-A.

34. Compare Complaint Counsel Exhibit 1115-C with Respondent Exhibit 1171-B where the "estimated economic return" of General Foods for the Boston and New York sales districts dropped to 9.0 percent and 6.8 percent respectively.

35. See George J. Benston, "The Validity of Profits-Structure with Particular Reference to the FTC's Line of Business Data," *American Economic Review* 75 (March 1985): 37–67.

36. See his initial opinion, 103 F.T.C. 204 (1984), 282–284.

37. Ibid., at 363. Miller's opinion covers many other economic issues that arose in this litigation and is not summarized here.

38. One of the earlier illustrations of the use of stock market data to measure expected profits is Sam Peltzman, "Entry in Commercial Banking," *Journal of Law & Economics* 8 (October 1965): 11–50. William G. Shepherd has a clear review of the concept and early literature in "The Elements of Market Structure," *Review of Economics and Statistics* 54 (February 1972): 25–37. A more recent variation on this theme (one that combines financial market data with accounting data) is the use of Tobin's *q*, which is the ratio of the market value to the replacement cost of a firm. A standard reference is Eric Lindenberg and Stephen Ross, "Tobin's *q* Ratio and Industrial Organization," *Journal of Business* 54 (January 1981): 1–32. For a more recent contribution, see Michael Smirlock, Thomas Gilligan, and William Marshall, "Tobin's *q* and the Structure-Performance Relationship," *American Economic Review* 74 (December 1984): 1051–1060.

39. Thomas F. Hogarty, "Economic Theory and Evidence on Cross-Subsidization of Retail Gasoline Operations," American Petroleum Institute Research Study #026R, October 1983.

40. Leonard W. Weiss, "Concentration and Price—A Possible Way Out of a Box" in Joachim Schwalbach, ed., *Industry Structure and Performance* (Berlin: Edition Sigma Rainer Bohn Verlag), 85–111 and "Concentration and Price—*Not* Concentration and Profits," unpublished manuscript, n.d.

41. Here Weiss draws upon the earlier work of Reuben A. Kessel. See Kessel's "A Study of the Effects of Competition in the Tax-Exempt Bond Market," *Journal of Political Economy* 79 (July/August 1971): 706–738, reprinted in R. H. Coase and Merton H. Miller *Essays in Applied Price Theory* (Chicago: University of Chicago Press, 1980), 233–265.

42. Ibid., 255.

43. Ibid., 250.

44. "The Concept of Monopoly and the Measurement of Monopoly Power," *Review of Economic Studies* (June 1943): 157–175. Reprinted in William Breit, Harold M. Hochman, and Edward Saueracker, eds. *Readings in Microeconomics* (St. Louis: Times Mirror/Mosby, 1986), 313–326.

45. Paul A. Samuelson, "A. P. Lerner at Sixty," *Review of Economic Studies* 31 (June 1964): 173 as reported in William Breit and Roger L. Ransom, *The Academic Scribblers*, rev. ed. (Chicago: Dryden, 1982), 140.

46. The notation has been changed somewhat from Lerner's original article. The index also equals $1/E_f$ where E_f is the elasticity of the firm's demand curve.

47. John T. Dunlop, "Price Flexibility and the Degree of Monopoly," *Quarterly Journal of Economics* 53 (August 1939): 522–534.

48. William M. Landes and Richard M. Posner, "Market Power in Antitrust Cases," *Harvard Law Review* 94 (March 1981): 937–996.

49. See "Landes and Posner on Market Power: Four Responses," *Harvard Law Review* 95 (1982): 1787–1874. The responses in order of appearance are: Richard Schmalensee, "Another Look At Market Power," 1789–1816; Louis Kaplow, "The Accuracy of Traditional Market Power Analysis and a Direct Adjustment Alternative," 1817–1848; Timothy J. Brennan, "Mistaken Elas-

ticities and Misleading Rules," 1849–1856; and Janusz A. Ordover, Alan O. Sykes, and Robert D. Willig, "Herfindahl Concentration, Rivalry, and Mergers," 1857–1874. Particular concern with the Lerner Index is found in the first and the last of these responses. The contribution of Ordover, Sykes, and Willig attempts to take the Lernerian approach beyond that of single-firm rivalry and apply it to oligopoly situations.

50. Schmalensee makes this point in "Another Look At Market Power," at 1787.

51. Charles A. Holt, "On the Use of Profit Data to Estimate the Social Cost of Monopoly Power in an Oligopoly," *Journal of Economics and Business* 34 (1982): 283–289.

52. Affidavit of Jerry A. Hausman, par. 9, March 18, 1986. The case is *American Floral Services* v. *Florists' Transworld Delivery Association and Teleflora, Inc.*, No. 84C1824 U.S.D.C. for North District of Illinois, Eastern Division. Judge Milton I. Shadur's grant of summary judgment dismissing the complaint of American Floral Service was issued February 13, 1986.

53. Ibid.

54. Bain, "The Profit Rate as a Measure of Monopoly Power," 292.

55. Robert Dorfman and Peter O. Steiner, "Optimal Advertising and Optimal Quantity," *American Economic Review* 44 (December 1954): 826–836.

56. Roger Sherman and Robert D. Tollison, "Advertising and Profitability," *Review of Economics and Statistics* 53 (November 1971): 397–407.

57. David R. Kamerschen, "An Estimation of the Welfare Losses from Monopoly in the American Economy," *Western Economic Journal* 4 (Summer 1966): 221–236.

58. Edward S. Mason, "The Current Status of the Monopoly Problem in the United States," *Harvard Law Review* 62 (June 1949): 1265–1285; reprinted in Richard S. Heflebower and George W. Stocking (eds.), *Readings In Industrial Organization and Public Policy* (Homewood, Ill.: Richard D. Irwin, 1958), 376–392.

59. David T. Scheffman and Charles A. Holt, "Strategic Business Behavior and Antitrust" (Chapter 2 herein), 39–82.

60. A. Michael Spence, "Entry, Capacity, Investment and Oligopolistic Pricing," *Bell Journal of Economics* 8 (Autumn 1977): 534–544.

61. The chronological development is apparent in Steven C. Salop, "Strategic Entry Deterrence," *American Economic Review* 69 (May 1979): 335–338; Steven C. Salop and David T. Scheffman, "Raising Rivals' Costs," *American Economic Review* 73 (May 1983): 267–271; Thomas G. Krattenmaker and Steven C. Salop, "Antitrust Analysis of Anticompetitive Exclusion: Raising Rivals' Costs to Achieve Power Over Price," *The Yale Law Journal* 96 (November 1986): 209–295. Another very useful paper on the conduct measure, written from a legal perspective but embracing an economic paradigm, is Robin C. Landis and Ronald S. Rolfe, "Market Conduct under Section 2: When Is It Anticompetitive?" in Franklin M. Fisher (ed.), *Antitrust and Regulation* (Cambridge: MIT Press, 1985), 131–152.

62. See Robert B. Shapiro, "Contestability and Strategy," *The Conference Board Research Bulletin* no. 195 (New York: The Conference Board, 1986), 114.

63. John A. Stuckey, *Vertical Integration and Joint Ventures in the Aluminum Industry* (Cambridge: Harvard University Press, 1983); Franklin M. Fisher, John J. McGowan and Joen E. Greenwood, *Folded, Spindled, and Mutilated: Economic Analysis and U.S. v. IBM* (Cambridge: MIT Press, 1983).

64. *Ball Memorial Hospital, Inc.* v. *Mutual Hospital Insurance, Inc.* No. 85–1481, slip op. at 12 (7th Cir. March 4, 1986).

65. F. M. Scherer, "The Posnerian Harvest: Separating Wheat from Chaff," *Yale Law Journal* 86 (April 1977): 974–1002 at p. 995. The elements are paraphrased from Scherer and their accompanying footnotes have been omitted.

2

Strategic Business Behavior and Antitrust

Charles A. Holt and David T. Scheffman

During the seventies business consultants and academics became interested in "business strategy" as an instrument for improving profitability. The emphasis of this approach was generally on actions that a firm could take to improve its long-run competitive position. At about the same time, there was a renewed interest by industrial organization economists and antitrust authorities in the possibility that monopoly power could be created or enhanced through predatory or limit pricing or through use of nonprice instruments such as investments, patents, contracts, and so forth. Finally, the renaissance of game theory that also began in the seventies spawned a renewed interest in theories of oligopoly that explicitly incorporated dynamic and "strategic" elements.

One attempt to bring the business school and industrial organization approaches together was the FTC conference summarized in Salop (1981). At that conference, the leading proponent of the business school strategy perspective, Michael Porter, was brought together with influential proponents of the industrial organization perspective, such as Michael Spence and Steven Salop, in an attempt to develop a synthesis that could be applied in an antitrust context. Although the FTC volume was very useful in stimulating discussion, it did not provide a clear conceptualization of strategic behavior or a framework for evaluating when strategic behavior would be anticompetitive.

Since the FTC conference, all three strands of literature on strategic behavior have mushroomed, and to a significant extent each has followed its own path. For example, Schmalensee's essay on the "new industrial organization" (Schmalensee 1982) and the recent surveys of advances in oligopoly theory (Dixit 1982, Fudenberg and Tirole 1986, and Shapiro 1986) pay little attention to the developing business school literature. As another example, a special issue of the *Journal of Economic Theory* (June 1986), devoted exclusively to strategic behavior, bore no obvious relationship to either the business school or industrial organization literatures. Finally, Michael Porter's recent books on business strategy pass over the other literatures very lightly.

One purpose of this chapter is to relate the antitrust implications of these literatures. We will focus primarily on the industrial organization literature, since that literature has the most to say about antitrust policy, although we will provide a conceptual framework that we believe provides some insight into all three literatures. Our aim has been to provide as technically simple a framework as is possible, consistent with the objective of distilling the antitrust implications of the more theoretical literature.

In the second section we develop a conceptual framework for the analysis of strategic behavior. The section concludes with a definition of strategic behavior. The third section examines the classic models of strategy considered in the antitrust literature: predatory pricing and limit pricing. One topic given considerable attention in this section is the concept of *credibility*, as developed in the game theory literature. In the fourth section the concept of strategic precommitment is developed, beginning with Spence's capacity expansion entry deterrence model. Other types of strategic precommitment are also discussed. The section ends with a discussion of the literature on reputation and entry deterrence. Various types of strategic actions that may facilitate collusion are considered in the fifth section. Finally, the sixth section attempts to summarize the antitrust implications of the recent literature on strategic behavior.

A CONCEPTUAL FRAMEWORK FOR THE ANALYSIS OF STRATEGIC BEHAVIOR

We begin by motivating the issues that arise in the choice of a conceptual framework for the analysis of strategic behavior. Any definition of strategic behavior cannot hope to be all inclusive of the many senses in which the term *strategy* has been used. Since the focus of this chapter and volume is antitrust policy, we will limit our attention to business conduct that could have implications for competition policy.

The primary concern of antitrust is the *direct* exercise of market power, that is, the possibility that a firm or group of firms may be able to reduce output below (or raise price above) the competitive level. The basic model of monopoly that identifies and quantifies the efficiency costs of exercised market power is now well known to both economists and antitrust practitioners.[1] Much of antitrust policy is concerned with simple horizontal conduct that restricts output and this conduct could not usually be termed strategic in any interesting sense. Whatever one takes strategic conduct to be, a price-fixing conspiracy does not generally involve conduct that would merit categorization as strategic.[2] Similarly, strategic conduct beyond the transaction itself is not usually a matter of significant interest in the antitrust analysis of a horizontal merger.[3]

The types of conduct of concern to antitrust that are more appropriately classified as strategic are generally actions that work to create, enhance, or protect market power, often by disadvantaging rivals. Predatory and limit pricing are examples that have received considerable attention. Another type of conduct that has historically been of concern in antitrust is "exclusionary" activity, one example being when a firm acquires control over an asset that is "essential" to its competitors' viability.[4]

We could limit our discussion of business strategies to conduct that injures rivals with the effect of creating or enhancing the market power of the perpetrator. This approach would, in principle, capture most types of strategic business behavior that have traditionally been the concern of the antitrust laws. One problem with this approach would be that it does not encompass all types of anticompetitive strategies, one example being those that *benefit* rivals by facilitating collusion. Would we not, for example, categorize as strategic sellers' adoption of provisions in sales contracts that facilitate collusion?[5]

However, even if we enlarge the scope of our inquiry to encompass some types of collusion-facilitating conduct, there is a more fundamental problem with attempting to limit the menu of actions to those that have anticompetitive effects: How do we determine when a particular strategy is anticompetitive? To understand the nature of this problem better, let us briefly describe the business school and antitrust economics literatures' approaches to business strategy and their relationship to developments in the literature on game theory.

The Business School Approach

The approach to strategy taken in the business school literature is typically based on a detailed consideration of a largely firm-specific historical development of a market. Important aspects of the internal organization of the firm often figure prominently in the analysis. The result is an institutionally rich, stylized model of a firm. What is missing in this approach, from an economic perspective, is a model that integrates the detailed exposition of a firm into an overall market equilibrium. At first glance, many of the strategies examined in the business strategy literature appear anticompetitive. However, it must not be forgotten that the effects of strategies are the result of an *equilibrium* involving the strategies of all the relevant actors in the market. The possibility of anticompetitive effects depends critically on the positions of the firm's actual or potential rivals. The institutional and structural environment faced by the firm places limits on the extent to which *any* type of conduct can be anticompetitive. After all, the essence of competition is to beat your rivals, and much business conduct that has the effect of injuring rivals is procompetitive (that is, improves market performance).[6]

The Antitrust Economics Approach

Naturally, "strategic behavior" as the concept is used in the business school literature can, in some circumstances, have anticompetitive effects. This possibility is the focus of the antitrust economics literature. However, the assumptions of the models of strategic behavior in the antitrust economics literature usually guarantee that the strategist has or can obtain market power, and that efficiency-driven motivations or effects of strategies are absent. This approach is typical in economic modeling, which usually strives for simplicity in assumptions.[7]

Unfortunately, the analysis required to discern the competitive implications of various strategies is much more complex than that used to demonstrate the inefficiency of monopoly pricing. In the simple predatory pricing story, for example, consumers benefit in the short run and only lose in the long run if the predator succeeds in driving out the rival. The efficiency implications of other types of business strategy are even more difficult to derive. Does a large firm that augments its R & D expenditures to foreclose potential rivals impair efficiency because of reduced competition or does it improve efficiency by hastening innovation? Does a firm that designs its products so that only a limited number of firms can produce compatible products injure rivals to the detriment of overall efficiency or does such a policy efficiently police free riding? As a final example, does a set of trading rules agreed upon by competitors that, in principle, restricts competition (for example, the New York Stock Exchange) reduce or improve economic welfare? Of course the antitrust laws generally recognize the ambiguity of the competitive effects of these types of conduct by requiring a rule-of-reason analysis.

It would be useful to catalogue the types of conduct discussed in the business strategy and economics literatures according to the conditions under which the conduct is likely to be anticompetitive. But this would

Figure 1
Residual Demand Model

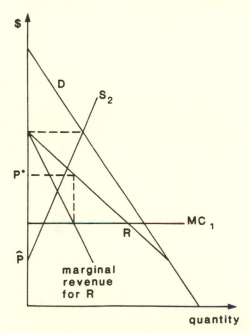

be a very major, if not impossible task; in any event, one that is beyond the scope of this modest survey. We will, however, provide some general discussion of the competitive implications of business strategy.

We will consider a broader category of strategies than those that are necessarily anticompetitive. The business strategy and antitrust economics literatures are primarily concerned with actions that individual firms can take that expand or protect "their demand," generally at the expense of actual or potential rivals, or actions that lower their costs relative to their rivals. A smaller strand of literature is concerned with conduct that could facilitate collusion.

This distinction between practices that disadvantage rivals and those that facilitate collusion can be illustrated with the standard residual demand model in figure 1. Here the market demand is D, the supply of the competitive fringe is S_2, and the horizontal difference between D and S_2 determines the residual demand, R, for the dominant-firm producer. The dominant firm, denoted G_1, will typically set a price, p^*, above its marginal cost, MC_1, as shown in figure 1, but no strategically interesting conduct is present.[8] Strategic actions would be those designed to shift the residual demand curve upward, which would be accomplished by shifting D or S_2. For example, the dominant firm might be able to shift S_2 by "overbuying" a critical input used by the fringe in order to raise that input's price, or by obtaining a cost-increasing regulatory change.[9] Alternatively, residual demand could be shifted if market demand, D, could be shifted, for example, by advertising or aggressive product promotion.[10] It is easily seen that strategic actions would be profitable if they result in a vertical shift in R that exceeds the vertical shift in the dominant firm's average cost.[11]

Besides strategies that disadvantage rivals, producers might find it profitable to engage in forms of conduct that facilitate collusion. Suppose, for example, that there are several producers in G_1, with a supply curve MC_1, who somehow get themselves to act as if their supply curve were a higher supply curve that intersected R at the price p^* in figure 1. If such a strategy were not too costly, it would obviously be profitable. How would such a strategy work? Intuitively, since a competitor's supply is governed by his marginal costs, the strategy should change the producers' marginal costs. One method to accomplish this would be to sign contracts with suppliers of a critical input with prices that increase with the quantity purchased, but that preserved the nonstrategic *average* input price.[12]

There are many other types of strategic actions that can be analyzed with the residual demand model. For example, if learning by doing causes a firm's costs to shift down over time, the dominant firm may wish to expand its own market share by cutting price below p^*.[13] A second example is predatory pricing; a price below p in figure 1 would result in the exit of fringe firms. Both of these examples are dynamic in nature, and will be discussed more fully later after the necessary game-theoretic concepts are introduced.

The Game Theory Approach

Although residual demand analysis can be used to model a variety of interesting strategies, it is limited in two important respects: the simplistic modeling of the "victim" of the strategy and the basically static nature of the analysis. Much of the economics literature has been concerned with dynamic, oligopolistic models of strategy. In his introduction to *Strategy, Predation, and Antitrust Analysis*, Salop (1981, 1–2) contrasts the dynamic oligopoly emphasis of the "strategic approach" with traditional analysis that "... focused on oligopolistic interaction at a single moment of time among sellers who ignored the responses of rivals." The residual demand analysis that we have described thus far depends critically on the assumption that the firms in group 2 acted independently and competitively. If the "fringe" producers act as oligopolists or strategically in a more general sense, we could no longer

Table 1
Profits

---

with p = 10-2(q$_E$+q$_I$) and AC$_i$ = 4
(profit for firm I, profit for firm E)

	q$_E$=0	q$_E$=1
q$_I$=1	(4,0)	(2,2)
q$_I$=1.5	(4.5,0)	(1.5,.5)
q$_I$=2	(4,0)	(0,0)
q$_I$=2.5	(2.5,0)	(-2.5,-1)

represent their behavior by a competitive supply curve such as S_2. Game theory provides a method for analyzing such a situation.

In traditional static oligopoly models a firm's behavior is summarized by a *best response function* that specifies the optimal decision of the firm as a function of decisions made by rivals.[14] For example, suppose that firms E and I produce quantities denoted by q_E and q_I, respectively, and that price is determined by an industry demand function: $p = 10 - 2(q_E + q_I)$. Firm E, the "entrant," has a capacity of 1 if it enters, and firm I, the "incumbent," has a capacity of 5/2. If each firm has constant average cost of 4, the profits for various output combinations are as shown in table 1. In the language of game theory, the table shows the relationship between the players' strategies (choice of outputs) and their payoffs (profits).

The best response for firm I is 1.5 if $q_E = 0$ and it is 1 if q_E is 1. The best response for firm E is 1 if q_I is less than 2 and 0 if q_I is greater than 2. As a matter of convention we assume that entry will not occur unless profits are *strictly positive*.[15] In table 1, profit levels for best responses are underlined, and it is apparent that the best responses for the two firms lead to an equilibrium in which each firm produces 1 unit. This is a *Cournot* equilibrium or, equivalently, a set of outputs that are consistent with these best response functions; that is, each firm's output is optimal given the outputs of the others, so no firm has an incentive to change its output *unilaterally*.[16]

Notice that each firm's best response in table 1 tends to decrease as

Figure 2
Cournot Model

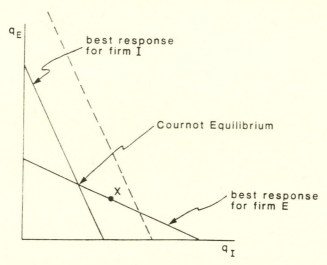

the other firm's output increases. If output quantities can be varied continuously, the best response functions for firms in a homogeneous product industry can be graphed as lines, and the Cournot equilibrium is depicted as the intersection of the duopolist's best response functions, as in figure 2.

One of the earliest formal models of strategy is the Stackleberg duopoly model. In that model one duopolist is able to make a binding output choice, which the other reacts to. Thus, the leader essentially chooses his preferred point on the follower's best response function. This point would typically give the leader a higher market share; point X in figure 2 could be such a point in which firm 1 is a leader. In table 1, the incumbent would lead with $q_I = 2$, since we assume that the entrant will not enter unless profits are strictly positive. Thus, the incumbent would earn a profit of 4 as a leader, as compared with a profit of 2 in the Cournot example. To become a Stackleberg leader, the firm would have to devise a strategic action that enables it to commit itself to an output first and then convey this information to the others.

It is easy to see how strategies of the type considered in our residual demand analysis can be modelled in a Cournot oligopoly model. A strategy that raises a rival Cournot oligopolist's costs would generally have the effect of shifting the rival's best response function in toward the origin, leading to higher profits for the other, "strategic," duopolist. Strategies that lower a firm's own costs shift its best response function out, expanding its share of the market.[17] Recent research has been concerned with how contracts between competitors or with buyers can facilitate responding profitability to interdependence, in essence by making the firms' best response functions explicitly take into account interdependence.

Although thus far we have considered only the Cournot model, it should be clear that the game-theoretic approach is easily generalized to other oligopoly models in which the strategic variables may be prices, advertising, and so forth. If there are strategies available to shift best response functions in these models, such strategies may be profitable, depending, of course, on the costs incurred in adopting such strategies and on the equilibrium outcome. Examples in the economics literature abound, although the models are generally dynamic.

The easiest way to bring in dynamic considerations is to model firms' activities as a two-stage game, where some strategic action is taken "today" in order to produce a result "tomorrow." At their core, such two-stage models are simply elaborations of the static oligopoly games that we have just discussed. The analysis of the second stage typically involves an oligopoly model of some sort, such as Cournot. The actions taken in the first stage determine the nature of the best response functions that, in turn, determine the equilibrium decisions in the second stage. For example, an expansion in capacity may shift a firm's own best response function outward at high output levels, enabling it to deter entry (by guaranteeing low postentry prices) and earn greater profits in future periods of increased demand. Alternatively, a firm may engage in cost-raising strategies that shift its rivals' best response functions.

A Definition of Strategic Behavior

The preceding discussion in this section suggests the following definition of strategic behavior: Strategic behavior involves actions that affect the best response functions of the "strategist" or of its rivals in a subsequent period. In game-theoretic terms, a strategic action affects the structure of the "subgame" that will be encountered in subsequent periods.

PREDATORY AND LIMIT PRICING

The Classical Approach

The strategy given the most attention in the antitrust literature is predatory pricing. The idea of driving one's competitors out of business by underpricing them in order to gain a monopoly is very old, certainly antedating the provisions in the Sherman Act that deal with this sort of conduct. Limit pricing is analogous to predatory pricing. The only difference is that an entrant must bear the costs of entering that have already been borne by incumbents. If none of the costs of entry are sunk, predatory pricing is exactly analogous to limit pricing.

Early notions of predation were based on the premise that the predator's power derived simply from its size relative to its victim. In essence, the model was of a bully who inflicted damage on his victim by price cuts. However, economists have long recognized that the predator needed some sort of cost advantage over its prey for price predation to be both successful and profitable.[18]

Naturally, if the predator has a sufficient advantage over its prey, predation will be both successful and profitable. However, in a situation in which the predator and prey have complete knowledge of demand and each other's costs, and the predator has a sufficient cost advantage that the net benefits of bankrupting the prey are positive, there is nothing in the predator's actions that is very interesting from a strategic perspective.[19] The predator's strategy simply involves a calculation of the relative profitability of predation and accommodation. Similarly, if the prey is fully cognizant of the facts that go into the predator's calculus, the only "strategy" of interest to the fringe is the most profitable method and time to exit. Indeed, given such a scenario, it is unclear why the prey was ever in the market.[20]

Besides the absence of an interesting strategic issue, this simple model of predatory pricing provides little to discuss from a policy perspective. Under some elaborations of this story, the source of the predator's cost advantage could justify an argument that its eventual monopoly was "thrust upon" it, so that its "predatory pricing" incurred no antitrust liability. Alternatively, independent of the source of its cost advantage, if the size of the predator's cost advantage were sufficiently large that the predatory price exceeded the predator's average variable costs, its actions would incur no antitrust liability under the Areeda-Turner rule.

Rather than focus on whether the predator has any advantage over the prey, other than size, some discussions of predatory pricing have suggested that it may be possible to obtain a monopoly by a "threat" to outlast the other firm(s) in a price war. In essence, the theory behind the predator's threat is that the threat can convince the prey that the predator will continue the price war at whatever cost, until the prey exits. In considering whether such a threat would be viable, the discussion generally focused on whether the predator had sufficient financial resources (for example, a "deeper pocket") to outlast the prey. Before we discuss the viability of such threats, it is useful to introduce a simple example that illustrates the strategic possibilities for the

Figure 3
Entry Deterrence Model

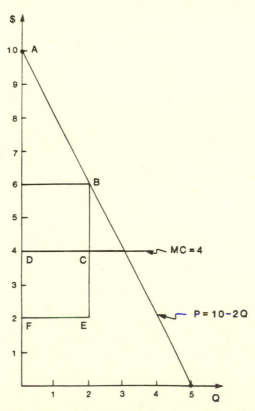

dominant firm with a size advantage. For expositional simplicity we will discuss the model in terms of limit pricing instead of predation, but we will show that the general results are applicable to predation.

We begin with a variation of the example of the previous section. As before, demand is linear: $p = 10 - 2Q$, as shown in figure 3. The outputs of the (potential) entrant and the incumbent are denoted by q_E and q_I, respectively. The incumbent is assumed here to have a sunk cost of $3/2$ and a constant marginal cost of $4 per unit of output. We assume that the entrant can only have a capacity of one unit, so the entrant's marginal cost curve becomes vertical at $q_E = 1$. It is also assumed that an entrant would incur a fixed cost (per unit of time) of $1, and that the entrant's marginal costs are also $4. Since the entrant's capacity cannot exceed 1, the only advantage of the incumbent is one of maximum size.

As a matter of convention, we again assume that entry will not occur

Table 2
Sylos Postulate Entry Deterrence Example

$$p = 10 - 2q_E - 2q_I$$

marginal cost of entrant = $4

fixed cost of entrant = $1

capacity of entrant = 1

apparent limit price = $5 (with $q_I = 5/2$, $V_I = 1$)

apparent limit price under Sylos = $7 (with $q_I = 3/2$, $V_I = 3$)

unless anticipated profits are strictly positive (rather than nonnegative). In this example, a price of $5 would appear to deter entry (or induce exit of the entrant) because, with a marginal cost of $4, there is no feasible output for the entrant that would yield operating profits in excess of the fixed costs of $1. The incumbent would sell 5/2 units of output at the limit price, which is above the output of 3/2 that maximizes profit in the absence of entry (as can be seen by subtracting the fixed cost from the incumbent's profit numbers in the left column of table 1).

Notice that a policy of maintaining the price at $5 in the event of entry means that the incumbent accommodates the entrant by keeping *industry* output constant in spite of entry. In other words, the incumbent reduces its output by the increment added by the entrant. Modigliani (1958) argued that it was not reasonable for the entrant to expect that the incumbent would reduce output in the event of entry; instead, the incumbent would be more likely to adopt a tough posture of maintaining its output at preentry levels, so that entry would raise industry output and lower price.[21] The assumption that the incumbent would maintain his preentry level of output is known as the *Sylos Postulate*. The analysis that follows from this postulate indicates that the incumbent firm will choose a preentry output level large enough that maintaining this level postentry does not permit profitable entry. In our numerical example, an output of 3/2, resulting in a price of $7, will apparently deter entry because the entrant's postentry output of one will reduce price to $5, a price that equals the entrant's fixed plus variable costs. Profits are denoted V_E and V_I.

Credibility and Price Strategies

What is critical to the success of either the simple limit pricing or Sylos-pricing policies is the entrant's forecast of the postentry price,

not the actual value of the preentry price. The connection made between beliefs and the preentry price is that in simple limit-pricing
models the entrant is assumed to believe that the preentry price (or
output, in the case of Sylos) will be the incumbent's postentry price
(or output). To examine the tenability of this assumption, let us make
some more assumptions about the entrant. Assume that the entrant's
fixed costs are sunk, that is, that he must incur a cost of one per period,
whether or not he produces, since the assets have no value outside this
industry. Assume further that there are no shut-down or start-up costs
for his plant.

Now consider what would happen if, for some reason, entry occurred
at either the limit or Sylos price. At any price above marginal cost ($4)
the entrant would produce its capacity output of 1. A price below $4
would reduce the entrant's production to zero, but the entrant would
not exit the industry, since, by assumption, all his costs are sunk. After
entry, the incumbent would face a residual demand obtained by shifting the market demand curve in figure 3 to the left by one unit for
any price at or above $4.[22] It is straightforward to show that the best
response of the incumbent to entry would be to select a price of $6 and
produce an output of one (the profit-maximizing response, given his
residual demand curve). One way to see this is to note that subtracting
fixed costs from the relevant entries in table 1 has no effect on the
incumbent's best response function.

If the potential entrant had this knowledge, what should he make
of the incumbent's threat to price at $5 post-entry? The threat to cut
price to $5 by producing an output of 3/2 in response to entry is not
credible since the incumbent's only rational response to entry would
be to select a price of $6 (because a $2 price-cost margin on 1 unit is
better than a $1 margin on 3/2 units). Notice that under the assump-
tions we have made in this example the preentry price is irrelevant to
the entrant's decision whether to enter. Unless the entrant is convinced
that the incumbent will act irrationally in the face of entry, entry is
profitable and cannot be deterred.

Credibility and the Concept of Subgame Perfect Equilibrium

The lesson of the preceding example is that threats are unlikely to
work unless they are credible, where by credible we mean that the
action taken by the firm at a specific time is in its own best interest
at that time, given both previous and anticipated actions of its rivals.
The rationality condition that requires that strategies be credible is
called "subgame perfectness" in the game-theoretic literature.[23] To
illustrate this concept further, consider a situation (formally, a game)
in which the entrant decides whether to enter, and then output deci-

Table 3
Strategies
(with a Noncredible Threat)

Incumbent's Strategy: if no entry, $q_I = 3/2$　(and p = $7)

if entry occurs, $q_I = 3/2$　(and p = $5)

Potential Entrant's Strategy: not to enter in the first stage,

$q_E = 0$ in the second stage.

sions are made based on the knowledge of whether entry has occurred. In game-theoretic terms a strategy for each firm will specify exactly what decision that firm will make in each possible contingency. Consider the strategies of the firms in table 3.

For these strategies to constitute an equilibrium, each strategy must represent a firm's best response to the other's strategy.[24] In other words, no *unilateral* change in either firm's strategy will increase its own profit. The strategies listed above are clearly an equilibrium in this sense; the entrant should not enter if the incumbent is going to maintain output in the event of entry, and the incumbent should produce an output of 3/2 if entry does not occur. (There is also another equilibrium which will be described below.)

Subgame perfectness requires a stronger condition for equilibrium. It requires that each action specified in each firm's strategy represents the best response of that firm to *any* action that is known to have been taken by its rivals, that is, that strategies are credible. For the strategies in table 3, the action specified by the incumbent's strategy in the event of entry ($q_1 = 3/2$) is not credible because this action is not the incumbent's best response if the potential entrant actually does enter. (Recall that q_1 is the best response to entry.)

The only subgame-perfect equilibrium for this example is one in which there is entry and both firms produce outputs of one in the second stage; this level of output is the profit-maximizing response for each firm to the output of one by the other firm. Recall that the incumbent's fixed cost is $3/2, and it operates with excess capacity in this equilibrium. Then, it follows from the relevant areas in figure 3 that the entrant's and incumbent's profits are, respectively, $V_E = 1$, $V_I = 1/2$. Welfare, measured as the sum of consumers' and producers' surplus, is 11/2, which is calculated by subtracting the sum of the fixed costs (1 + 3/2) from the area ABCD in figure 3 (area ABCD = 8). Letting W denote aggregate net welfare, we can summarize this analysis (table 4):

Table 4
Subgame Perfect Equilibrium

Entrant's Strategy: enter in first stage

$$q_E = 1$$

Incumbent's Strategy: if no entry, $q_I = 3/2$ (and p = $7)

if entry occurs, $q_I = 1$ (and p = $6)

Equilibrium Outcome: $q_E = q_I = 1$

$p = \$6, W = 11/2, V_E = 1, V_I = 1/2.$

The analysis of this example illustrates the general result that price itself cannot be used as a weapon to deter entry of a firm if the incumbent's best response in the face of entry is to accommodate. This will always be the case if the potential entrant is as efficient as the incumbent, unless, of course, natural monopoly problems require that there be only one firm in the market. Similarly, a predatory pricing strategy will not be a credible strategy for forcing the exit of an equally efficient firm. However, the discussion of "reputation" models later in this chapter will show that a price-cutting response to entry can deter future entry if the entrant is uncertain about the incumbent's costs.

To sum up, predatory or limit-pricing strategies as threats are not likely to be credible unless there are some significant asymmetries between the incumbent and the entrant. Strategies that result in successful predation or limited entry are more likely to involve nonprice instruments. We begin our discussion of such instruments in the next section.

CREDIBLE STRATEGIES THAT DETER ENTRY

Strategic Investment

Antitrust experts have been concerned with capacity expansion at least since Judge Learned Hand's famous dictum in *Alcoa*: "Nothing compelled it [Alcoa] to keep doubling and redoubling capacity before others entered the field."[25] In his seminal analysis of strategic behavior, Spence (1977) presented a formal analysis of a strategic investment in capacity that would alter an incumbent's costs in a manner that deterred entry.[26] An investment of this kind fits our definition of a stra-

Table 5
Incumbent's Postinvestment Position in the Event of Entry

	$6	$5	$4
price			
quantity	1	3/2	2
variable cost	2	3	4
fixed (sunk) cost	11/2	11/2	11/2
incumbent's profit	-$3/2	-$1	-$3/2

tegic action because, by taking an action that alters its own costs, the firm alters *its own* ex post incentives in a manner that benefits itself. To see how this would work, consider the following modification of our earlier example.

Suppose now that the incumbent can make an *irreversible* investment that costs $2 per unit of capacity and that results in a marginal cost of $2.[27] This new investment has a higher fixed cost and a lower marginal cost than the existing capacity. We will show that there is an equilibrium in which the incumbent invests in two units of new capacity and thereby successfully deters entry. Since investments are irreversible, the incumbent retains the fixed cost of the old, unused capital, and so the incumbent's fixed cost following the strategic investment would be $11/2 (per unit of time).[28]

The model now has three stages. In the first stage the incumbent makes a decision on an irreversible investment; in the second stage the entrant observes whether the investment is made and decides whether to enter; then, outputs are selected by firms in the market in the final stage. To derive the equilibrium of this model, first consider what would happen if both investment and entry occurred. Recall that the entrant will produce at his capacity of one unit if price exceeds his marginal cost of $4. Using this information, it is straightforward to show the incumbents' opportunities (see table 5).Thus, once the investment is made, the incumbent has an incentive to respond to entry by maintaining output at 3/2 and letting price fall to $5. The incumbent's profit is negative at this output, but profit would be even lower at all other outputs, since the investment is irreversible.[29]

The effect of strategic investment in this example is to change the incumbent's best response function, and the result is that the incumbent's incentives are altered in a manner that makes it credible to charge the entry-deterring price even if entry occurs. The only equilibrium that satisfies the subgame-perfect criterion now involves investment, no entry, and an output of two (which is the monopoly output for the incumbent with a marginal cost of $2). The resulting price will be $6 and the incumbent's profit will be $5/2, and so the strategic investment permits the incumbent to deter entry and raise profit above the level that would result in the subgame-perfect equilibrium without the investment.[30]

Irreversible investment makes an entry-deterring strategy credible because it alters the incumbent's best response in the face of entry. However, notice that we assumed in our example that there is a cost-effective way of reducing marginal costs to two. Naturally, the viability of such strategies depends on their costs. Besides the cost-effectiveness issue, this sort of strategic investment assumes the ability to preempt, that is, that the incumbent can take an action prior to the entrant, since if entry occurred prior to the incumbent's strategic investment, that investment would no longer be profitable.[31] Although the incumbent would seem to have a natural "first-mover" advantage, he may also have some disadvantages. The entrant, in principle, has the advantage of more flexibility, being able to decide everything from scratch. This can make strategic investment risky for the incumbent if technology or other market conditions change. We will discuss these issues further when we summarize the antitrust implications of strategic behavior.

The welfare implications of strategic investment in this section's example are quite interesting. It is easily shown that the strategic equilibrium results in aggregate net welfare of 13/2 (per unit of time).[32] This level of welfare is *greater* than the level of welfare of 11/2 in the subgame-perfect equilibrium with no strategic investment, which is given in table 4. To see why welfare has improved, notice that industry output (two units) and price ($6) are the same in each equilibrium (leaving consumer surplus unchanged), but producer surplus has increased from $3/2 to $5/2. Producer surplus is higher in the strategic equilibrium because the investment enables the incumbent to be more efficient than the entrant, and this gain more than offsets the cost of the increased capacity.[33] Of course, the welfare effect depended on the costs of the strategic investment. If, for example, the $4 incremental costs of the strategic investment were instead assumed to be between $5 and $6, the investment would still profitably deter entry, but welfare would fall because producer surplus would fall below 3/2.

Strategic Underinvestment

The typical preemptive capacity expansion model predicts precommitment to low variable costs through overinvestment as a method of

Figure 4
Bertrand Model

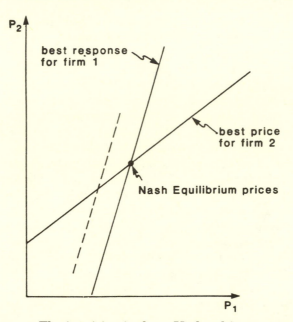

entry deterrence. The intuition is clear: Under this assumption a strategy that reduced one of the firm's marginal costs would shift his best response function out, resulting in a decrease in his competitor's output in equilibrium, and this could increase the strategist's profits if the costs of reducing marginal costs were sufficiently low.

However, this intuition is not always valid; the profitable strategy in some situations results in the equivalent of *under*investment. Needless to say, this complicates the policy application of strategic models, an issue we will return to below. Suppose, for example, that instead of a Cournot duopoly, the duopolists are price setters with differentiated products. We assume here that the price setters take the price of their competitor as given. The best response functions of the duopolists can now be drawn in a graph where the prices of the two producers are measured on the axes, as in figure 4. Notice that price-setting duopolists (assuming the products are substitutes) have upward sloping best response functions, that is, the optimal price of one duopolist is an increasing function of the price charged by the other.

Consider now our earlier analysis of strategic investment: an investment for one firm that lowers its marginal cost shifts out its best response function, causing the rival's output to shrink, in a *Cournot* duopoly. In a price-setting duopoly, however, lowering one's own marginal costs results in lower best response prices for you (as shown by the dashed line for firm 1 in figure 4), leading one's rival to lower his price in equilibrium (and, therefore, increase his output). The result is an equilibrium with greater output for both firms. Thus, investment that, for example, simply reallocates some variable costs to fixed costs, may hurt the price-setting duopolist, since the result is greater output by both him and his rival.

Similarly, although actions that raise the rival's costs can be powerful strategies (if cost effective), sometimes raising your costs relative to your rivals is a profitable strategy, since it may commit you to a high-price strategy that they will follow. These effects are analyzed in more detail in Fudenberg and Tirole (1984).

There are other reasons why a profitable strategy may involve underinvestment. Consider, for example, R & D as a strategic instrument. An incumbent with large sunk costs may have less of an incentive to innovate, ceteris paribus, than an entrant with no sunk costs, and therefore he may have an incentive to accommodate an innovating entrant.[34] In order to credibly deter entry through R & D expenditures then, it may be profitable for the incumbent to underinvest, since that strategy credibly maximizes the incumbent's incentives to respond aggressively to the threat of an R & D race.

Strategic Effects of Long-term Contracts: Meet-or-Release and Most-Favored-Customer-Contracts

Long-term contracts, like sunk investments, under some conditions can deter entry. As an example, suppose that the incumbent has signed a contract in which buyers agree not to divert purchases from the incumbent to an entrant as long as the incumbent matches a lower price offered by the entrant. Such clauses are known as "meet or release" provisions. In addition, we assume that the contract contains "most favored customer" provisions that preclude preferential discounts, that is, a discount offer given to one buyer must be given to all. The competitive effects of such contractual provisions has received considerable attention recently. Salop (1986), for example, noted that meet-or-release provisions may provide the incumbent with a credible contractual method of maintaining output in the face of entry. In *Ethyl*, the FTC argued that most-favored-customer clauses deterred aggressive discounting.[35]

We will illustrate the effects of these contractual provisions in the context of the Sylos postulate entry deterrence example of table 2. Recall that the incumbent with a marginal cost of four can deter entry with the "Sylos price" of seven and the corresponding output of 3/2, provided that this output is protected by meet-or-release clauses.

But when the long-term contracts expire, the entrant may be able to compete on an equal footing, so contracts with meet-or-release clauses may not deter entry permanently. This possibility can be illustrated in the context of the example summarized in table 2. For simplicity, we alter the example by allowing only one size plant, that with a capacity of 3/2 and a fixed cost of 3/2. Since fixed cost equals capacity and marginal cost equals four for each firm, the long run competitive price is five. The issues to be analyzed are whether entry can be deterred and whether price can be maintained above the competitive level.[36]

Suppose that the incumbent has announced in advance that its list price will be six, which is between the Sylos and competitive levels. If the potential entrant decides to enter he will not announce a higher list price since he would get no business. We assume that the entrant matches the list price of six but retains the option of offering a subsequent list price reduction, which we will call a discount. The entrant in this example has three choices: not enter and earn a profit of zero, enter with a list price of six and not discount, and enter with a list price of six and offer a discount price of five (a price below five would never be profitable). If entry occurs, we assume that each firm contracts to sell one unit, which is half of the market demand at the common list price of six. Then each firm decides whether to discount before knowing the other's discount decision. Thus, a discount in this example is a unilateral, across-the-board reduction in list price, which also must be offered to existing buyers with most-favored-customer clauses. The discount decisions are simultaneous, although because of meet-or-release clauses in sales contracts, each firm has the contractual right to retain its own sales if it subsequently matches the other's discount.

In order to decide what to do, the potential entrant must consider what happens if entry occurs. If entry is observed, there are four outcomes that can occur since each firm then decides whether to discount from the common list price. If neither discounts, each sells one unit at a price of six and incurs a variable cost of four and a fixed cost of 3/2, so profits are 1/2 each, as shown in the upper left-hand box of table 6. If both firms discount to five and the additional market demand of one-half unit is divided equally between them, their profits will be −1/4 each. If one firm discounts and the other does not, the discounter obtains all of the additional market demand (one-half unit), but the other firm is able to retain all of its contract sales (one unit, at the price it must meet, five), which permits it to cover some of its fixed cost. Since the discounter has to offer the discount price of five on both the previously contracted sales of one unit and the new sales of one-half unit, the discounter earns a profit of zero. The firm that did not initiate the discount earns a profit of −1/2 because it operates with excess capacity.

Table 6 illustrates the way in which contracts with meet-or-release

Table 6
Entry Subgame

(entrant's profit, incumbent's profit)

incumbent's decisions:

		not discount	*discount*
entrant's decisions:	*not discount*	(1/2, 1/2)	(-1/2, 0)
	discount	(0, -1/2)	(-1/4, -1/4)

and most-favored-customer clauses may result in supracompetitive list prices that are stable with respect to unilateral across-the-board discounts; if one firm thinks that the other will not discount, then it is in his own interest not to discount.[37] In other words, unilateral discounts from a list price of six will be unprofitable in the entry subgame in table 6. And if neither firm discounts, profits are positive, so one subgame-perfect equilibrium outcome is entry with no discounting.[38]

Refinement of Subgame Perfectness

In the last several years game theorists have realized that the notion of subgame perfectness needs to be refined because it often admits "too many" equilibria, some of which are not sensible. For example, note that simultaneous discounting is also an equilibrium in table 6, since if a firm thinks that its rival will discount, then its best response is to discount. Thus, there are two outcomes in the subgame of table 6 that are equilibria in the sense that a unilateral deviation by either firm is unprofitable. The discounting equilibrium in the entry subgame results in negative profits, so one subgame-perfect equilibrium for the game as a whole is for the potential entrant to stay out and for the incumbent to discount in the event of entry.[39] (Remember that a strategy specifies what a player will do in each contingency, so the incumbent's strategy specifies what he will do in the face of entry, *even though entry does not occur in equilibrium.*)

How can we choose between the two quite different equilibrium outcomes? This question is related to the issue of what beliefs in the post-entry game are reasonable. The subgame-perfect equilibrium with discounting and no entry is not "sensible" in that the only reason to enter the market would be to earn positive profits, which is not possible if the entrant discounts. Thus, it would be reasonable for the incumbent, having observed entry, to infer that the entrant will not offer a discount in this example.

In essence, the entrant is able to make the following "speech" to the incumbent: "We both know that, by entering, I gave up the option to earn a zero (economic) profit with certainty, and I would not have done this unless I expected to do better in competition with you, so you should infer that I will not discount, and therefore you should not discount." It is important to note that the analysis of the entry subgame here depends on an event, entry, that occurred *previously*.[40]

Other Models of Strategic Entry Deterrence[41]

The simple model of strategic investment discussed above exhibits the essential feature of one type of strategic-entry-deterrence model— the incumbent makes irreversible commitments that affect *his* costs sufficiently that the postentry price would be unprofitable for the entrant. In terms of the analysis of the second section, this type of model involves the incumbent making an irreversible commitment that changes his postentry best response function. In a one-incumbent model that action results in the market being a natural monopoly. In a model with more than one incumbent, strategic precommitments by the incumbents may result in the exit of some incumbents and entry deterrence against potential entrants, thereby enhancing or protecting profits in an oligopoly equilibrium.

We will now briefly summarize some of the other main strategic instruments of entry deterrence that have been considered in the literature. The central feature of these strategies are that they are designed to increase the strategist's profitability at the expense of his (actual or potential) rivals. These other strategies include:

1. Learning by Doing. In this type of model current costs are a decreasing function of past cumulative output. The incumbent increases production to get further down the learning curve, lowering his marginal costs and the postentry price.

2. R & D Investment and Preemptive Patenting. Here, the incumbent races to beat potential entrants to technologies with which they could enter and compete by developing and patenting them first. Some of the R & D models are similar to the learning-by-doing models in that the incumbent speeds up R & D to lower his costs. In the preemptive-patenting models the incumbent may not lower his own costs (for example, in the case of "sleeping patents") but he raises the costs of entry.

3. Product Selection. The incumbent may "fill up" product space through product or brand proliferation, or locational preemption, leaving no viable niche

for an entrant. Another possibility is to create a "fighting brand" to raise the marketing costs of a new entrant.

4. Advertising. If there are economies of scale in advertising, the incumbent might engage in "excessive" advertising if this can raise the unit costs of an entrant more than his own unit costs.

5. Cost-Increasing Input Purchases. One method by which an incumbent can convert variable into fixed costs is by contracting for inputs in a way that converts input costs into fixed costs. Requirements of "take or pay" contracts have this effect. The result is to lower marginal costs by converting some variable costs into fixed costs. Another strategy involves overpurchasing inputs to increase their price to the entrant. For example, if the incumbent is partially vertically integrated, raising the "market" price of his produced input raises the entrant's marginal costs more than the incumbent's average costs. Such a strategy might be accomplished either by continuously overbuying inputs in the market, or foreclosing access to inputs by buying up their suppliers. Entrants' costs can also be raised by regulations that "grandfather" incumbents or by preempting otherwise cost-efficient choices of entrants.

This list is not exhaustive, but it does summarize the most prominently considered strategic instruments that we have not already discussed in more detail. Although the instruments differ substantially, they all have the same effect: they change either the incumbent's or entrants' best response function (or both). As discussed in the second section, strategies that shift the strategist's or his rivals' best response functions can be profitable even if they do not result in predation or entry deterrence, and so any of the strategies we have enumerated could be profitable strategies even if they don't deter all entry or cause rivals to exit. Finally, however, as discussed above, without more structure and institutional detail, the nature of the profitable precommitment is generally ambiguous; a profitable strategy may involve the equivalent of either over- or underinvestment.

Incomplete Information and Reputation

All of the strategic actions discussed above involve *nonprice* instruments that alter the *structure* of the subsequent subgames (that is, the strategic actions changed at least some of the best responses of the participants in the game). Strategies based on price alone did not deter entry because these strategies did not alter the structure of the subsequent subgames. In this section we will show that it may be possible to deter entry without using a nonprice instrument by "fighting" attempted entry, if the entrant is uncertain about the incumbent's costs.

The discussion will be based on the following example. Suppose that there are just two kinds of incumbents. "Weak incumbents" are not

Table 7
Profits for Relevant Output Combinations

Outcome	Profits of entrant (FC=3/2, MC=4)	Profits of "weak" incumbent (FC=3/2, MC=4)	Profits of "strong" incumbent (FC=11/2,MC=2)
no entry (monopoly q_I)	0	3 (q_I=3/2)	5/2 (q_I=2)
entry accommodated (q_E=1, q_I=1)	1/2	1/2	-3/2
entry contested (q_E=1, q_I=3/2)	-1/2	0	-1

willing to fight an entrant by holding their output at preentry levels if entry occurs. But "strong incumbents," like the one who made the strategic investment in our earlier example, have marginal costs sufficiently low to make such a fighting response credible. If the entrant does not know with certainty which type of incumbent he is facing, then a multiperiod setting a *weak* incumbent may fight any entrant in early periods in order to establish a "reputation" of being tough and to thereby deter subsequent entry.[42] Models with such reputation effects were first analyzed in Kreps and Wilson (1982) and in Milgrom and Roberts (1982b).

The effects of reputation can be illustrated in the context of our ongoing numerical example of strategic entry deterrence. Suppose now that the entrant can enter with a fixed cost of 3/2 per period that is *not* a sunk cost.[43] Suppose, further, that the entrant knows that there are only two types of incumbents, and a weak incumbent has a fixed cost of 3/2 and a marginal cost of four, while a strong incumbent has fixed cost of 11/2 and a marginal cost of two.[44] The entrant's beliefs about the strength of the incumbent are summarized by the probability that the entrant is strong, denoted X. The incumbent, of course, knows with certainty whether he is strong or weak.

Again, using the demand function $p = 10 - 2q_I - 2q_E$, we can compute firms' single-period profits for aggressive ($q_I = 3/2$) and for accommodating ($q_I = 1$) responses to entry. The firms' profits for the relevant output combinations are given in table 7.

Consistent with our earlier discussion of this example, table 7 shows that a weak incumbent will prefer to accommodate entry, but a strong incumbent will not. It is straightforward to show that a potential entrant will not enter in a one-period game (or in the final period of a longer game) if the probability that the incumbent is strong is greater than one-half.

Now consider a two-period model in which the entrant holds the belief that the incumbent is strong with a probability X that is greater than one-half. We will take this probability to represent the entrant's beliefs at the beginning of period 1. The entrant could consider entering in period 1 in an effort to determine the incumbent's type. If the incumbent accommodates entry, this response would obviously reveal the incumbent to be weak, and thereby induce entry again in the final period, since a weak incumbent will always accommodate in the last period. Following Kreps and Wilson, assume that an entrant who observes the fighting response ($q_I = 3/2$), will not revise his prior beliefs of the probability (X) that the incumbent is strong.[45] Therefore, a fighting response to entry in the first period will also deter entry in the second period because the entrant believes that the incumbent is more likely to be strong and hence that the profit of $-1/2$ is more likely than the profit of $1/2$.

Even a weak incumbent in this example will wish to fight entry in the first period because his profits of zero in the first period would rise to the monopoly profit of three in the final period, which yields a greater total profit than the profit of $1/2$ in each period that results from accommodating entry. (Recall that accommodation in the first period will also induce entry in the second.) Thus, there is an equilibrium in which both types of incumbents contest entry in the first period, and the entrant does not enter in either period. The conclusion is that the entrant's uncertainty about the incumbent's cost type can result in an equilibrium in which the incumbent would fight entry in an early stage in order to build a reputation that deters entry in a later stage.[46]

The implications of models such as this one are unclear. These models typically have many possible equilibria, including both entry and deterrence, and the structures of the models sometimes provide little insight into what equilibrium will be attained. The problem here is partly a technical one, involving what is the appropriate definition of equilibrium. However, perhaps the most interesting development in modern oligopoly theory is the growing consensus that institutional details and especially, industry history, are critical determinants of what sort of equilibrium an industry will reach.[47] Thus, although oligopoly theory is becoming increasingly technical, it is moving in the direction of the business school literature in its emphasis on institutional and historical detail. Until it has moved much farther, the literature on reputation and uncertainty provides little that is applicable to policy issues.

COLLUSION-FACILITATING PRACTICES

Up until now, the focus of our discussion has been on strategies that injure rivals such as predation and entry deterrence. Strategies that benefit rivals by facilitating collusion are also possible. Such strategies fall into two categories. First, firms can commit to high prices by changing the mixture of their costs in a way that raises marginal costs. Of course such a strategy will generally have to be effected in concert (explicitly or tacitly) to be successful. (In addition, a high marginal cost strategy leaves the firms more vulnerable to entry.) The second type of collusion-facilitating strategy involves commitments that result in more "interdependent" best response functions. A strategy that commits a firm to follow a competitor's price cuts changes its and its competitors' best response functions. As shown above, the use of meet-or-release and most-favored-customer provisions in long-term contracts may have this effect.[48] An example that has long been thought to be a method of facilitating collusion is adoption of basing-point pricing.[49] Basing-point pricing changes the firms' best response functions for prices at particular locations. Another example that has concerned antitrust authorities is "price signaling" through advance announcement of price changes in the media. Finally, some recent research has examined the effect of interfirm exchange agreements on tacit coordination.[50]

Antitrust economists are interested in identifying and analyzing facilitating practices for two reasons. First, there is the possibility of challenging the use of practices under Section 1 of the Sherman Act as a restraint of trade. Second, in merger cases the use of facilitating practices is considered a "plus factor" that makes it more likely that the government will challenge a merger under the 1984 Department of Justice *Merger Guidelines*.[51]

Of the researchers concerned with business strategy, game theorists have given the most attention to strategies that could facilitate collusion. One recent example is Green and Porter (1984), who develop a "trigger pricing" model of enforcing a collusive agreement. This type of model has firms building into their best response functions "punishment strategies" that are triggered by prices below the collusive level. In their duopoly model, Green and Porter's firms select output quantities and price is determined by the quantities selected and by a random demand shock. It is assumed that the firms cannot observe either the shock or their competitor's quantity directly, so they use the observed price to infer something about their competitor's quantity. Firms maximize the expected value of profits over an infinite horizon.

There is a range of equilibria in the Green and Porter model, involving quantities each period that are, on average, below the Cournot equilibrium quantities, yielding a price that is, on average, above the price that results in a Cournot equilibrium in a single period or stage of this infinitely repeated game. These equilibria are supported by punishments of the following form. If either firm observes that the price has fallen below some "trigger price" level, then it increases its output to the Cournot equilibrium level for the single stage of the game for a fixed number of periods. The length of the punishment must be long enough to deter either firm from deviating from the low equilibrium outputs, that is, the single-period gain from such a deviation must be swamped by the effects of lower earnings during the punishment period. In this way collusive prices can result from purely noncooperative behavior in a dynamic game, although the maximum price level that can be sustained depends on firms' discount rates and other factors. The antitrust implications of this type of model are derived from the *equilibrium* relationship between the maximum price level that can be sustained with such strategies and the variables, such as the number of firms, that might be affected by antitrust policy. Also, any effort to write punishment strategies directly into sales contracts could have a strong anticompetitive effect, although this would be a red flag to the antitrust enforcement agencies.

Friedman (1971) and others have analyzed similar equilibria in infinite period "super games" in which firms choose prices, not quantities.[52] In general, there are many supra-competitive price levels that can be supported in equilibrium. At an equilibrium, each firm is deterred from cutting price unilaterally because the one-period gain is swamped by the lower earnings during the "punishment period." Obviously, the quicker a deviation is detected in these models, the lower the gain from deviation and the higher the price that can be supported in equilibrium. Thus, an industry practice or institution that forces quick revelation of discounts should receive careful antitrust scrutiny. Also, as Stigler (1964) noted, selective discounts are harder to detect. Thus, any practice that results in uniform pricing tends to make a unilateral price cut less attractive in an equilibrium in which punishments follow detection. Another antitrust implication of these models is that any practice that enables a firm to commit itself to cutting price for a fixed minimum period of time may thereby enable it to "announce" exactly the kind of punishment strategy that supports "collusive" price outcomes in a supergame. It is ironic to note that Baumol (1979) proposed *institutionalizing* such a punishment strategy by adopting an antitrust policy that would require a firm that cuts price in response to entry to keep price down for a specified period of time (for example, 6 months) if exit occurs. Although such a policy would punish the firm making a predatory price cut, it might also facilitate entry deterrence in equilibrium because the predator is not permitted to revert quantity to an accommodating posture.[53]

Although game theorists have developed a number of new models of oligopoly, very little advance has been made thus far in identifying collusion-facilitating strategies that could be prosecuted under the antitrust laws. Should these modern oligopoly theories be developed sufficiently to provide empirical implications, they may shed light on the circumstances under which a merger in a concentrated industry is likely to be anticompetitive.[54] However, it would appear that we may still be a long way from any significant contribution of this type.

BUSINESS STRATEGY AND ANTITRUST

We have now completed our survey of the strategic literature. What remains is to evaluate the policy implications of this literature. To begin, it is worth restating Michael Spence's oral remarks at the 1980 FTC conference on business strategy: "All business behavior is strategic." Real world competition involves direct rivalry between competitors, and rivalry cannot exist without recognition of interdependence and without winners and losers (among the competitors). The fundamental problem for antitrust is to determine when rivalry reduces aggregate net efficiency.[55]

In the industrial organization literature it was once argued that discerning anticompetitive conduct was fairly easy. It is now difficult to find such an optimistic outlook, as Kenneth Elzinga's contribution to this volume indicates.[56] Economists have demonstrated that a variety of strategies can result in predation, entry deterrence, or oligopoly pricing. The same strategies, however, can also lead to the exit of inefficient producers, efficient expansion of capacity, efficient speeding of R & D, and so forth. As a general theoretical matter, the competitive effects of business strategies are ambiguous. This is also an obvious empirical conclusion, since we can find variants of most types of strategies being used by firms without market power in largely competitive industries. Next we will summarize the major problems that arise in any attempt to derive useful policy conclusions from the business strategy literature.

First Mover Advantage versus the Risks of Precommitment

The models of predation and strategic entry deterrence generally assume, at least implicitly, that the incumbent is able to act before the entrant. In reality, this assumption may presume more advantage than the incumbent often has. Sometimes, the entrant (or competitor) may be able to preempt any action of the incumbent, thereby ensuring the incumbent's best response is to accommodate entry. In our illustration of preemption by capacity expansion, for example, if the entrant is able to make an irreversible investment first, the equilibrium will involve entry. Most of the models in the literature build in an implicit first mover advantage for the incumbent and so do not allow the possibility of a preemptive strategy for the entrant.

In most cases the models of business strategy do not feature the inherent risks of precommitment in the analysis. By definition, precommitment to some extent "ties your hands" with respect to what actions you will take in certain contingencies. As we have seen, such self-imposed restrictions can have benefits. However, such restrictions also leave a firm at risk if its expectations about the future state of an industry and one's competitors are not borne out. For example, a strategy of investing in excess capacity to deter domestic entry into widget production will turn out to be a bad strategy if movements in exchange rates or the efficiency of foreign competitors opens up the domestic market to foreign competition. Such a strategy will also turn out to be undesirable if gadgets, a good substitute for widgets, are invented, resulting in a significant decline in the demand for widgets. Similarly, raising industry costs through regulation may benefit some competitors in short run, but may have undesirable long-run consequences. Finally, making precommitments to facilitate collusion are likely to increase the likelihood of future entry. The business strategy models usually make static assumptions about future market conditions, so that the literature on "anticompetitive strategies" probably overestimates the profitability of strategic precommitment.

The Qualitative Relationship between Strategy and Its Consequences

As discussed above, the recent literature on business strategies shows that the *qualitative* relationship between strategic instruments and their competitive effects can be ambiguous, with the ambiguity depending critically on the form that competition takes in the market of interest. *Under*investment (or its equivalent) may, in some cases, be the profitable entry-deterring strategy, if the market is characterized by differentiated products and price-setting oligopolists. The ambiguity of the qualitative relationship between strategies and their consequences obviously complicates the problem of deriving policy implications.

Welfare Analysis

To begin our discussion of the welfare implications of business strategy, recall that the strategic investment example of an earlier section showed that strategic behavior that deters entry does not necessarily reduce market efficiency,[57] even in an incumbent-monopoly model that does not allow any efficiency-augmenting effects of the strategy.[58] Although the example is simple, the conclusion is valid in more sophisticated models of business strategy. Therefore, assuming that antitrust is concerned with economic efficiency, it should be clear that policing business strategy by antitrust regulation is inherently complicated.[59] One of the primary reasons for this complexity is that strategies often provide a gross, if not net, benefit to customers. For example, building more capacity benefits customers by assuring future supply. Similarly, speeding up R & D is likely to speed up innovations of benefit to customers. Finally, meet-or-release and most-favored-customer clauses in sales contracts are provisions that customers would value, ceteris paribus. In a nutshell, the problem is how to use observed industry data to determine in a specific case whether the strategist is simply better at responding to his customers current and future needs or, instead, is engaging in welfare-reducing strategic entry deterrence. The models in the literature generally do not confront this calculus because they typically rule out any gross benefits by implicitly assuming them away.

"Second Best" Problems

Another reason for the ambiguity of welfare conclusions arises directly from what is termed the problem of the "second best."[60] Simply put, for our purposes the main result of the theory of the second best is that an increase in market power for a firm that already has some market power does not necessarily reduce welfare.[61] Therefore, if the strategist has market power absent the strategic activity, the theory of the second best shows that as a theoretical matter, it is very difficult to establish that aggregate (or even consumer) welfare is necessarily reduced by the strategic activity. The simple example of entry deterrence by capacity expansion discussed above illustrates the principle. In that example the strategist preserves his monopoly position as a result of the strategy that forestalls entry, but welfare is nonetheless enhanced.

THE APPLICATION OF STRATEGIC THEORY TO ANTITRUST ANALYSIS: THE EXAMPLE OF DUPONT

In this section we will discuss the application of strategic theory to antitrust. For purposes of illustration we will base most of our discussion on the FTC's case charging DuPont with monopolizing the titanium dioxide (TiO_2) market.[62] In many ways this was the most straightforward of the strategic monopolization cases brought by the government in the 1970s. The strategic theory was a relatively simple version of the strategic capacity expansion theory that we discussed above.

Beginning in the 1960s, DuPont pioneered a technology for the production of TiO_2 that was different from that of its competitors. For a while, this technology placed DuPont in about the same cost position as its competitors. However, because of changes in relative input costs and environmental regulations, DuPont had a significant cost advantage over its competitors by the late 1960s. At about the same time DuPont and the industry were projecting that there would be a significant growth in demand for TiO_2 in the 1970s. As a result, DuPont set out on an aggressive capacity expansion program. It also refused requests from its competitors to license its technology. From 1972 to 1976 DuPont's share of sales in the (domestic) TiO_2 market grew from 30 percent to 42 percent. Its share of capacity grew even faster, since the anticipated demand growth was not realized because of the slowdown of the American economy.

In 1978 the FTC issued a complaint charging that DuPont had been engaged in an attempt to monopolize the titanium dioxide market for at least the preceding six years.[63] The FTC's basic argument was that DuPont had engaged in capacity expansion in order to deter investment by its existing competitors in the TiO_2 market, and that the effect of this action was that DuPont would be able to raise prices without threat of capacity expansion by its rivals.

As discussed above, the basis of such a strategic entry deterrence theory is that the creation of excess capacity by the incumbent makes the threat of low postentry prices credible, thereby forestalling entry. If the strategy is successful, the incumbent is sheltered from the threat of entry and can act as a monopolist or dominant firm.

One significant problem with this line of argument is that, as in any predatory theory that involves significant costs for the predator, recoupment must be shown to be plausible. Recoupment becomes less plausible, other things equal, the longer and more costly and predatory period. At the time the FTC suit was brought, DuPont had already been engaged in a capacity expansion program for six years, the result of which was that prices had fallen throughout the period. Thus, establishing that DuPont would be likely to be able to recoup its short-run losses would not be an easy task.

Although the FTC's theory was strategic capacity expansion, it did not deal satisfactorily with the credibility problem.[64] Rather, the FTC made a standard predatory pricing argument—that is, that because of its excess capacity DuPont would necessarily discipline its rivals if they attempted to expand capacity. But as we have seen, for a capacity expansion strategy to be credible, it must be the case that expansion of capacity by the competitors would be likely to lead to prices below their long run average costs. Assuming, as argued by the FTC, that DuPont was a dominant firm, then the central issue in assessing the credibility of DuPont's strategy is whether accommodation or price competition would be the most profitable strategy for DuPont to adopt if a competitor had increased its capacity.[65]

Although the model of strategic investment discussed above pertained to the case of a potential new entrant, it can be reinterpreted as a case of potential capacity expansion by an existing competitor. This is because the demand function in the example could be taken to represent residual demand, that is, market demand adjusted for the supply behavior of fringe competitors. With that interpretation the example shows that a cost-reducing investment by the dominant firm may deter capacity expansion by the fringe competitors. And even if capacity expansion is deterred, as we saw above, the welfare effects depend on the degree of the cost and capacity advantage enjoyed by the dominant firm, which are empirical issues that would have to be resolved in any strategic-capacity-expansion monopolization case.

It is probably obvious to the reader that establishing that capacity expansion by DuPont's rivals would be likely to lead to prices below their long-run average costs would not be a trivial matter. Arguments would have to be based on the structure of the market and, in particular, on relative costs and capacity conditions. Obviously, a necessary condition for low prices to result if DuPont's competitors expanded their capacities is that the size of increments in capacity be sufficiently large relative to the overall market that they would have a significant depressing effect on price. In a market with static demand and in which increments of capacity must be of significant size relative to the market, such a theory is plausible. It is less plausible in a market in which there will be growth in demand and in which increments in capacity might come from "stretching" existing capacity instead of from new plants. These are issues that would have had to be addressed if the FTC had recognized the credibility problem in its predation theory.

Even if the FTC had recognized and dealt with the credibility problem, *DuPont* would have been a very difficult case. As discussed above, the modern strategic models typically make implicit or explicit assumptions that may be critical to the analysis. Perhaps the most difficult issue in *DuPont* is that the FTC conceded that DuPont had a significant proprietary cost advantage over its competitors. If DuPont is firm I in the Cournot example in figure 3, the "fortuitous" cost reduction would shift DuPont's best-response function to the right, as indicated by the dashed line.[66] This shift would raise DuPont's market share and lower price.[67] Thus, DuPont would be expected to be the major capacity expander in such a situation, regardless of the degree of market power that it had. This raises the very difficult issue of how much expansion by DuPont would have been procompetitive. The strategic literature provides no guidance here.

The fact that DuPont's exploitation of its cost advantage by capacity expansion resulted in lower prices and a higher market share for DuPont for a significant period of time was difficult for the FTC administrative law judge (ALJ) to reconcile with a predation argument. In his opinion (issued in 1980), the ALJ stated:

I am not convinced that DuPont was required to take actions different than those it did take. DuPont's cost advantage was the result of business foresight, intelligent planning, dedicated technological application to a most difficult production problem, the taking of economic risk, and its competitors' choice [to stay with an alternative technology]. . . .

I do not believe that DuPont was required to price its TiO_2 products high enough to insure its less efficient competitors sufficient revenue to finance expansion. . . .

The lowest cost producer's choice to expand capacity in a situation of short supply, is sound business judgment that is economically justified. (693–94).[68]

Although some version of the facts in *DuPont* could support a theoretically valid predatory capacity expansion theory, the litigation in *DuPont* made clear that it is very difficult to distinguish competitive from predatory behavior—particularly in a situation in which the predator's actions involve taking advantage of a cost advantage derived from its own efforts. The FTC attempted to finesse this issue by arguing that, although DuPont had pioneered an alternative technology that had resulted in significantly lower costs, DuPont should not be able to exploit its superiority to the disadvantage of its competitors because the lower costs derived largely from "fortuitous" changes in input costs and regulation. Needless to say, this approach, if upheld, could have very far-reaching implications for successful innovative firms. Under the FTC's theory, a large innovative firm that gained a significant advantage over its rivals because of fortuitous circumstances could not consciously exploit its advantage too much at the expense of its rivals.[69] Indeed, the FTC's theory was perhaps broad enough to reach nonfortuitous circumstances—such as innovations specifically undertaken to gain advantage over rivals by producing a better product.

The FTC staff's proposed remedy in *DuPont* would have required that DuPont license its superior technology to its competitors on terms favorable to the competitors. The ALJ rejected such a remedy, although on somewhat narrow grounds:

DuPont was not required to license its ilmenite technology to its competitors (or potential entrants, if any).... There is not showing on this record that competitors could not develop that technology, if they had chosen to take that course of action. The fact that these competitors found themselves five to ten years behind DuPont in 1972 did not obligate DuPont to give up its technological advantage. (p. 694).

The language of the ALJ's decision could be read as conceding that if a dominant firm had an advantage that could not be duplicated by its competitors, it might be required to offer licenses to its competitors. This theory however has not thus far been upheld in the courts.

In summary *DuPont* illustrates much of the difficulty inherent in bringing a monopolization case under strategic theories. Strategic capacity expansion to preempt actual or potential rivals is a fairly simple theory. Nonetheless, establishing an anticompetitive effect will generally be very difficult, particularly if, as in *DuPont*, the capacity expander has a cost advantage over his rivals, and the apparent interim impact of capacity expansion is lower prices.

DuPont was probably the simplest strategic monopolization case. The FTC's case against the breakfast cereals companies and the Justice Department's case against IBM were much more complex. The basic lesson, however, from the strategic monopolization cases appears at this point to be that economics may not be able to sufficiently distinguish between procompetitive and anticompetitive strategic conduct for the courts to conclude that such conduct violates the antitrust laws. The richness of evidence presented in a monopolization case cannot generally be easily fit into a strategic model. And if the suspect strategic actions relate to basic competitive advantages of the respondents (for example, pioneering a lower cost technology, making a better breakfast cereal, and so on), it will necessarily be difficult for economics to conclude that those actions are anticompetitive. Thus, although the strategic literature offers many useful insights to antitrust analysis, the literature still seems a long way from being able to provide tests that are useful to the courts.

SUMMARY OF ANTITRUST ANALYSIS OF BUSINESS STRATEGY

In economic terms, the antitrust analysis required to evaluate the legality of business strategy is analogous to rule-of-reason analysis of vertical and horizontal restraints. However, the prevailing view in antitrust economics indicates that vertical restraints should probably be legal in most cases, and that horizontal restraints that significantly restrict competition are suspect, at this point theory gives us almost no guidance on presumptions about the strategies considered in the antitrust economics literature. In addition, these strategies usually have a more prospective character than does conduct more typically dealt with in a rule-of-reason analysis.

The traditional approach to diagnosing anticompetitive conduct in antitrust has been to determine whether the firm engaging in the conduct has or can attain market power. That focus, of course, provides a useful initial screen for conducting the analysis of the competitive consequences of particular conduct.[70] Unfortunately, the market power "test" provides only an initial screen, since the strategic literature indicates that many types of conduct can be procompetitive, even when the firm has market power.[71] This is for the two reasons discussed above: Gross customer benefits accompany most strategies, and passing the market power test puts us in the very complicated world of the "second best."

Demonstrating that the activities of a naked cartel are anticompetitive is fairly straightforward.[72] A much more sophisticated and empirically based analysis is required to determine that a firm's aggressive expansion of capacity is an example of inefficient entry deterrence,[73] or that a firm's attempt to minimize compatibility with competitors' products is inefficient predation,[74] or that brand proliferation is an entry-deterring strategy that harms consumers,[75] or that the common adoption of contractual provisions in an industry facilitates collusion with no out-weighing efficiency.[76] The prominent strategic antitrust cases of the seventies make clear the difficulties that courts, regulatory bodies, and even economists have in proving that a particular set of strategies has an anticompetitive effect, even in the context of a particular case with vast empirical and institutional detail.[77]

In conclusion, although the business strategy literature has increased our understanding of the ways in which firms actually compete, discerning the circumstances in which consumers do not gain from such forms of competition remains a very formidable task. If the business strategy literature is to make a useful contribution to antitrust policy, this deficiency will have to be remedied.

NOTES

The views expressed here are those of the authors, not necessarily those of the Federal Trade Commission. This research was supported, in part, by the National Science Foundation under grant SES–8720105. The authors are grateful to Richard Higgins, Kenneth Elzinga, James Langenfeld, Robert Porter, and Roger Sherman for helpful comments.

1. See Scherer (1980) and Posner (1976).

2. However, some types of conduct, that we will call strategic, facilitate collusion. We will discuss such conduct below.

3. Department of Justice *Merger Guidelines* (1984). Occasionally, some form of conduct that could be dignified by being termed strategic may be an issue in a horizontal merger investigation.

4. See Krattenmaker and Salop (1986).

5. See Holt and Scheffman (1987) for an analysis of such contracts.

6. The textbook economic models of competition largely fail to address such rivalry. These models typically treat demand and costs as exogenous and describe competition as arising from simple profit maximization in a context in which there is no apparent need or role for strategic behavior. Firms in these models simply deliver their output to the "market," having chosen the output level that maximizes profits. Most "real world" firms are faced with the task of finding a market for their output (often by stealing their rivals' customers) or finding a way of obtaining a cost advantage relative to their rivals (sometimes by engaging in actions that raise the relative costs of their rivals), so that much of business behavior is inherently strategic.

7. Economic modelling also tends to concentrate on anticompetitive explanations of business conduct. "If an economist finds something—a business practice of one sort or another—that he does not understand, he looks for a monopoly explanation." (Coase [1972]).

8. If G_1 were a group of firms operating as a cartel, it would take R as its demand curve, acting as a monopolist with respect to that demand curve, charging a price of p^*, so that the elasticity of the residual demand curve R would be a critical parameter in assessing the extent of market power possessed by the first group. See Landes and Posner (1981), Baker and Bresnahan (1985), and Scheffman and Spiller (1987).

9. For more discussion see Salop and Scheffman (1983).

10. For example, the strategic business literature is concerned with such issues as "product positioning," which envisages a market with differentiated products. Most of the interesting strategic aspects of such promotion cannot be captured in our simple model of homogeneous good market, and so for the time being we will not consider further actions that would shift *market* demand.

11. For the details of the analysis see Salop and Scheffman (1983).

12. Of course this story leaves unresolved why the suppliers of the input would find it in their interest to have such contracts, since the effect would be to reduce their sales. It would be possible, in principle for them to be compensated by the strategic group.

13. The semiconductor industry is one commonly cited example.

14. Best response functions are sometimes called "reaction functions," but the word *reaction* is misleading because all decisions are simultaneous in a static model.

15. Alternatively, we could have made E's fixed costs of entry slightly larger, so E's profit in the situation $q_I = 2$, $q_E = 1$ is negative (and all other entries for E for the case $q_E = 1$ would be slightly smaller).

16. In essence, each firm assumes that the demand facing it is the market demand minus a fixed supply by its rivals. More specifically, each firm's reaction function gives its profit maximizing output decision for each level of output of the rival. The firm is assumed to postulate that its output decisions

do not alter the output decisions of its rival, as is the case when outputs are selected simultaneously. Thus, for any given output level of the rival, say $\hat{q}$, the firm perceives that the demand it is facing is the market demand minus $\hat{q}$. Notice that the simultaneity inherent in this approach differs from the residual demand analysis in which the dominant firm knows what the fringe will do for any action of the dominant firm, which would be the case if the dominant firm announces its price *before* fringe firms choose their outputs.

17. As we will see below, the relationship between changes in costs and shifts in the reaction functions depends critically on the particular oligopoly model.

18. For one thing, the relative size of the predator works against him in that any given reduction in price imposes more costs on him than it does on the prey, although the predator, if successful, will reap the monopoly gain.

19. By net benefits here we mean that the profits of a bankruptcy strategy exceed the profits of a strategy of accommodation.

20. A more interesting story can be told in a dynamic context, where, for example, the static picture we have depicted arose from exploitation of learning curve effects. We will return to dynamics presently.

21. "...As long as we are dealing with homogeneous oligopoly, it is hard to find a well-defined sensible alternative" (Modigliani [1958], 230).

22. This would be the postentry residual demand curve facing the incumbent.

23. This concept was introduced by Selten (1965). A nontechnical discussion of this and related concepts can be found in Meyerson (1986).

24. Formally speaking, a *Nash* equilibrium.

25. *U.S. v. Aluminum Company of America.* 148 F.2d 416 (2nd Cir. 1945).

26. In Spence's first model, the investment only affects the firm's capacity. Our analysis most closely matches Spence's second model in which investment affects both capacity and marginal cost. One difference is that there is only one incumbent firm in our analysis; Spence considered the case in which there were several incumbent firms that colluded perfectly prior to entry but behaved noncooperatively in their postentry price choices (that is, entry changed the equilibrium concept).

27. It is critical to the analysis that the investment is irreversible. Otherwise, the best response in the face of entry would be to reverse the investment, making the investment not credible.

28. This is $4 for the strategic investment plus $3/2 for the existing sunk investment.

29. If the incumbent had only installed one unit of new capacity, then the cost and profit rows of table 5 show that the incumbent's best postentry quantity is one, so a threat to let the postentry price fall to $5 would not be credible for this smaller level of investment. Conversely, the incumbent would not acquire more than two units of new capacity, since two is the monopoly profit-maximizing output in the absence of entry.

30. Another method of achieving the no-entry equilibrium described in our example would be to prepay for variable inputs, reducing their variable cost by $2 per unit of output. Finally, a postentry output of 3/2 could be made credible if the incumbent could enter into long-term contracts with buyers that

commit him to sell (and buyers to accept) 3/2 units of output. We will discuss these and other methods of precommitment further below.

31. This assumes that the entrant has sunk costs of entry.

32. Welfare after the investment is the difference between the area *ABEF* in figure 3 and the incumbent's postinvestment fixed cost of 11/2.

33. The result does not depend on output remaining unchanged due to strategic investment. The example can be changed so that output falls but the gain in producer surplus exceeds the loss in consumer surplus that arises from the decline in output.

34. For further discussion of the possibility of strategic underinvestment see Fudenberg and Tirole (1984) on the "fat-cat effect" and the "lean and hungry look."

35. See Holt and Scheffman (1985) for a discussion of the case and a complete version of the following analysis.

36. These issues are analyzed in more generality in Salop (1985) and Holt ad Scheffman (1986).

37. Of course, in this example, no potential efficiency-enhancing properties of meet-or-release or most-favored-customer provisions in sales contracts were considered.

38. The analysis of Holt and Scheffman (1986), applied to this example, implies the unprofitability of any (possibly small) discount from any (possibly noninteger) common list price below six in this example.

39. There is also a third equilibrium in the entry subgame that involves randomization, but it can be shown that the entrant's expected profits are also negative in this "mixed strategy" equilibrium.

40. This type of reasoning has been called "forward induction" by Kohlberg and Mertens (1986); it is different from the usual "backward induction" method of first analyzing the final stage (here the entry subgame) and then analyzing the first-stage decision. Cho and Kreps (1987) have used this type of reasoning to eliminate "bad" equilibria in signaling models; and Kohlberg and Mertens have proposed a formal equilibrium solution concept that would rule out the no-entry equilibrium in our example. There have been several previous attempts to develop a satisfactory equilibrium concept that prunes equilibria that are not sensible; among these are the notions of a sequential equilibrium, a perfect equilibrium, and a proper equilibrium. These concepts have been widely discussed and used by theorists, but none of these would rule out the no-entry equilibrium in our example. By their own admission, the works of Cho and Kreps and of Kohlberg and Mertens are incomplete, but we anticipate that the developing theory of equilibrium for noncooperative games will have important implications for the analysis of strategic behavior in industry. Brandts and Holt (1987) report results of laboratory experiments that are supportive of the Cho and Kreps analysis.

41. Although our discussion here will focus on strategic entry deterrence, there are analogous models of predation.

42. That is, he does not know the incumbent's costs.

43. The presence of significant sunk costs for the entrant would make it more difficult for the incumbent to drive the entrant out of the market.

44. In this model the incumbent's technology is predetermined by a random

event. The strong incumbent cannot liquidate the additional investment and a weak incumbent cannot alter its type by making a strategic investment.

45. Kreps and Wilson calculate a "sequential equilibrium" in which the beliefs are endogenous, and as they note, there may be many such equilibria, some of which are more reasonable than others.

46. Kreps and Wilson (1982) work with multiperiod examples in which there are equilibria in which the firms randomize over possible decisions. In such equilibria, there is a positive probability that entry actually occurs, so reputation building is observed along the equilibrium path. There would be an equilibrium in randomized strategies in our example if the probability of a strong incumbent were smaller than 1/2.

47. See Kreps and Spence (1985), Fudenberg and Tirole (1986), and Shapiro (1986).

48. For a full discussion see Holt and Scheffman (1987).

49. However, see Haddock (1982).

50. See Holt and Scheffman (1986).

51. A plus factor is a structural or behavioral characteristic in a market that increases the likelihood of collusion in that market.

52. See Kreps and Spence (1985), Fudenberg and Tirole (1986), and Shapiro (1986) for critiques of the supergame approach to collusion.

53. Isaac and Smith (1985) report the result of a series of laboratory experiments in which the imposition of a variation of Baumol's rule resulted in higher prices and lower market efficiency.

54. An analysis of the implications of modern oligopoly theory for merger analysis has essentially not yet been conducted. We are currently developing such an analysis.

55. And when this rivalry violates the antitrust laws.

56. One thing, however, the recent strategic literature does make clear is that traditional theories of predatory pricing are untenable. Predation is more likely to be the result of non-price strategies such as "raising rivals' costs."

57. For a discussion of models in which limiting entry can lead to increases in welfare see von Weizsacker (1980).

58. For example, the example does not allow the possibility and effects of increased assurance of supply.

59. Or even with only consumer welfare (see Lande [1982]).

60. See Scherer (1980).

61. In its original form, the theory of the second best showed that in an economy with competitive and imperfectly competitive sectors, restoring competition to one of the imperfectly competitive sectors could result in the economy's net welfare being reduced. The result here is even stronger, in that it states that increases of market power within an individual market may improve welfare in that market, independent of competitive conditions in other sectors of the economy. For the typical model in the strategic-entry-deterrence literature featuring a dominant firm, the technical result is that the relevant comparative statics results in dominant firm models are generally ambiguous. See Salop and Scheffman (1987) for examples. For examples of second best problems in oligopoly models see von Weizsacker (1980).

62. Titanium dioxide is a white chemical pigment employed primarily by

the manufacturers of paints, paper, synthetic fibers, plastics, ink, and synthetic rubber to make them white or opaque.

63. *In the matter of E. I. DuPont*, docket no. 9108, complaint filed April 10, 1978.

64. Of course, the necessity of credibility was not fully developed in the economic literature at that time.

65. This was a somewhat dubious proposition given DuPont's share in the TiO_2 market.

66. For the case of price competition, the cost reduction shifts the firm's best-response function to the left, as shown in Figure 4. The resulting price reductions would cause the quantity sold to expand, as was the case in Figure 3 when the best-response function shifted to the right.

67. In particular, total quantity will rise and price will fall if the best-response function of firm E has a slope of greater than -1.

68. The FTC upheld the ALJ's decision on appeal by the FTC staff.

69. The commission's economic expert, Professor W. G. Shepherd testified that "DuPont should have done whatever it wanted to do, subject to the proviso that it not choose a strategy whose effect was to transform the TiO_2 industry into a virtual monopoly," (CX 218 pp. 65–66). Shepherd's explicit complaint was that DuPont had kept prices too low and had refused to license its technology.

70. Although, it is sometimes important to discern what the market power is derived from. For example, it can be profitable for firms without market power in the market they sell in to raise their rivals' costs. (See Salop and Scheffman [1987] and Salop, Scheffman, and Schwartz [1984].) The market power in that example is the power to affect the costs of their rivals.

71. Recall that in our example of entry deterrence by capacity expansion, entry deterrence was efficient, even though it resulted in the incumbent having a monopoly.

72. Although, as with everything, it may not be as easy as was once thought. See, for example, Bittlingmayer (1982).

73. *In the matter of E. I. DuPont*, docket no. 9108, complaint filed April 10, 1978.

74. *U.S. v. IBM*, S.D. New York, complaint filed January 17, 1969.

75. *In the matter of Kellog Co. et. al.*, docket no. 8883, complaint filed January 24, 1972.

76. *Ethyl Corp. et al.* 101 FTC 423 (1983) (Docket No. D9128); *E. I. DuPont DeNemours and Co. v. FTC.* 729F2d. 128 (2d Cir. 1984).

77. See, for example, Fisher, McGowan, and Greenwood (1983).

REFERENCES

Baker, J., and T. Bresnahan (1985) "The Gain from Merger of Collusion in Product-Differentiated Industries." *Journal of Industrial Economics* 33: 427–444.

Baumol, W. (1979) "Quasi-Permanence of Price Reductions: A Policy for Prevention." *Yale Law Review* 89:1–26.

Bittlingmayer, G. (1982) "Decreasing Average Cost and Competition: A New

Look at the Addyston Pipe Case." *Journal of Law and Economics* 25: 201–229.

Boyer, M., and M. Moreaux (1983) "Consistent Versus Non-consistent Conjectures in Duopoly Theory: Some Examples." *Journal of Industrial Economics* 32: 97–112.

Brander, J. and B. Spencer (1983) "Strategic Commitment with R&D: The Symmetric Case." *Bell Journal of Economics* 14: 225–235.

Brandts, J., and C. Holt (1987) "An Experimental Test of Equilibrium Dominance in Signaling Games." Documents De Discussion, working paper 78.87, IAE, Autonomous University of Barcelona.

Bulow, J., J. Geanakoplos, and P. Klemperer (1985) "Multimarket Oligopoly: Strategic Substitutes and Complements." *Journal of Political Economy* 93: 488–511.

Cho, I., and D. Kreps (1987) "Signalling Games and Stable Equilibria." *Quarterly Journal of Economics* 52: 179–221.

Coase, R. (1972) "Industrial Organization: A Proposal for Research." In *Policy Issues and Research Opportunities in Industrial Organization*, ed. V. Fuchs, 57–73. New York: Columbia University Press.

Cooper, T. E. (1986) "Most-Favored-Customer Pricing and Tacit Collusion." *The Rand Journal of Economics* 17: 377–388.

Cournot, A. (1927; originally, 1883) *Researches into the Mathematical Principles of the Theory of Wealth.* New York: MacMillan.

Davidson, C., and R. Deneckere (1986) "Long-Run Competition in Capacity, Short-Run Competition in Price, and the Cournot Model." *The Rand Journal of Economics* 17: 404–415.

Dixit, A. K. (1979) "A Model of Duopoly Suggesting a Theory of Entry Barriers." *Bell Journal of Economics* 10: 20–32.

Dixit, A. K. (1980) "The Role of Investment in Entry Deterrence." *Economic Journal* 90: 95–106.

Dixit, A. K. (1982) "Recent Developments in Oligopoly Theory." *American Economic Review* 17: 12–17.

Dixit, A. K., and C. Shapiro (1986) "Entry Dynamics with Mixed Strategies." In *Strategic Planning*, ed. L. G. Thomas, 63–79. Lexington, Mass.: Lexington Books.

Eaton, B. C., and R. G. Lipsey (1979) "The Theory of Market Preemption: The Persistence of Excess Capacity and Monopoly in Growing Spatial Markets." *Economica* 46: 149–158.

Eaton, B. C., and R. G. Lipsey (1981) "Capital Commitment, and Entry Equilibrium." *Bell Journal of Economics* 12: 593–604.

Encaoua, D., P. Geroski, and A. Jacquemin (1984) "Strategic Competition and the Persistence of Dominant Firms: A Survey." In *New Developments in the Analysis of Market Structure*, ed. F. Mathewson and J. Stiglitz, Boston: MIT Press.

Fisher, F., J. McGowan, and J. Greenwood (1983) *Folded Stapled and Mutilated: Economic Analysis and U.S. v. IBM.* Cambridge: MIT Press.

Friedman, J. (1971) "A Noncooperative Equilibrium for Supergames." *Review of Economic Studies* 38: 1–12.

Fudenberg, D., R. Gilbert, J. Stiglitz, and J. Tirole (1983) "Preemption, Leapfrogging, and Competition in Patent Races." *European Economic Review* 22: 3–31.

Fudenberg, D., and J. Tirole (1982) "Capital as a Commitment: Strategic Investment to Deter Mobility." *Journal of Economic Theory* 31: 227–250.

Fudenberg, D., and J. Tirole (1983) "Learning by Doing and Market Performance." *Bell Journal of Economics* 14: 522–530.

Fudenberg, D., and J. Tirole (1984) "The Fat Cat Effect, the Puppy-Dog Ploy and the Lean and Hungry Look." *American Economic Review* 74: 361–366.

Fudenberg, D., and J. Tirole (1986) "Dynamic Models of Oligopoly." In *Theory of the Firm and Industrial Organization*, ed. A. Jacquemin. New York: Harwood Academic Publishers.

Gaskins, D. (1971) "Dynamic Limit Pricing: Optimal Pricing Under Threat of Entry." *Journal of Economic Theory* 3: 306–322.

Gilbert, R., and R. Harris (1984) "Competition with Lumpy Investment." *Rand Journal of Economics* 15: 197–212.

Gilbert, R., and D. Newbery (1982) "Preemptive Patenting and the Persistence of Monopoly." *American Economic Review* 72: 514–526.

Green, E., and R. Porter (1984) "Noncooperative Collusion under Imperfect Price Information." *Econometrica* 52: 87–100.

Grossman, G., and C. Shapiro (1987) "Dynamic R&D Competition." *Economic Journal* 97: 372–387.

Haddock, D. (1982) "Basing-Point Pricing: Competition vs. Collusion Theories." *American Economic Review* 72: 289–306.

Holt, C. A., and D. Scheffman (1985) "The Effects of Advance Notice and Best-Price Policies: Theory, with Applications to *Ethyl*." FTC working paper.

Holt, C., and D. Scheffman (1986) "A Theory of Input Exchange Agreements." FTC working paper.

Holt, C. A., and D. Scheffman (1987) "Facilitating Practices: The Effects of Advance Notice and Best-Price Policies." *Rand Journal of Economics* 18: 187–197.

Isaac, Mark R., and V. Smith (1985) "In Search of Predatory Pricing." *Journal of Political Economy* 93: 320–45.

Kohlberg, E., and J. Mertens (1986) "On the Strategic Stability of Equilibria." *Econometrica* 54: 1003–1037.

Krattenmaker, T., and S. Salop (1986) "Competition and Cooperation in the Market for Exclusionary Rights." *American Economic Review* 76: 109–113.

Krattenmaker, T., and S. Salop (1987a) "Analyzing Anticompetitive Exclusion." *Antitrust Law Journal* 56: 71–108.

Krattenmaker, T., and S. Salop (1987b) "Anticompetitive Exclusion: Raising Rivals' Costs to Achieve Power Over Price." *Yale Law Journal* 96: 209–293.

Kreps, D., and J. Scheinkman (1983) "Quantity Pre-commitment and Bertrand Competition Yield Cournot Outcomes." *Bell Journal of Economics* 14: 326–337.

Kreps, D., and A. M. Spence (1985) "Modelling the Role of History in Industrial Organization." In *Issues in Contemporary Microeconomics and Welfare*, ed. G. Feiwel. Albany: State University of New York at Albany Press.

Kreps, D. M., and R. Wilson (1982) "Reputation and Imperfect Information." *Journal of Economic Theory* 27: 253:279.

Kreps, D., and R. Wilson (1985) "Sequential Equilibria." *Econometrica* 50: 863–894.

Lande, R. (1982) "Antitrust: The Efficiency Interpretation Challenged." *Hastings Law Journal* 34: 65–150.

Landes, W., and R. Posner (1981) "Market Power in Antitrust Cases." *Harvard Law Review* 94: 937–983.

Lieberman, M. (1984) "The Learning Curve and Pricing in the Chemical Processing Industries." *The Rand Journal of Economics* 15: 213–228.

Meyerson, R. (1987) "An Introduction to Game Theory." In *Studies in Mathematical Economics*, ed., Stanley Reiter, 25:420 MAA Studies in Mathematics.

Milgrom, P., and J. Roberts (1982a) "Limit Pricing and Entry under Incomplete Information: An Equilibrium Analysis." *Econometrica* 50: 443–459.

Milgrom, P., and J. Roberts (1982b) "Predation, Reputation, and Entry Deterrence." *Journal of Economic Theory* 27: 280–312.

Modigliani, F. (1958) "New Developments on the Oligopoly Front." *Journal of Political Economy* 66: 215–232.

Porter, M. F. (1980) *Competitive Strategy*. New York: Free Press.

Porter, M. F. (1985) *Competitive Advantage*. New York: Free Press.

Porter, R. H. (1983) "A Study of Cartel Stability: The Joint Executive Committee, 1880–1886." *Bell Journal of Economics* 14: 301–314.

Posner, R. (1976) *Antitrust Law: An Economic Perspective*. Chicago: University of Chicago Press.

Prescott, E., and M. Visscher (1977) "Sequential Location among Firms with Foresight." *Bell Journal of Economics* 8: 378–374.

Reinganum, J. (1983) "Uncertain Innovation and the Persistence of Monopoly." *American Economic Review* 73: 741–748.

Rosenthal, R. (1981) "Games of Imperfect Information, Predatory Pricing and the Chainstore Paradox." *Journal of Economic Theory* 25: 92–100.

Salop, S. (1979a) "Monopolistic Competition with Outside Goods." *Bell Journal of Economics* 10: 141–156.

Salop, S. (1979b) "Strategic Entry Deterrence." *American Economic Review* 69: 335–338.

Salop, S. (1986) "Practices that Credibly Facilitate Oligopoly Coordination." In *New Developments in the Analysis of Market Structure*, ed. Joseph Stiglitz and Frank Mathewson, 265–290. Cambridge: MIT Press.

Salop, S., ed. (1981) *Strategy, Predation and Antitrust Analysis*. Washington, D.C.: Federal Trade Commission.

Salop, S., and D. Scheffman (1983) "Raising Rivals' Costs." *American Economic Review* 78: 267–271.

Salop, S., D. Scheffman, and W. Schwartz (1984) "A Bidding Analysis of Special Interest Regulation: Raising Rivals' Costs in a Rent Seeking Society." In *The Political Economy of Regulation: Private Interests in the Regulatory Process*, ed. R. Rogowsky and B. Yandle. Washington, D.C.: Federal Trade Commission.

Salop, S., and D. Scheffman (1987) "Cost-Raising Strategies." *Journal of Industrial Economics* 36: 19–34.

Scheffman, D., and P. Spiller (1987) "Geographic Market Definition under the Department of Justice Merger Guidelines." *Journal of Law and Economics* 30: 123–148.

Scherer, F. M. (1980) *Industrial Market Structure and Economic Performance.* Chicago: Rand McNally.

Schmalensee, R. (1978) "Entry Deterrence in the RTE Cereal Industry." *Bell Journal of Economics* 9: 305–327.

Schmalensee, R. (1982a) "The New Industrial Organization and the Economic Analysis of Modern Markets." In *Advances in Economic Theory*, ed. W. Hildebrand, 253–285. Cambridge: Cambridge University Press.

Schmalensee, R. (1982b) "Product Differentiation Advantages of Pioneering Brands." *American Economic Review* 72: 349–365.

Schmalensee, R. (1983) "Advertising and Entry Deterrence." *Journal of Political Economy* 90: 636–653.

Selten, R. (1965) "Spieltheoretische Behandlung eines Oligopolmodels mit Nachtragetvagheit." *Z. ges. Staatwiss* 12: 301–324, 667–689.

Selten, R. (1978) "The Chain-Store Paradox," *Theory and Decision* 9: 127–159.

Shapiro, C. (1987) "Theories of Oligopoly Behavior," Discussion paper #126, Woodrow Wilson School of Public and International Affairs, Princeton University. In *Handbook on Industrial Organization*, ed. R. Schmalensee and R. D. Willig, forthcoming.

Shubik, M. (1959) *Strategy and Market Structure.* New York: John Wiley.

Spence, A. M. (1976) "Product Selection, Fixed Costs, and Monopolistic Competition." *Review of Economic Studies* 43: 217–235.

Spence, A. M. (1977) "Entry Capacity, Investment and Oligopolistic Pricing." *Bell Journal of Economics* 8: 534–544.

Spence, A. M. (1979) "Investment Strategy and Growth in a New Market." *Bell Journal of Economics* 10: 1–19.

Spence, A. M. (1981) "The Learning Curve and Competition." *Bell Journal of Economics* 12: 49–70.

Stanford, W. (1986) "Subgame Perfect Reaction Function Equilibria in Discounted Duopoly Supergames Are Trivial." *Journal of Economic Theory* 39: 226–232.

Stigler, George (1964) "A Theory of Oligopoly." *Journal of Political Economy* 72: 55–59.

U.S. Department of Justice. *Merger Guidelines.* June 14, 1984.

von Weizsacker, C. C. (1980) *Barriers to Entry: A Theoretical Treatment.* Berlin: Springer-Verlag.

Yelle, L. E. (1979) "The Learning Curve: Historical Review and Comprehensive Survey." *Decision Sciences* 10: 302–328.

3

Merger Policy in the 1970s and 1980s

F. M. Scherer

If the possibility that competition will fail is considered sufficiently serious to take remedial public policy measures, there are two main alternative approaches. One is to monitor and if need be to regulate conduct, for example, by imposing penalties when collusion occurs or, when an industry tends persistently toward monopolistic pricing, to fix maximum prices by regulatory commission. The other approach is to regulate structure, intervening to maintain sufficiently fragmented market structures that competitive conduct follows virtually automatically. Merger policy is the principal instrument of the second approach. Unless one believes that noncompetitive conduct is naturally rare and fleeting in duration, it is the less interventionist of the alternatives, since minimal monitoring is required and, if intervention proves warranted, it can be episodic. It is not too far fetched to say that merger policy is to pricing conduct policy as surgery is to continuing drug therapy.

Mike Mann was a structuralist. It shows in his research, which other contributors to this volume describe. It also shows in his approach to competition policy problems as director of the Federal Trade Commission's Bureau of Economics between early 1971 and mid–1973. In what may be the closest thing available to a final public report on his stewardship at the FTC, there is a distinct note of pride:[1]

In one policy area, antitrust, many economists . . . are advocating a forceful policy stance: placing greater emphasis on market structure and less on market conduct. And it is the case...that the Bureau of Economics played a strong role in the emergence and character of the [breakfast] cereals and Xerox antitrust cases; and that our efforts on behalf of policy planning have gently nudged the Commission toward looking at industries with particular structural characteristics.

STRUCTURAL ANTITRUST AT THE FTC

With 20–20 hindsight we know now that the Mann era was perhaps the zenith of structuralism at the FTC. The Xerox antitrust case was settled with a patent licensing decree that fell considerably short of the structural divestiture remedy originally contemplated. The result appears to have been successful, with the FTC action deserving direct credit.[2] However, the Xerox history also suggests that we may have to modify Clair Wilcox's old saw, "The formula for competition is simple: add one part of Sears Roebuck to twenty parts of oligopoly," replacing Sears with Japan, Inc.[3] The cereals case was not only a serious loss for the FTC. In the decision that spelled its demise, the Commission conceded that its aggressive structure-busting days were over:[4]

... While there may be a legitimate concern about the anticompetitive effects of the exercise of oligopoly power, it is rarely true that these concerns will mandate an administrative agency to restructure an industry, short of a legislative warrant to that effect.

What remains on the structural dimension is merger policy, which, unlike breakfast cereals and Xerox, is reactive, not assertive, seeking to hold back new tides of concentration rather than reversing them. Although the FTC's merger enforcement efforts during the Mann era were less dramatic than the "big" structural cases, they were at least as vigorous as might befit the trough between two merger waves. Between January 1971 and June 1973, the FTC issued 23 antimerger complaints, of which more than three-fourths led to abandonment of the merger or at least some divestiture of the acquired assets.

The 9.2 merger complaints issued per year during the Mann era can be compared with the FTC's average of 7.25 per year during 1981–1985, when, by my calculations, the volume of manufacturing and mining merger activity in constant dollar terms was seven times the level of 1971–1973.[5] Thus, in terms of merger complaints brought per inflation-adjusted dollar of merger activity, the FTC of Mike Mann's period appears to have been more aggressive by something approximating a factor of nine. Evidently, there has been retrenchment on that dimension too. In much of what follows, I shall attempt to explain what happened to induce the change.

MIKE MANN'S ROLE AS SCHOLAR–POLICY ADVISER

First, however, I must make what may seem a digression, but one that will prove germane to the main story. Mike Mann was not only an antitrust policy structuralist. His work at the Federal Trade Commission reveals another facet that may have had less impact in the short run but more in the long run. Mike was acutely conscious of the limitations of economic knowledge, including his own, for purposes of formulating and implementing policy. This scholarly caution had at least four significant manifestations.

First, he played an important role in making the Bureau of Economics a balance wheel during the 1970's, checking the tendency of aggressive young lawyers to take actions on the basis of legal and/or economic theories that, however strongly held in the past, were poorly supported by solid analysis. In the structuralist speech quoted above, he noted "a certain negativism in the posture of the Commission's economists" and reported that he and his staff "find it easier to argue against policy initiatives than to support them."[6] In what must have been his maiden communication to the commission as bureau director, he argued against divestiture following the conglomerate acquisition of a major meat packer. He observed inter alia that economic theory "gives us no idea at what level of aggregate concentration mutual forbearance is likely to take place," that it "would take quite an incautious line of reasoning to argue that aggregate concentration in [the food industry] comes close to a level encouraging mutual forbearance," and that theories of predatory cross subsidization "do not, either in their logic nor with any known supporting empirical evidence, constitute a solid basis for divestiture."[7]

A second important characteristic was his continuing concern over the inadequacy of the information on which relevant economic theories were grounded and on the basis of which specific FTC enforcement decisions were taken. He saw as an important foundation for structural antitrust the statistical association observed by scholars, including himself, between market concentration and profitability. Yet in his "structuralist" speech, he recognized "there is no doubt that any empirical test of the relationship between concentration and profitability is hindered by a variety of liabilities, the most notable of which are poor data."[8] Discussing before a congressional committee the difficulties the FTC had obtaining data, he exclaimed: "I am appalled by the kind of responsibilities this agency has with respect to the kind of data base with which it has to work, for me as an economist and for the Bureau of Economics."[9] And in testimony on the FTC's investigation of energy market boundaries and how they affected the evaluation of energy industry mergers, he lamented:[10]

If I had my d'ruthers, I would rather make public policy with the best
information that one could possibly bring to bear. But we have never had that
state of perfection. We have to guess at times that we are doing the right
thing.

Third, however, he not only lamented information gaps, he did something about them. One step was the initial implementation of a quantitative "policy planning model," through which the FTC would
evaluate the performance of industries and assess the benefits and costs
of policy intervention. I confess that I was skeptical whether such a
"numbers-crunching"approach could ever work, and as Mike's succes-
sor at the FTC I did not support it. Mike recognized that the data
needed for such a model, if it were ever to be feasible, did not exist.
To move the policy planning model nearer realization and to obtain
the data he considered necessary to advance our understanding of
structure-performance relationships, he set in motion two major data
collection programs: a "corporate patterns" survey that sought five-
digit product line sales and market share data from the 1,000 largest
manufacturing corporations and the more ambitious "line of business"
program, asking large corporations to report profitability, research and
development, advertising, and other financial data broken down to the
level of highly disaggregated industry categories. The programs were
immensely controversial and had to be fought to the Supreme Court
before being implemented successfully. Later, those who, unlike Mike,
divined "truth" without the benefit of data chose to discontinue them.
But for a brief period, the programs yielded a rich harvest for the
analysis of structure-performance relationships and much else. On this,
more in a moment.

Finally, at about the time he was leaving the Federal Trade Commission, Mike organized (with Harvey Goldschmid and J. Fred Weston)
a conference that proved to be a watershed in the debate over structure-
performance relationships.[11] The conference brought together most of
the leading scholars of the structure-conduct-performance school and
the revisionist "Chicago" school for state-of-the-art surveys and head-
to-head debate on economies of scale, concentration and profits, advertising, technological innovation, "administered prices," and the implications of knowledge on those matters for antitrust policy. Mike's
role, I am told by "middleman" Goldschmid, was not merely to represent his own structuralist school. He also actively augmented Fred
Weston's suggestions to ensure that the "Chicago school" was represented as strongly as possible. That both schools claimed victory at the
conference's conclusion is tribute to the organizing committee's care
and skill as well as to the closeness of the issues.

CHANGES IN ECONOMIC KNOWLEDGE

"Soon or late," said Keynes in the last sentence of his greatest work, "it is ideas, not vested interests, which are dangerous for good or evil."[12] At the 1974 "New Learning" conference, the previously well-accepted structure-conduct-performance paradigm entered a crisis stage, suggesting that conditions were ripe for the emergence of new ideas and theories.[13] Numerous anomalies had come to light. Perhaps the most important was articulated by Harold Demsetz. In an earlier paper and also in his "New Learning" paper, he showed that the positive correlation between industry seller concentration and profitability held up only for the largest sellers and not for fringe competitors.[14] If high concentration led to elevated prices, as postulated in the accepted paradigm, why didn't all sellers, large and small, benefit under the price umbrella? Surely, Demsetz continued, the smaller firms in concentrated industries must be less efficient than industry leaders, producing at higher unit cost and/or offering inferior product quality, and so a correlation between size and efficiency must exist. Moreover, in industries where the largest sellers *are* more efficient, one might expect them more or less rapidly to win larger market shares, so that rising concentration should follow when leading firms are particularly efficient. And one more step: if the most concentrated industries are those in which the largest firms enjoy particularly great efficiency advantages, then their supranormal profits (really, efficiency rents) will be weighted especially heavily in the profit aggregates for the most concentrated industries. In industry aggregate studies, this could lead to the possibly spurious inference that the higher profits associated with higher concentration come from price raising rather than cost reduction. Reacting to Demsetz's challenge, Leonard Weiss wrote in his companion "New Learning" paper: [15]

The correct test for the hypothesis that high concentration merely reflects high market shares which derive from the same source as high profits would seem to be a study that takes both market share and concentration into account at the same time. Market share should capture the effect of economies of scale, superior products, or superior management—and then some. At least in the case of dominant firms, it would also show the effect of control over price. If there is any effect left for concentration, this would surely reflect the ability of concentrated industries to act collusively. Indeed, the effect of concentration would probably be understated, since market shares of leading firms and concentration are sure to be correlated.

He noted some empirical support for the hypothesis that even after controlling for market share, concentration still had a positive influence on profits. He also listed reasons why high market shares and high concentration might coincide to confer monopoly power from which only the largest sellers reaped supranormal profits. But the data available at the time were, as Mike Mann recognized, much too meager to permit confident empirical tests.

More than a dozen years later we have advanced a few important steps beyond the unsatisfactory state of knowledge in 1974. To test the Weiss formulation properly, one needs profit and market share data disaggregated to the level of individual seller operating units in specific industries. The line of business data whose collection Mike Mann initiated are nearly ideal for that purpose, as are the similar PIMS (Profit Impact of Market Strategy) data collected on a less systematic sampling basis by the Strategic Planning Institute. Tests with both data sets for the (possibly atypical) 1970s show that industry concentration has little or no explanatory power, except perhaps, as already noted by Weiss, in the food products sector, while profitability is positively and strongly correlated with market share. These results support the Demsetz emphasis on scale economies, superior products, and superior management—plus Weiss's "then some." Using PIMS data, Gale and Branch have shown that the higher profitability associated with large market shares comes partly from lower costs and partly from higher prices, the latter linked in turn to superior product images stemming from both real quality differentials and the advantages from being a "first mover."[16] Using FTC line of business data, Ravenscraft confirmed that the market share–profitability relationship interacts with industry advertising/sales ratios, suggesting product differentiation advantages, and capital intensity, suggesting scale economies.[17] He and Kwoka have gone farther to show that the relationship differs between leading sellers and their followers and is stronger in industries with larger leading plant sizes, suggesting that scale economies and the way the leader chooses to exercise its cost-price leadership are important.[18]

Work is only beginning toward the next essential step: dynamic analyses investigating whether a leading firm with some advantage over smaller rivals opts to maintain high prices (a hallmark of monopoly power), sheltering smaller rivals under its umbrella, or prices aggressively to squeeze out higher-cost rivals.[19] Meanwhile, Leonard Weiss has counterattacked by leaping over the profits-concentration-market share nexus and attempting to relate *prices* directly to concentration across geographically or otherwise segmented markets with similar products but different structures.[20] For a handful of such cases, he finds a significantly positive price-concentration relationship. And along a completely different line, two studies have examined the *stock price* movements of the competitors to firms that have consummated horizontal mergers sizable enough to have been challenged by the U.S.

antitrust authorities.[21] Their results indicate that such mergers are accompanied by competitor stock price increases, implying the expectation of concentration-induced product price increases, although the authors of the studies fallaciously draw an opposite conclusion.

In sum, economic knowledge has advanced appreciably since Mike Mann was involved in merger antitrust enforcement at the FTC in 1971–1973. The old, simple structure-conduct-performance paradigm has been shaken. No simple new paradigm has decisively emerged to take its place. We know at least that structure-performance links are complex: that higher concentration can bring either greater efficiency (manifested in lower costs or the provision of superior value to consumers) or more monopoly power (manifested in elevated prices) or both, in some mix whose exact proportions remain undiscovered.[22] Much more remains to be learned, although here, as in most other areas of federal government statistical activity, collection of the data most needed to illuminate the relationships has been cut back. Meanwhile, one might suppose that changes in merger policy might accompany changes in the underlying intellectual foundations. And that, as the statistics on merger complaint frequency presented earlier indicate, has in fact occurred.

THE CHANGES IN MERGER POLICY

Although ideas are what count in the long run, in the short run it is men and women with power, usually applying old theories, who make the difference. Antitrust activities directed toward controlling mergers was vigorous during the 1970s (and 1960s) in part because Congress articulated a strong mandate in passing the Celler-Kefauver Act of 1950 and partly because of tough antimerger precedents issued by a Supreme Court inclined to support vigorous government intervention against what it perceived to be the augmentation (or abuse) of private business power.[23] Markets were defined so as to resolve the benefit of the doubt against mergers, trends toward rising concentration and market share thresholds were interpreted in such a manner that "the government always wins,"[24] and economic or social trade-offs were abjured to focus, as the Supreme Court stated in its *Philadelphia Bank* opinion, on preventing merger-related concentration increases:[25]

We are clear . . . that a merger the effect of which "may be substantially to lessen competition" is not saved because, on some ultimate reckoning of social or economic debits and credits, it may be deemed beneficial. A value choice of such magnitude is beyond the ordinary limits of judicial competence, and in any event has been made for us already, by Congress when it enacted the amended Section 7. Congress determined to preserve our traditionally competitive economy. It therefore proscribed anticompetitive mergers, the benign and the malignant alike, fully aware, we must assume, that some price might have to be paid.

However, the Court's position changed as new and more conservative justices replaced the "liberals" appointed by Presidents Roosevelt, Eisenhower, Kennedy, and Johnson. When President Nixon's fourth appointment, William Rehnquist, was installed in late 1971, the balance shifted. The antitrust enforcement agencies suffered their first substantive defeat on merger matters before the Court in 1974 when it rejected, in a five-four split decision, a government appeal against the lower court's chosen method of measuring market shares.[26] In its opinion, the majority favored a thorough evaluation of the economic and other circumstances affecting producers' present and future "ability to compete" in place of a mechanical recitation of past market shares. The message sent to lower courts and antitrust enforcers was that market structure measurements had to be well supported by economic evidence or they would fail. In the same year, the Court, divided five to three, greatly expanded the role careful economic analysis had to play in determining whether the acquisition by one firm of another which was only a potential competitor, not an actual competitor, violated the law.[27] Three years later, the Supreme Court again stressed the necessity for a thorough "rule of reason" analysis to assess the competitive consequences of manufacturer-dealer contract restrictions.[28] From that decision, direct analogies could be drawn to the vertical mergers it had condemned earlier without inquiring into their possible economic benefits.[29]

The Reagan Revolution

Within the less populist, more analytic framework established through new Supreme Court pronouncements, enforcement of the merger laws continued to be vigorous during the Nixon, Ford, and Carter administrations. In this respect, a strong bipartisan tradition was continued. However, with the Reagan administration came a clear change. Key antitrust enforcement positions were filled by individuals directly identified with, or openly sympathetic to, the Chicago school view that, within broad bounds, high market concentration has few negative consequences and that mergers tend in the vast majority of cases to be efficiency increasing and seldom competition reducing.[30] Under virtually any broad statutory and judicial mandate, the antitrust agencies have considerable discretion in choosing when to prosecute and (especially) when not to. That choice is affected by a complex mixture of mandate, ideology, and the attitudinal filters applied to supposedly objective facts. The filter applied by Reagan appointees was different. Many mergers that almost surely would have drawn a challenge from past administrations were let through; and the number of challenges issued per year by the two enforcement agencies declined by half relative to 1960–1980 averages despite all-time peak levels of merger activity.[31]

Accompanying the change in enforcement vigor was the issuance of new statements on how the antitrust agencies would evaluate mergers—for the Justice Department, new *Merger Guidelines*, published on June 14, 1982 and amended two years later; for the FTC, a June 1982 "Statement Concerning Horizontal Mergers." The Department of Justice *Guidelines* are more comprehensive, so I shall emphasize them. Continuing the tradition established earlier, they took a basically structural approach to the merger question. Within this framework, they had several noteworthy features.

Prior to their issuance, how one went about defining "the relevant market" impacted by a merger was codified in no clear and consistent way. What existed was a hodgepodge of court precedents, often based on shallow or defective economic reasoning and sometimes conflicting. The 1982 *Guidelines* sought to bring greater coherence and economic rationality to the process. They stated that the explicit goal of merger policy was to fend off monopoly power consolidations permitting sellers to "maintain prices above competitive levels for a significant period of time."[32] They then went on to recognize that one could not meaningfully delineate a market in most instances without making a value judgment as to *how much* price elevation would be tolerable if its occurrence failed to trigger price-eroding substitute competition.[33] They resolved the value question by stating that as a first approximation, the department would hypothesize a 5 percent price increase and ask how many buyers would shift to other products or more distant suppliers within one year. The market would then be broadened until it encompassed sufficient products and geographic sources so that a 5 percent price increase would no longer induce significant defection of buyers to "outside" sources.

Once markets are defined, it is but a mechanical problem (assuming subpoena power) to calculate market shares and concentration ratios. The 1982 *Guidelines* substituted for the four-seller concentration ratios used in most prior merger litigation the more exotic Herfindahl-Hirschman Index (HHI), derived by summing the squares of each seller's market share. Although certain theories of oligopoly behavior favor the HHI over concentration ratios, neither has consistently outperformed the other in empirical studies. Quantitative standards for judging the structural impact of horizontal mergers were then articulated by the *Guidelines*: for example, merger challenges were "unlikely" if post-merger HHIs fell below 1,000; a challenge "was more likely than not" when the postmerger HHI was between 1,000 and 1,800 and the merger per se had added more than 100 points; and a challenge was "likely" if the postmerger HHI exceeded 1,800 and the merger added 100 points or more.

Having set these seemingly precise "magic numbers," the *Guidelines* then backed off from them by listing numerous "other factors" that would be considered, including the ease of new competitive entry, the heterogeneity of products and seller locations, the lumpiness of orders, the amount of information available to market participants on rival price quotations, and the sellers' past record of conduct—that is, collusive or competitive. The 1982 *Guidelines* announced that the Justice Department would not ordinarily consider efficiencies as a defense for mergers that would otherwise be challenged; the FTC differed by pledging to consider efficiencies in deciding whether to challenge a merger but not in litigating challenges.[34] In 1984 the Department of Justice changed its position, offering to consider "significant efficiencies" if merger is reasonably necessary to achieve them and if the parties establish their likelihood by "clear and convincing evidence."[35] The 1984 revision also made clear that foreign competition would be viewed in the same manner as domestic competition when markets were defined, although special consideration had to be given to import quotas and other trade barriers.

Further 1982 Department of Justice *Guideline* provisions squared the treatment of potential competitor acquisitions with the main horizontal merger guidelines and the latest judicial precedents, and indicated that vertical mergers would be challenged only under narrowly prescribed conditions.[36]

In their explicit recitation of market definition principles and HHI thresholds, the 1982 *Merger Guidelines* propelled antitrust enforcement toward a somewhat more lenient stance. The *Guidelines* attempted, and probably did help, to reduce the risk of "Type I" errors stemming from economically unsound flights of fancy in defining markets so narrowly as to imply high concentration when it does not meaningfully exist.[37] However, the 5 percent price elevation criterion is arbitrary. It makes it likely that market boundaries will be drawn broadly, possibly permitting mergers to go through even though they offer no social benefits and, if sizable, harm consumers by a quantitatively substantial amount.[38] Confronted with the same issue, Judge Manos in *Marathon* v. *Mobil* concluded that persisting price differentials of approximately 1 percent between geographic regions and unexplained by transportation cost differentials were sufficient to establish the regions as relevant markets.[39] The HHI thresholds articulated in the 1982 *Guidelines* were slightly more lenient than those set by the

Department of Justice in 1968 *Merger Guidelines*, especially for markets with relatively equal-sized sellers, and considerably more lenient than those actually applied by the courts in litigated cases. Of 94 prior litigated mergers on which data were available, according to calculations by Professor Kauper, at least 29, many of which were found illegal, would not have qualified for challenge under the 1982 *Guidelines*.[40]

The *Guidelines'* list of "other factors" allows the Department of Justice even more discretion in choosing not to challenge mergers even when they breach the quantitative thresholds. This is not really new; the antitrust agencies possessed broad discretion in choosing (or rejecting) cases long before the *Guidelines* were published. What is significant is that the combination of the *Guidelines* plus an attitude of general reluctance to intervene against mergers makes it possible to weaken enforcement substantially while claiming that the new stance is rooted in careful, objective economic analysis.

Whether this is a good or bad thing is not for me to decide. Strong value judgments are demanded, and, however the market is defined, I can claim no monopoly on correct values. Certainly, the Department of Justice *Merger Guidelines* are a vast improvement analytically over the earlier amorphous body of doctrine. Equally certainly, many of the challenges brought by earlier administrations and (less often) sustained in litigation were, in hindsight, trivial. Where values become important is on the seriousness of, and relative weight to be placed on, avoiding Type I errors (challenging mergers when they are benign or cost reducing) as compared to Type II errors (letting undesirable, for example, price raising, mergers go through). Here the "New Learning" conflicts continue.

"Chicagoans" see mergers as preponderantly efficiency increasing and seldom monopoly power enhancing. Others are more willing to believe that mergers can, by concentrating market structures sufficiently and/or bringing price cutters under firm control, lead to higher prices. And they are more skeptical about the cost reduction benefits. My own statistical research and case studies with David Ravenscraft show, for example, widespread inefficiency resulting from mergers during the 1960s and early 1970s, when many managements bit off far more than they could chew.[41] The average profitability of acquired units fell relative to premerger levels, especially when relatively small firms were acquired, and thousands of acquired units were subsequently sold off after their operating profits turned negative on average. The decline in profitability was evident both for horizontal and conglomerate acquisitions, although the more serious problems leading to sell off were primarily associated with conglomerate acquisitions— that is, those for which the acquiring company's management had the least relevant experience. Although it also identified significant success stories, our research raised strong doubts as to whether mergers are efficiency enhancing *on average*, as Chicagoans claim.

The task of sorting out the evidence on merger costs and benefits and settling value conflicts belongs to Congress. Like the economists, Congress has been of a divided mind about mergers and many other facets of antitrust. Its longstanding ambivalence was not unlike that of President Theodore Roosevelt, characterized so well in the words of the immortal Mr. Dooley:[42]

"Th' trusts," says [Roosevelt] "are heejoous monsthers built up be th' enlightened intherprise iv th' men that have done so much to advance progress in our beloved country," he says. "On wan hand I wud stamp thim undher fut; on th' other hand not so fast."

The Celler-Kefauver Act of 1950 was one of the rare occasions when Congress stated its antitrust values forcefully: If it would not stamp the "trusts" under foot, it would at least nip their growth in its incipiency by denying them the high protein nutritional supplement of mergers. Since then, Congress has shown no inclination to reenter the substantive value-setting arena and clarify its 1950 intent, strengthening the presumption against mergers (as proposed in diverse 1970s bills to control conglomerate acquisitions more fully) or drawing back to a less vigorous policy.

New Legislation?

In 1986, the Reagan administration sought a more decisive statement from Congress. It proposed a set of five antitrust law reform bills, two of which directly affected mergers. One bill would grant (with certain limitations) five-year exemptions from merger antitrust for industries found to be injured by import competition. The merger exemptions would be granted in lieu of more conventional import injury remedies such as special tariffs or import quotas, which had to be foresworn by the affected industry for 10 years. The other bill, the proposed Merger Modernization Act of 1986, was more closely related to the central thread of this chapter. It would in effect codify the Reagan administration's policies, preventing a return, cynics observed, to more aggressive policies should Democrats or, worse yet, middle-of-the-road Republicans regain control of the White House in 1989.

The Merger Modernization Act had three main components. First, for the Celler-Kefauver Act's prohibition of mergers whose effect "may be substantially to lessen competition, or to tend to create a monopoly," it would substitute a prohibition of mergers where "there is a significant probability that such acquisition will substantially increase the ability to exercise market power." Consistent with the 1982 and 1984 *Guidelines*, another section defined the ability to exercise market power as "the ability of one or more firms profitably to maintain prices above competitive levels for a significant period of time." The apparent intent of these two provisions was to raise the burden of proof borne by antitrust enforcers (for example, the substitution of "there *is* a significant probability" for "may be" and "tend to") and to focus merger enforcement more narrowly on price-raising effects and away from the "fragmented markets for their own sake" goals imputed to Congress in early Supreme Court pronouncements.[43]

The merger law reform proposal was received coolly by a Congress whose Democratic leaders were concerned about the administration's weak enforcement policy in the face of a massive merger wave. Critical reactions were also engendered by the lack of substantiation for the administration's main supporting argument: that the effort to interdict mergers could interfere (and presumably had already done so) with "the ability of American firms freely to reorganize through mergers and acquisitions that enhance productivity, innovation, and worldwide competitiveness."[44]

When asked for actual cases in which U.S. companies' international competitiveness had been inhibited by the merger laws, Secretary of Commerce Malcolm Baldrige could come up with only one example: the fear by heavy truck makers Paccar, Mack, White, and Freightliner that mergers among themselves would be challenged, as a result of which Mack linked up with Renault, White with Volvo, and Freightliner with Daimler-Benz.[45] Following these foreign alliances, Secretary Baldrige continued, some of the U.S. manufacturers turned overseas for their diesel engines, and domestic engine maker Cummins lost half of its business. There may be other flaws in the Secretary's story, but two are manifest. The links to foreign companies allowed the domestic heavy truck specialists to broaden their lines with imported medium-size trucks—an advantage they could not have realized as directly through merger among themselves. More importantly, I have reliable hearsay evidence that the chief executive officer of Cummins Engine, when asked about the loss of sales to foreign manufacturers, conceded that the foreign engines were simply a better buy.

There were other gaps. To say the least, it was disingenuous for the Reagan administration to single out merger laws as a cause of U.S. industry's manifest import competition problems when by far the most important cause was the extraordinarily high value of the U.S. dollar between 1982 and 1985, which in turn followed directly from the fiscal and monetary policies adopted by the administration. Moreover, the administration's argument considered only one side of the linkage between mergers, market structure, and international competitiveness and totally ignored another side. Many of the industries visibly distressed by import competition—for example, steel, automobiles, antifriction bearings, zippers, and electric motors—got themselves into trouble by exploiting monopoly power (sometimes in tandem with their labor unions) to raise prices above sustainable levels and by neglecting appropriate attention to product quality.[46] It is far from clear that the merger cure proposed by the administration would not have side effects worse than the structural rationalization opportunity losses that might occasionally be alleviated.

Because of these shortcomings, as well as from the intrinsic politics of a Congress in which Democrats held a clear majority after 1986, the Reagan administration's merger law reform proposals died in committee. This is in one respect a pity, for the U.S. merger law is imperfect, and there are problems that could feasibly be solved. Two could be wounded (but not killed) with a single stone.

A major behavioral defect is that far too many mergers are ill thought out in advance and turn out to be efficiency reducing, not efficiency enhancing.[47] At the same time, *some* mergers, including some that might be stopped under a strict structuralist antitrust policy, could indeed be efficiency enhancing. The Celler-Kefauver Act provides no defense for cost-reducing mergers with an incipient tendency toward monopoly, and the Supreme Court merger case precedents are either hostile or neutral to cost-saving effects.[48] Thus, the administration's commendable policy of considering efficiency claims is without statutory or judicial support. Revising the law to incorporate an efficiencies defense would put the policy on firmer footing and eliminate the most serious losses associated with traditional merger antitrust. It is not necessary to weaken the structural criteria, on the basis of which a prima facie case against mergers would be established. Rather, once incipient tendencies toward monopoly or lessened competition were shown, the presumption of illegality would be rebuttable by clear evidence of significant efficiencies attainable uniquely through merger. Needless to say, the burden of proof would have to be borne by the merging parties, for only they have the essential inside knowledge. Recognizing that they would have to bear such a burden under cross examination if their merger were challenged would have another highly desirable effect: It would force managers critically to evaluate *in advance* how their operations would be fused and rationalized and what problems might lie in the path to efficiency gains. By focusing managerial attention on the efficiency increase opportunities and obstacles, such a policy would goad companies into avoiding ill-starred, efficiency-reducing mergers.

The principal objection to such proposals is that the U.S. courts and administrative tribunals have always experienced great difficulty separating the wheat from the chaff on complex economic and technological matters. There are several possible solutions. One would be to establish a special judicial tribunal (analogous to the U.S. Tax Court) with expertise for considering disputed merger efficiency questions. A milder proposal would be to have judges retain experienced economists, business management specialists, or other "experts" as clerks for the duration of a disputed merger efficiencies case. A third possibility would be to give disputed mergers a "trial run" of two or three years, during which managers would be challenged to deliver the efficiencies they have promised but cannot prove in advance. This is much less radical than it seems, for when a merger promises unique and substantial efficiencies, the merger partners have strong incentives to contest a government challenge and delay resolution for years through protracted litigation.[49] To make it work, the court hearing the merger case and any preliminary injunction motions would have to stipulate the contours of a future divestiture action if the efficiencies do not in fact materialize.[50]

In sum, there are problems of merger law and policy that still need solution. They can be solved, and they should be solved. The Reagan administration bungled the opportunity to do so by reaching for value judgments Congress was unlikely to accept and by stressing in its legislative justifications ideology and sloganeering rather than careful analysis of the actual problems. One hopes that the next administration will learn from its mistakes and do better on the next round.

CONCLUSION

Much has happened since Mike Mann participated in merger antitrust enforcement at the Federal Trade Commission during the early 1970s. We have learned a lot, in part thanks to his efforts to facilitate dialogue and secure better data. The policies have changed. But complacency is not warranted. We still have much to learn, and the policies and enforcement apparatus can be improved. To move forward on both the knowledge and policy fronts is what Mike would have wanted.

NOTES

1. H. Michael Mann, "A Structuralist Direction for Antitrust: The View of a Policy Advisor," speech before a conference of the Minnesota State Bar Association and the University of Minnesota, April 28, 1973, p. 2.

2. See Timothy F. Bresnahan, "Post-entry Competition in the Plain Paper Copier Market," *American Economic Review* 74 (May 1984): 15–19.

3. Clair Wilcox, "On the Alleged Ubiquity of Oligopoly," *American Eco-*

nomic Review 40 (May 1950): 71. By the time the replacement is accepted, it will no doubt be obsolete too, with Brazil and Korea comprising the new substitute team.

4. Final dismissal order *In the Matter of Kellogg et al.*, 99 Federal Trade Commission Reports 269, 290 (1982).

5. The merger volume data are extended from my figure 4.5, *Industrial Market Structure and Economic Performance*, 2d ed. (Boston: Houghton Mifflin, 1980), 120. The merger complaint data are drawn from a study by Willard F. Mueller, *The Celler-Kefauver Act: The First 27 Years*, printed by the House Committee on the Judiciary, Subcommittee on Monopolies and Commercial Law (December 1978), and from an FTC tabulation of "Competition Consents and Complaints," current through March 31, 1985.

6. Mann, "A Structuralist Direction," 2.

7. Memorandum to the commission regarding the acquisition by United Brands Company of John Morrell & Co., January 8, 1971, signed by Mike Mann as incoming director of the Bureau of Economics. This and another memorandum were released to me under a Freedom of Information Act request.

8. Mann, "A Structuralist Direction," 7.

9. Testimony before the House Committee on the Judiciary, Subcommittee on Monopolies and Commercial Law, Hearings, *Food Price Investigation* (June 28, 1973), 55.

10. Testimony before the House Select Committee on Small Business, Subcommittee on Special Small Business Problems, Hearings, *Concentration by Competing Raw Fuel Industries in the Energy Market and Its Impact on Small Business* (July 1971), p. 18.

11. Harvey J. Goldschmid, H. Michael Mann, and J. Fred Weston, eds., *Industrial Concentration: The New Learning* (Boston: Little, Brown and Co.,1974).

12. John Maynard Keynes, *The General Theory of Employment Interest and Money* (New York: Harcourt Brace, 1936), 384.

13. Compare Thomas S. Kuhn, *The Structure of Scientific Revolutions* (Chicago: University of Chicago Press, 1962), chapter 7.

14. Harold Demsetz, "Industry Structure, Market Rivalry, and Public Policy," *Journal of Law & Economics* 16 (April 1973): 1–10; idem, "Two Systems of Belief about Monopoly," in Goldschmid, Mann, and Weston, eds., *Industrial Concentration*, especially 177–184.

15. Leonard W. Weiss, "The Concentration—Profits Relationship and Antitrust," in Goldschmid, Mann and Weston, eds., *Industrial Concentration*, 225–226.

16. Bradley T. Gale and Ben S. Branch, "Concentration versus Market Share: Which Determines Performance and Why Does It Matter?" *Antitrust Bulletin* 27 (Spring 1982): 83–106.

17. David J. Ravenscraft, "Structure-Performance Relationships at the Line of Business and Industry Level," *Review of Economics and Statistics* 65 (February 1983): 22–31.

18. John Kwoka and David J. Ravenscraft, "Collusion vs. Rivalry: Price-Cost Margins by Line of Business," *Economica* 53 (August 1986): 351–363.

19. Richard E. Caves, Michael Fortunato, and Pankaj Ghemewat, "The De-

cline of Dominant Firms," *Quarterly Journal of Economics* 99 (August 1984): 523–546.

20. Leonard W. Weiss, "Concentration and Price—A Possible Way Out of a Box," in Joachim Schwalbach, ed., *Industry Structure and Performance* (Berlin: International Institute of Management, 1985), 85–112.

21. Robert Stillman, "Examining Antitrust Policy toward Horizontal Mergers," and B. Espen Eckbo, "Horizontal Mergers, Collusion, and Stockholder Wealth," *Journal of Financial Economics* 11 (1983): 225–273.

22. If prices are raised owing to enhanced monopoly power following mergers, the efficiency with which resources are allocated may be reduced. A distinction is made here between efficiency in the allocation of resources and efficiency in the *use* of resources, for example, in achieving minimum production and distribution costs. If mergers decrease the efficiency of resource allocation but increase the efficiency of resource use, a trade-off may be required. See Oliver E. Williamson, "Economies as an Antitrust Defense: The Welfare Tradeoffs," *American Economic Review* 58 (March 1968): 18–36. If on the other hand, as suggested below, mergers reduce the efficiency of resource use, no trade-off problem is posed.

23. On the main motions, the bill passed 223–92 in the House of Representatives and (16 months later) 55–22 in the Senate. In the Senate, 40 Democrats voted for and none against the bill; 15 Republicans voted for and 22 against.

24. Dissent of Justice Potter Stewart in *U.S.* v. *Von's Grocery Co. et al.*, 384 U.S. 270, 301 (1965).

25. *U.S.* v. *Philadelphia National Bank et al.*, 374 U.S. 321, 371 (1963).

26. *U.S.* v. *General Dynamics Corp. et al.*, 415 U.S. 486 (1974).

27. *U.S.* v. *Marine Bancorporation et al.*, 418 U.S. 602 (1984). Justice Douglas, who dissented in *General Dynamics*, abstained.

28. *Continental T.V. Inc. et al.* v. *GTE Sylvania, Inc.*, 433 U.S. 36 (1977).

29. See *Brown Shoe Co. et al.* v. *U.S.*, 370 U.S. 294 (1962).

30. Indeed, one of the most impressive achievements of the Reagan administration was the thoroughness with which it imposed ideological screens in filling management positions throughout the government. President Nixon aspired to purge the bureaucracy, but was not nearly as thorough. Mike Mann and I—nominally Nixon appointees who had to be cleared through the White House—were both "liberal" Democrats. I knew of no ideological screen imposed in the antitrust agencies below the bureau director level. Both of my key division chiefs, inherited from Mike Mann, received their graduate education at the University of Chicago. They were chosen not because of that, but because they were the most able people we could find for the jobs.

31. One ought not make such statements without being specific and hence open to criticism. Examples in which I was directly involved as consultant include Mobil-Marathon (1981) (provisionally approved by the FTC staff conditional upon a divestiture agreement that would have gutted the Marathon wholesale operation's strength, but enjoined by a U.S. district court); Eaton's acquisition of Clark's truck transmission operations (1985); and Heileman-Pabst (1985–1986) (approved by the Justice Department, but enjoined by a U.S. district court). My view of the last merger is that it should have been

approved because the alternatives were inferior, but it would probably not have been approved under pre-1980 rules.

32. U.S. Department of Justice, *Merger Guidelines*, June 14, 1982, p. 2.

33. Ibid., 4, 10. Compare Scherer, *Industrial Market Structure and Economic Performance*, 549, note 111.

34. In issuing a complaint against certain acquisitions and joint ventures by antifriction bearing maker SKF, the Federal Trade Commission in 1975 instructed its staff that an efficiencies defense was to be invited. The published preliminary decision and final order show no trace that one was offered or accepted. See *In the matter of SKF Industries et al.*, 94 Federal Trade Commission Reports 6 (1979).

35. U.S. Department of Justice, *Merger Guidelines*, June 14, 1984, p. 22.

36. The single theory on which vertical mergers are to be challenged is distinctly "non-Chicago," having been formulated originally by William S. Comanor in "Vertical Mergers, Market Power and the Antitrust Laws, *American Economic Review* 57 (May 1967): 259–262.

37. I formulate the null hypothesis here as stating that a merger is not in fact anticompetitive.

38. Compare William M. Landes and Richard A. Posner, "Market Power in Antitrust Cases," *Harvard Law Review* 94 (March 1981): 954–955.

39. *Marathon Oil Co.* v. *Mobil Corporation et al.*, Memorandum of Order and Opinion, Case C81–2193 (November 30, 1981), above footnote 11, referring to testimony establishing the magnitude of the differentials and observing that they were significant "when compared to a petroleum company's profits."

40. Thomas E. Kauper, "The 1982 Horizontal Merger Guidelines: Of Collusion, Efficiency, and Failure," in Eleanor M. Fox and James T. Halverson, eds., *Antitrust Policy in Transition: The Convergence of Law and Economics* (Chicago: American Bar Association: 1984), 174, note 8.

41. David J. Ravenscraft and F.M. Scherer, *Mergers, Sell-offs, and Economic Efficiency* (Washington, D.C.: Brookings Institution, 1987), chapters 4, 5, 6, and 7.

42. From a Finley Peter Dunne column quoted in William Letwin, *Law and Economic Policy in America* (New York: Random House, 1965), 205.

43. *Brown Shoe Co. et al.* v. *U.S.*, 370 U.S. 294, 344 (1962).

44. U.S. Department of Justice, "Merger Modernization Act of 1986," Analysis (n.d.).

45. House Committee on Banking, Finance, and Urban Affairs, Subcommittee on Economic Stabilization, Hearings, *Structuring American Industry for Global Competition* (March 11, 1986), 33–34.

46. For case studies on three of these, see my testimony before the House Committee on the Judiciary, Subcommittee on Monopolies and Commercial Law, Hearings, *Corporate Initiative* (1981), 35–46.

47. See again Ravenscraft and Scherer, *Mergers*, especially chapter 7.

48. See *Brown Shoe Co.* v. *U.S.*, 370 U.S. 294, 344 (1962); and *U.S.* v. *Philadelphia National Bank et al.*, 374 U.S. 321, 371 (1963). Federal Trade Commission decisions viewing expected cost savings as an affirmative ground for prohibiting mergers include *In the matter of Procter & Gamble Company*,

63 F.T.C. 1465, 1581–1582 (1963); and *In the matter of Foremost Dairies, Inc.,* 60 F.T.C. 944, 1084 (1962).

49. See Kenneth G. Elzinga, "The Antimerger Law: Pyrrhic Victories," *Journal of Law & Economics* 12 (April 1969): 43–78.

50. This is also not radical. Roughly one-third of all acquisitions end in sell-offs, the vast majority of which are not induced by antitrust decrees. See Ravenscraft and Scherer, *Mergers,* 164–166. An important change in merger enforcement has come from the greatly increased willingness of managers to carry out divestiture programs. This permits microsurgical correction of structural antitrust problems and also saves face in poorly litigated cases.

4

The Revolution in Antitrust Analysis of Vertical Relationships: How Did We Get from There to Here?

Lawrence J. White

If a Rip Van Winkel of antitrust had gone to sleep in the late 1950s and had then awakened almost three decades later in the mid–1980s, he would find many areas of antitrust thought and philosophy relatively unchanged. Price fixing and market allocations among horizontal competitors are still strongly and near universally condemned.[1] Mergers among horizontal competitors in concentrated industries where entry is difficult are still disapproved, although views have changed as to what constitutes high concentration, difficult entry, or appropriate market definition. Monopoly, in principle, is still condemned, although the lengthy litigation of the federal government's suits against IBM and AT&T have altered many observers' views as to the wisdom of direct, frontal, structural antitrust attacks on entrenched positions of market power. And most economists and many lawyers continue to believe that the Robinson-Patman Act's prohibitions on price discrimination are largely anticompetitive and should be scrapped.

But in the area of vertical relationships Mr. Winkel would find a revolution in antitrust economics and legal thinking. In the late 1950s, just before dozing off, he would have found a general suspicion of, and in some instances an outright hostility to, vertical integration and vertical restraints between business firms in the marketplace. Major antitrust legal decisions had condemned (or would soon do so) vertical mergers, tying arrangements, exclusive dealing, full-line forcing, resale price maintenance, and territorial restrictions as anticompetitive and illegal. Although the hostility expressed toward vertical relation-

ships that were other than arm's length was frequently tempered by
some acknowledgment of the possibilities of increased efficiency
through these arrangements, the prevailing mood could be characterized as one of suspicion and fear that most vertical restraints and
explicit efforts at vertical integration were aimed at (and had the effect
of) achieving monopoly power by excluding rivals or restricting competition. The efficiency enhancements were clearly thought to be sec-
ondary.

Upon awakening in the mid–1980s, he would now find the presumptions concerning these practices virtually reversed: Their efficiency-enhancing aspects are usually discussed first in much greater
detail, and then their anticompetitive possibilities are mentioned. Judicial opinions have shown greater acceptance for many of these arrangements; the Antitrust Division of the U.S. Department of Justice
has issued a set of guidelines indicating its wide tolerance of these
practices.

How did we get from there to here? Highlighting and explaining
that course of progression will be the task of this chapter. The remainder of this chapter will proceed as follows: As background, the
second section will offer a brief description of what is meant by vertical
integration and vertical restraints and discuss important ambiguities
in these concepts. The third section will then offer some landmarks to
indicate the progression. The fourth section will try to explain how
and why the revolution took place and will also discuss briefly the
"counterrevolution" that has cautioned that vertical restraints may be
somewhat less benign that the "revolutionists" have claimed. The fifth
section will offer a brief conclusion.

SOME DEFINITIONS

At first glance, the concepts of vertical integration and vertical restraints appear simple. Closer examination, however, reveals ambiguities that have plagued legal policy (and are likely to continue to do
so). To understand vertical integration and restraints, one must first
begin with vertical relationships generally.

Vertical Relationships

A vertical relationship is fundamentally the business relationship
between a seller and a buyer. Thus, the separate relationships between
the wheat farmer and the storage elevator, the elevator and the flour
mill, the mill and the bakery, the factory and the wholesaler, and the
wholesaler and the grocery store are all the familiar examples of vertical relationships.

These relationships are frequently described in terms of "upstream" and "downstream" parties (relative to the stream of materials flowing from "upstream" original producers—for example, farmers—to "downstream" final consumers). But an important ambiguity immediately arises as to who is the "buyer" and who is the "seller" in these relationships, since alternative contracting arrangements can reverse the buying and selling positions of the parties and the apparent direction of the flow between the parties. For example, the farmer may *sell* his crop to the storage elevator operator, who takes possession for future resale to the flour mill; or the farmer may simply rent storage space—in essence, *buy* storage services—from the elevator operator, with the farmer's retaining possession of the wheat for future resale to the flour mill. The same parties and services are involved in the two arrangements, but the identities of the "buyer" and the "seller" have been reversed (as has the identity of who bears the risk of subsequent fluctuations in the price of the wheat).

Vertical Integration

Vertical integration implies the encompassing within one firm of production activities that previously were (or in principle could be) located in two separate firms and had involved the selling of the output of one firm in an arm's-length transaction to the other. Thus, to continue the previous example, any merging of the farmer with the grain elevator, or the elevator with the flour mill, and so forth, either through a formal combination or through one entity internally expanding its activities so as to encompass the activities of the other, would be an act of vertical integration. This definition, though, immediately reveals a second important ambiguity: Virtually any production process can be decomposed into vertically related subprocesses yielding interim products or services that in principle could be (and in practice often are) bought and sold in arm's-length transactions among independent firms. Any time a firm faces a "make or buy" decision, any time the firm could either contract out for a service or generate it internally, vertical integration (the "make" alternative) is a possibility.

In essence, *all* firms consist of bundles of vertically related production processes that in principle are divisible. Thus, with virtually limitless possibilities of divisibility of vertical production processes, there is no "natural" level of vertical integration that could serve as a benchmark for legal judgments. Firms will make their individual choices with respect to vertical integration so as to achieve efficiency advantages and to exercise market power (if the opportunities for the latter are present). Inherent talents, market opportunities, and the state of technology will all influence these choices. Changes in these underlying conditions are likely to change the extent of vertical integration chosen.

Vertical Restraints

Vertical restraints are conditions imposed by one firm with respect to another firm that is vertically related to the first as a condition of sale or purchase. Familiar forms of vertical restraints include:[2]

1. *Tying*: A seller requires that, as a condition to buying one item, the purchaser must buy a second item as well.
2. *Full-line forcing*: A seller requires that, as a condition to buying any individual item, the purchaser must also buy the seller's full line of products.
3. *Requirements (or loyalty) contract*: A seller requires that, as a condition to buying an item, the purchaser must commit to buying all (or a specified percentage) of its production requirements of that item from the seller.
4. *Exclusive dealing*: A seller requires that, as a condition of buying an item, the buyer agrees to buy only the items sold by the seller.
5. *Territorial (or customer) restraints*: A seller requires that, as a condition to buying an item, the purchaser (for example, a distributor) agrees to resell the item only to customers located in specified geographic areas (or to customers meeting other specific criteria) or to resell from a specified location.
6. *Resale price maintenance (or "fair trade" or "vertical price fixing")*: A seller requires that, as a condition to buying an item, the purchaser agrees to resell the item only at or above a specified price.[3]

Four important characteristics of vertical restraints are worth noting. First, they are a way, through contracts among independent firms, of inducing some of the behavior that could otherwise be achieved through vertical integration. If manufacturing and retailing operations are combined under single ownership and control, the executive of the combined entity can direct the managers of the retail outlets to take their supplies only from the in-house manufacturing operations, to sell only from specific locations, or to sell only to specific classes of customers. (Similarly, the manager of the manufacturing operation can be directed to sell only through the in-house retail outlets, and so forth.) Vertical restraints among independent entities are thus a way of achieving partial vertical integration.

Second, examples 1–4 above have a basic similarity of logic: In each case they condition the purchase of some quantities of an item on purchase of further quantities of the same or other items, and they implicitly or explicitly exclude other sellers.

Third, examples 5 and 6 are alternative means of restricting competition among the distributors of the seller's product and are likely to have similar (upward) effects on distributor gross margins and on the ultimate selling price of the item.

Fourth, to enforce the vertical restraint, the seller must implicitly or explicitly have the power to refuse to deal with the buyers who refuse to abide by the restriction; equivalently, the seller must be able to deal exclusively with those who agree to the restrictions.

Again, important ambiguities arise. First, *all* contracts between buyers and sellers restrain and exclude. An agreement that A will buy B's product, in a specified quantity or for a specified period of time, restrains A and B (at least temporarily) from buying and selling elsewhere and thus (at least temporarily) excludes or forecloses the C's of the world from making these sales or purchases. The restraints listed above are really just part of a larger continuum.

Second, virtually all products and services are, in principle, nearly infinitely divisible into components and thus inherently involve tying components (or variants on tying). All shirts sold at retail have buttons tied (literally) to them; all autos have radiators, windshields, and paint attached to them; hospitals provide medical services, nursing services, linen services, and food services as a package. In general, as products and services move downstream toward their final use, more components are tied together into bundled packages sold to purchasers. Again, there is no "natural" level of untied or unbundled product that could serve as a benchmark for judgments. Instead, firms will offer products with greater or less degrees of tying so as to achieve greater efficiencies in production or use or to exploit market power. And as technology, tastes, and market opportunities change, tying and bundling practices will change.

The concepts of vertical relationships, integration, and restraints are thus more slippery and ambiguous than might appear at first glance. And this slipperiness has persistently bedeviled antitrust policy.

SOME LANDMARKS

Having established a foundation (albeit of a somewhat uncertain footing), we will now document our initial claim that legal and economics antitrust thinking about vertical relationships has changed markedly over the past three decades. We will provide examples from major policy documents, significant legal decisions, and a few leading texts.

We begin in 1955 with the *Report* of the Attorney General's National Committee to Study the Antitrust Laws.[4] The committee, cochaired by Stanley N. Barnes and S. Chesterfield Oppenheim, totaled 63 members. Among the list were familiar names in the law and economics of antitrust: Walter Adams, Morris A. Adelman, John Maurice Clark, Milton Handler, Edward F. Howrey, Alfred E. Kahn, Eugene V. Rostow,

Louis B. Schwartz, Bernard G. Segal, Whitney North Seymour, William Simon, Sumner H. Slichter, John Paul Stevens, and George J. Stigler. The *Report*, as an introduction to a recent reprinting recounts, "had a profound influence on both the judiciary and the Congress and thereby influenced the course of antitrust decisions and antitrust legislation over the next two and a half decades."[5]

The *Report* ran 405 pages including dissents. Only a small fraction of these pages were devoted to vertical topics, but these few pages are instructive for our purposes. In its first mention of a vertical problem, the committee concluded

that where an exclusive dealership forms part of an attempt to monopolize... it should be held a violation. On the other hand, where an exclusive dealership is merely an ancillary restraint, reasonably necessary to protect the parties' main lawful business purposes, such a dealership should be upheld where its effect is not unreasonably to foreclose competition from the dealer's market (p. 43).

The *Report*'s view of tying was a deeply suspicious one:

Ordinarily, the manufacturer's goodwill is adequately safeguarded by reasonable specifications of the supplies his main product requires, thereby for the most part obviating the need for a "tying" contract automatically disqualifying all his competitor's goods. Apart from protection of goodwill, the sole apparent rationale of a monopolistic tying agreement is to exploit a power position in the market for the "tied" product beyond the consumer acceptance it would rate if competing independently on its merits and on equal terms (p. 159).

And the *Report* endorsed the Supreme Court's decision in the 1947 *International Salt* case, which had dealt harshly with tying.[6]

The *Report* was somewhat more balanced in its approach to requirements contracts and exclusive dealing.

Unlike monopolistic tying clauses, exclusive arrangements may in fact promote vigorous competition and need not signal coercive market power in the seller. ... Exclusive arrangements may, on the other hand, seriously clog competition in channels of distributions.... The central inquiry, we believe, is whether a system of challenged exclusive arrangements in fact "forecloses" competitors from a substantial market (pp. 159–160).

The *Report*, though, endorsed the Supreme Court's decision in the 1949 *Standard Stations* case, which dealt harshly with full-line forcing.[7]

The *Report* condemned the Miller-Tydings and McGuire Acts, which had permitted resale price maintenance on a state-option basis. "The throttling of price competition in the process of distribution that attends 'Fair Trade' pricing is, in our opinion, a deplorable yet inevitable concomitant of federal exemptive laws" (p. 168). A few committee members dissented, however, arguing that loss leader sales could debase manufacturers' trademarks and goodwill and that small retailers needed protection.

Finally, the *Report* endorsed (with some dissents) the rights of a patent holder to impose restrictions on use (for example, with respect to field of use or geographical area of use). But when tying or resale restraints were raised, the *Report* condemned them.

In the next few years, the Supreme Court showed a hostility to vertical mergers in its 1957 *DuPont*[8] decision and continued its hostile approach to tying in its 1958 *Northern Pacific*[9] decision.

The next major landmark was the 1959 publication of Carl Kaysen and Donald Turner's *Antitrust Policy*, which served as a primary text in many antitrust courses in law schools and graduate economics departments and a frequent source of reference and citation over the next decade.[10] Although only a small fraction of this 345-page book was devoted to vertical issues, the discussion was again instructive.

Kaysen and Turner's first treatment of vertical relations was a discussion of vertical integration. They devoted a third of a page to the presence of vertical integration where there are "real economies of transfer within the firm"; they then devoted two and a half pages to showing how it can also be "related to the achievement, maintenance, spread, or exploitation of market power"(p. 120). They endorsed vertical divestitures "under the standards applicable to horizontal dissolution" (p. 126), and they proposed that vertical mergers that involve "an acquisition of a relatively substantial customer or supplier by a firm with 20 percent of its primary market" should be "prima facie illegal" (p. 133).

They were quite hostile toward tying, concluding that "a flat rule against tying arrangements, regardless of whether they serve a useful purpose, appears justified"(p. 159). And they echoed the attorney general's committee in enthusiastically endorsing the repeal of the Miller-Tydings and McGuire Acts (pp. 212–213).

The 1960s saw a number of major Supreme Court decisions in merger cases, starting with the 1962 *Brown Shoe* case, that voided mergers between horizontal competitors and between vertical partners, even when market shares were comparatively small.[11] The same decade saw the Court first say, with respect to territorial restrictions in the 1963 *White Motor* case, "We do not know enough of the economic and business stuff out of which these arrangements emerge...."[12] Then, in the 1967 *Schwinn* case, the Court ruled that this vertical restraint was per se illegal.[13] And the Court, in its 1960 *Parke Davis*,[14] 1964 *Simpson*,[15] and 1968 *Albrecht* [16] decisions, continued its condemnation of resale price maintenance.

Seeking to codify the Court's merger decisions and offer guidance to the antitrust bar, U.S. Department of Justice's Antitrust Division in 1968 issued its first set of *Merger Guidelines*.[17] The *Guidelines* indicated the circumstances under which the division was likely to bring suit. The division devoted a quarter of the document to vertical mergers, emphasizing their possible anticompetitive consequences. The *Guidelines* indicated that the division would challenge vertical members between supplier and customer firms when the supplier firm had 10 percent or more of its market and the customer firm had 6 percent or more of its market, unless "there are not significant barriers to entry into the business of the [customer] firm" (p. 16).

In that same year, the White House Task Force on Antitrust Policy, chaired by Phil C. Neal, delivered its *Report*.[18] The 12-person committee included William F. Baxter, Robert H. Bork, William K. Jones, Paul W. MacAvoy, James W. McKie, and Lee E. Preston. The *Report*'s 28 pages dealt with vertical issues only secondarily. But it did recommend that a patent holder, if he chose to license his patent, could not grant an exclusive license but rather "must license all qualified applicants on equivalent terms" (p. 10). The *Report* recommended the repeal of the Miller-Tydings and McGuire Acts, since "the case against resale price maintenance has been made so often and persuasively that we think no further elaboration is necessary" (p. 12).

One dissent to the report, though, was a leading indicator of the changes to come. Robert Bork wrote that " ... the proposal that a patentee who licenses one applicant must license all on equal terms seems ill-advised. ... It assumes ... that there are no valuable efficiencies in an exclusive dealing policy. ... Our present information suggests that this requirement is a mistake"(p. 26). Further, he wrote,

the case against resale price maintenance is not at all persuasive. ... There is a case against resale price maintenance when it is no more than a cover for a dealer cartel, but there is a strong case for the practice when a manufacturer desires to use it to improve his dealers' performance. I would recommend federal legislation approving the latter form of resale price maintenance ... as entirely consistent with the purposes and spirit of antitrust ... (p.26).

The next year, 1969, the Task Force on Productivity and Competition, appointed by the newly inaugurated Nixon administration and chaired by George J. Stigler, delivered its *Report*.[19] The task force had nine members, including Ward S. Bowman, Jr., Ronald H. Coase, Kenneth W. Dam, Richard A. Posner, and Peter O. Steiner.

The *Report* confronted the issue of vertical mergers head on: "Our task force is of one mind on the undesirability of an extensive and vigorous policy against vertical mergers: vertical integration has not been shown to be presumptively noncompetitive and the Guidelines err in so treating it" (p. 5042). The *Report* also contained a separate statement, "Vertical Integration by Merger or by Contract," by Ward Bowman, who wrote,

...The notion that vertical arrangements can, by foreclosing or excluding rivals, create or maintain monopoly has been misconceived by legislators, antitrust prosecutors and courts.... On the contrary, this form of integration, whether by merger or by various forms of contractual arrangements, can and does enable the integrating firm...to attain efficiencies in production and distribution (p. 5045).

The next few years saw the Supreme Court decide the 1969 *Fortner I* [20] case, showing a continued hostility to tying, and the 1972 *Ford Motor Co.* [21] case, showing a continued hostility to vertical mergers. But in 1977, the Court's decision in two cases indicated a less hostile attitude toward vertical arrangements. In *Sylvania*, a case concerning territorial restraints, the Court reversed its harsh per se rule of *Schwinn* and instead imposed the more tolerant rule of reason test on these arrangements. [22] And in *Fortner II*, the Court found that combining the sale of prefabricated housing with credit financing of that sale was not an illegal tie. [23]

The next major landmark was the publication in 1978 of the first three volumes of Phillip Areeda and Donald Turner's *Antitrust Law*, [24] to be followed by two volumes [25] in 1980 and two volumes [26] authored only by Areeda in 1986. Like the Kaysen-Turner book of 1959, these volumes quickly became a frequently assigned and cited text. Unlike the earlier text, however, Areeda and Turner were more sympathetic to vertical arrangements. Some examples follow: "The prospect that monopoly at one stage of production may be used to create monopoly at earlier or later stages sounds ominous, but...a prohibition on such vertical integration should be the exception rather than the rule" (vol. 3, p. 197). "With some exceptions, tying arrangements do not reinforce the firm's market power in the tying product.... A tying arrangement will not significantly affect competition even in the tied product market when, as is commonly the case, the tied sales are only a small portion of the total market..." (vol. 3, p. 258). "Apart from the possible entry barrier effect..., it would be rare to find a vertical merger that caused a significant decline in competition in the first or second market..." (vol. 4, p. 225). "Unlike horizontal agreements between competitors, which are relatively rare, vertical agreements between actual or would-be suppliers and customers are everywhere. Sales, licenses, franchises, employment, and information arrangements are commonplace. This ubiquity suggests that only a few of them will be of antitrust concern" (vol. 7, p. 3).

It is worth noting, however, that Areeda and Turner recommended that vertical mergers be prohibited where the largest four firms account for 75 percent or more of sales in the upstream and downstream markets, where the merging entities account for 15 percent or more of the sales in each market, and where barriers to entry in both markets are "substantial" (vol. 4, pp. 269–270).

In 1982,[27] the Antitrust Division issued a new set of *Merger Guidelines*.[28] This time less than a fifth of the document was devoted to vertical mergers, and the tone was much less harsh than had been true 14 years earlier. The division indicated that it would usually challenge vertical mergers only when the upstream market has a Herfindahl-Hirshman Index of 1,800 or above (which empirically is roughly equivalent to the largest four firms' accounting for 70 percent or more of the market[29]—a cutoff point quite similar to that of Areeda and Turner) and other limiting conditions are present.[30] At approximately the same time, the Federal Trade Commission issued a *Statement on Horizontal Mergers*.[31] No mention at all was made of vertical mergers in this latter document.

In 1983, the division filed amicus briefs with the Supreme Court in the *Monsanto*[32] and *Jefferson Parish*[33] cases, urging the Court to reconsider its harsh per se prohibitions on resale price maintenance and tying, respectively, and instead to adopt rule of reason approaches.

The following year, the Court ruled in *Monsanto* that it would continue its per se ban on resale price maintenance, but it stressed the importance of preserving *Sylvania*'s more lenient approach to territorial vertical restraints.[34] Also in 1984, the Court decided *Jefferson Parish* in a way that eased prohibitions on tying, though the Court did not explicitly retreat from its per se approach, despite a strong dissent by four justices urging the majority to adopt a rule of reason approach.[35]

Finally, in 1985 the division issued a set of *Vertical Restraints Guidelines*.[36] The *Guidelines* indicated a tolerant view toward territorial customer restraints, exclusive dealing arrangements, and tying. The division stated that it would not challenge the first two categories of restraints if the firm employing the restraint has a market share of 10 percent or less, if the market shares of the firms employing the restraint sum to less than 60 percent, or if their squared market shares sum to less than 1,200. Further, if entry is easy in the relevant markets or other factors make the exercise of market power unlikely, the division is unlikely to challenge.

With respect to tying, the division indicted that it would not challenge a tying arrangement if the tying party's market share for the tying product is 30 percent or less. Further, even in instances of market shares above the level, the division will employ further analysis to determine whether the arrangement was likely to be anticompetitive.

Thus, from 1955 through 1985, the nature of antitrust analysis of vertical restraints moved from one of suspicion and distrust to one of much greater tolerance.

THE REASONS FOR THE CHANGE

The previous section documented the "there," the "here," and the major landmarks on the path between them. In this section we try to explain why this change occurred.

To explain this change, however, we first must describe the system of beliefs, and their sources, that formed the basis for the prevailing antitrust views of the late 1950s. As usual, a number of influences shaped this system.

First, Edward Chamberlin's *The Theory of Monopolistic Competition*[37] and Joan Robinson's *The Economies of Imperfect Competition*,[38] both published in the 1930s, provided theoretical structures for understanding markets in terms other than the models of perfect competition and simple monopoly that preceded them. Both authors' theories stressed the importance of product differentiation as a possible source of sub-optimal market performance.

Second, Chamberlin's book[39] and William Fellner's *Competition among the Few*[40] provided explicit models of oligopoly behavior and explained how and why that behavior might approximate monopoly behavior.

Third, Joe Bain's *Barriers to New Competition* provided the theoretical and empirical underpinnings for how and why monopolists and oligopolists could persist in their anticompetitive behavior.[41] Among Bain's four important sources of barriers to entry were product differention and access to scarce resources (such as patents).

Fourth, patents, trademarks, and copyrights were seen as important sources of monopoly power and of likely to be deleterious product differention.[42]

Fifth, the data revealed by the postwar *Censuses of Manufactures* indicated that a significant fraction of American manufacturing industries had relatively high rates of seller concentration.[43] And the early empirical studies indicated a positive correlation between industrial concentration and profit rates.[44] Thus, there appeared to be empirical support for the Chamberlin-Fellner-Bain theories.

Sixth, markets were thought to be fragile. Large firms might use the sheer size of their financial resources to create barriers to entry (for example, through advertising and other measures of product differentiation) and/or to intimidate, discipline, or eliminate smaller firms through predatory or quasi-predatory behavior, especially "below cost" price cutting. Tying and other vertical restrictions were similarly seen as tools for larger firms to exclude and foreclose their smaller rivals and thereby "leverage" and enhance and expand their market power. Vertical integration was seen to provide the same opportunities for exclusion and leverage.

Seventh, much of the prevailing antitrust and microeconomics thought embraced the "inhospitality tradition": If a business practice's effects and implications were not well understood, economists and lawyers commonly ascribed a monopoly motive to it.[45] And, since markets appeared to be fragile, observers believed that prohibition of the practice would be safer than permitting experimentation.

Finally, many observers recognized that the amendments to the antitrust laws that had been passed in the 1930s—the Robinson-Patman Act and the Miller-Tydings Act—were fundamentally anticompetitive in intent. The Robinson-Patman Act strengthened the price discrimination prohibitions of the Clayton Act; the Miller-Tydings Act allowed the individual states to have the option of exempting transactions involving resale price maintenance within their state from the reach of the Sherman Act. Both pieces of legislation had been passed largely at the behest of small retailers and distributors, who feared the growth of larger retailers and chains and also feared vertical integration by larger retailers and manufacturers. It was surely the protectionist intent underlying the Miller-Tydings Act that kept many economists and lawyers suspicious of resale price maintenance for decades afterward.[46]

These, then, were the major facets of the mindset that underlay mainstream antitrust thinking and especially underlay the suspicion of vertical arrangements in the late 1950s.

What changed, so as to bring about the changes in thinking about vertical arrangements documented in the previous section? Again, there were a number of influences. It is worth noting, however, that many of them stemmed from academic lawyers or economists who taught or had been trained at the University of Chicago and had had direct or indirect contact with Aaron Director of the University of Chicago Law School.[47]

First, authors such as Robert Bork, Ward Bowman, John McGee, and Richard Posner attacked the basic notion that vertical integration could have exclusionary or leveraging effects that would extend or enhance market power.[48] Using a model of fixed proportions among inputs, they demonstrated that a monopolist can fully capture the available monopoly profits while remaining at one stage of production.

There are no extra profits to be gained from exclusion or leverage. Hence, these authors argued, monopolization is unlikely to be a motive for vertical integration, leaving efficiency gains as the primary (or sole) motive. Applying the same logic to tying and similar vertical restraints, they reached the same conclusion. They acknowledged that vertical integration might provide an opportunity for an upstream monopolist to practice price discrimination and thereby enhance its profits, but the net social welfare consequences of price discrimination are ambiguous. Also, vertical integration might increase barriers to entry by requiring that an entrant (to assure itself of a source of supply or of distribution) has to enter production at both the upstream and downstream levels, thereby increasing capital and management requirements. But most of these authors doubted that this increase in entry barriers would be a significant problem in many (if any) empirical circumstances.

Second, a new analysis of tying by Ward Bowman[49] and Meyer Burstein[50] showed that tying can serve as a vehicle for metering the use of the tied product and thereby serve as an alternative mechanism for practicing price discrimination. Again, the social welfare consequences of price discrimination are ambiguous.

Third, Lester Telser showed that resale price maintenance (RPM) need not be motivated only as an anticompetitive dealers' cartel.[51] Instead, he demonstrated that a manufacturer might wish to impose RPM on its dealers so as to encourage the latter to provide point-of-sale services (for example, information) for which the dealers cannot directly charge and that might be subject to "free riding" among the dealers themselves and might thereby not otherwise be provided at levels that the manufacturer deems appropriate. Since the manufacturer would not otherwise gain from restricting competition among its distributors,[52] there is a strong presumption that the manufacturer's free-willed use of RPM improves efficiency.[53] Telser's argument has since been extended to other dealer services.[54] The free rider problem can, in a similar fashion, be used to provide an explanation for a manufacturer's wanting to impose territorial restraints on its dealers[55] or to insist on a policy of exclusive dealing.[56]

Fourth, a number of authors questioned whether markets are as fragile and as fraught with anticompetitive elements as had been thought. Harold Demsetz, Yale Brozen, Sam Peltzman, and others questioned the robustness and validity of the relationship between industrial concentration and profit rates, and they suggested that influences other than market power, such as the greater efficiency of companies with larger market shares, might be the explanation for any positive relationship between concentration and profits.[57] They also questioned whether entry barriers are as much of a problem as had been thought. They focused much more on long-run incentives rather than on short-run considerations. Two important indications of this change were the shift in the discussion of patents, copyright, and trademarks to a characterization of them as "intellectual property" rather than as automatic monopolies and the greater concern about the long-run incentives for this intellectual property to be produced and protected.

This reorientation of thinking with respect to vertical relationships has not gone unchallenged. Beginning in the early 1970s, John Vernon and Daniel Graham,[58] George Hay,[59] Richard Schmalensee,[60] Frederick Warren-Boulton,[61] and Fred Westfield[62] demonstrated that vertical integration could enhance a monopolist's market power.[63] When input proportions are variable (rather than fixed), integration downstream prevents the downstream entities from altering their relative use of the monopolist's product and thus reducing their demand for the monopolist's product. Even in this event, however, there is an efficiency gain (the downstream entities no longer inefficiently switch away from the monopolist's product) as well as an enhancement of market power, and the social welfare consequences (and even the net effect on the final price of the downstream product) are ambiguous.[64]

Further, David Scheffman and Steven Salop[65] demonstrated that if vertical restraints (including vertical integration) had the effects of "raising rivals' costs," the consequences could be anticompetitive.[66] William Comanor and H. E. Frech provided a similar analysis to show that exclusive dealing could raise rivals' costs and thus be anticompetitive.[67] And William Comanor[68] and F. M. Scherer[69] have provided analyses of retail price maintenance that undercut Telser's presumption of efficiency consequences. Drawing on an earlier insight by Michael Spence,[70] they point out that a manufacturer, in imposing RPM so as to induce more services from its dealers, responds primarily to the demands of consumers at the margin. If inframarginal consumers receive no benefits from the extra services but nevertheless have to pay for them, net social welfare might decrease rather than increase, even though the RPM-induced services cause the manufacturer's output to increase (because of the response of the marginal consumers).[71]

Thus, the vertical "revolutionists" have not wholly won the day. The "counterrevolutionists" have indicated proper areas of continuing antitrust concern in vertical relationships. But as the excerpts in the third section of this chapter indicate, the tone and the presumptions of the dialogue have shifted substantially over the past few decades.

CONCLUSIONS

Vertical relationships among firms continue to provide a fruitful field for economic and legal analysis. The revolution in antitrust analysis of vertical relationships over the past three decades has surely pushed antitrust policy in a sensible direction, but the counterrevolutionists' contribution has also been worthwhile. A dialectic process between the two groups is likely to continue and to yield a better understanding of and better policy toward vertical relationships. It is surely a healthy process.

NOTES

I would like to thank Marilyn Frankel, Robert Larner, and James Meehan for helpful suggestions on an earlier draft.

1. Possible exceptions would include Donald Dewey, "Information, Entry and Welfare: The Case for Collusion," *American Economic Review* 69 (September 1979): 587–594; and Domenick T. Armentano, *Antitrust and Monopoly: Anatomy of a Policy Failure* (New York: Wiley-Interscience, 1982).

2. Though the examples in the text are described in terms of the seller's imposing restrictions on the buyer, analogous restrictions could be imposed by the buyer on the seller.

3. The usual form of resale price maintenance that has been observed (and analyzed) is the requirement of a minimum price. But it could also take the form of a required maximum price. See *Albrecht* v. *Herald Co.*, 390 U.S. 145 (1968).

4. Attorney General's National Committee to Study the Antitrust Laws, *Report* (March 31, 1955); reprinted in *The Journal of Reprints for Antitrust Law and Economics* 11 (1980): 1–405.

5. James M. Clabault, "Introduction," reprinting of Attorney General's National Committee to Study the Antitrust Laws, *Report*, iii.

6. *International Salt Co., Inc.* v. *United States*, 332 U.S. 392 (1947).

7. *Standard Oil Co. of California* v. *United States*, 337 U.S. 293 (1949).

8. *United States* v. *E. I. DuPont de Nemours & Co.*, 353 U.S. 586 (1957).

9. *Northern Pacific Railway Co.* v. *United States*, 356 U.S. 1 (1958).

10. Carl Kaysen and Donald F. Turner, *Antitrust Policy: An Economic and Legal Analysis* (Cambridge: Harvard University Press, 1959).

11. *Brown Shoe Co.* v. *United States*, 370 U.S. 294 (1962).

12. *White Motor Co.* v. *United States*, 372 U.S. (1963).

13. *United States* v. *Arnold, Schwinn and Co.*, 388 U.S. 365 (1967).

14. *United States* v. *Parke, Davis & Co.*, 362 U.S. 29 (1960).

15. *Simpson* v. *Union Oil Co.*, 377 U.S. 13 (1964).

16. *Albrecht* v. *Herald Co.*, 390 U.S. 145 (1968).

17. U.S. Department of Justice, *Merger Guidelines* (May 30, 1968); reprinted in U.S. Senate, Committee on the Judiciary, Subcommittee on Antitrust and Monopoly, *Economic Concentration Hearings*, part 8, "The Conglomerate Merger Problem" (November 4, 1969 to February 19, 1970), 5126–5152.

18. White House Task Force on Antitrust Policy, *Report* (July 5, 1968); reprinted in *Antitrust and Trade Regulation Report* no. 411, Special Supplement, part 2 (May 27, 1969), 1–28; in U.S. Senate, *Economic Concentration*

Hearings, 5053–5082; and in *Journal of Reprints for Antitrust Law and Economics* 1 (Winter 1969).

19. Task Force on Productivity and Competition, *Report* (1969); reprinted in *Antitrust and Trade Regulation Report* no. 413 (June 10, 1969), 1–28; in U.S. Senate, *Economic Concentration Hearings*, 5034–5052; and in *Journal of Reprints for Antitrust Law and Economics* 1 (Winter 1969).

20. *Fortner Enterprises, Inc.* v. *United States Steel Corp.*, 394 U.S. 495 (1969).

21. *Ford Motor Co.* v. *United States*, 405 U.S. 562 (1972).

22. *Continental T.V.* v. *GTE Sylvania*, 433 U.S. 36 (1977).

23. *United States Steel Corp.* v. *Fortner Enterprises*, 429 U.S. 610 (1977).

24. Phillip Areeda and Donald F. Turner, *Antitrust Law: An Analysis of Antitrust Principles and Their Application*, vols. 1–3 (Boston: Little, Brown, 1978).

25. Phillip Areeda and Donald F. Turner, *Antitrust Law: An Analysis of Antitrust Principles and Their Application*, vols. 4–5 (Boston: Little, Brown, 1980).

26. Phillip Areeda, *Antitrust Law: An Analysis of Antitrust Principles and Their Application*, vols. 6–7 (Boston: Little, Brown, 1986).

27. The 1979 *Report to the President and the Attorney General* of the National Commission for the Review of Antitrust Laws and Procedures did not address vertical issues, and this report is not included as part of the progression.

28. U.S. Department of Justice, *Merger Guidelines* (June 14, 1982); reprinted in Bureau of National Affairs, *Daily Report for Executives*, DER no. 114, Special Supplement (June 14, 1982): 506–514; in *Antitrust Bulletin* 27 (Fall 1982): 633–665; and in *Journal of Reprints for Antitrust Law and Economics* 16 (1986): 133–165.

29. This simple equivalence was determined through simple ordinary least-square regressions of the four-firm concentration ratio against the Herfindahl-Hirschman Index for a sample of 100 industries. See also John E. Kwoka, Jr., "The Herfindahl Index in Theory and Practice," *Antitrust Bulletin* 30 (Winter 1985): 915–947.

30. When the *Merger Guidelines* were revised in 1984, less than a sixth of that document was devoted to vertical mergers. See U.S. Department of Justice, *Merger Guidelines* (June 14, 1984); reprinted in *Antitrust and Trade Regulation Report* no. 1169, Special Supplement (June 14, 1984): 510–516; in *Antitrust Bulletin* 29 (Winter 1984): 735–773; and in *Journal of Reprints for Antitrust Law and Economics* 16 (1986): 77–115.

31. U.S. Federal Trade Commission, *Statement on Horizontal Mergers* (June 14, 1982); reprinted in Bureau of National Affairs, *Daily Report for Executives*, DER no. 114, Special Supplement (June 14, 1982): 514–518; and in *Journal of Reprints for Antitrust Law and Economics* 16 (1986): 173–185.

32. Brief for the United States as *Amicus Curiae* in Support of Petitioners, *Monsanto Co.* v. *Spray-Rite Service Corp.* (May 1983); reprinted in *Journal of Reprints for Antitrust Law and Economics* 16 (1986): 907–935.

33. Brief for the United States as *Amicus Curiae* in Support of Reversal, *Jefferson Parish Hospital District No. 2* v. *Edwin G. Hyde* (May 1983).

34. *Monsanto Co.* v. *Spray-Rite Service Corp.*, 104 S. Ct. 1464 (1984).

35. *Jefferson Hospital District No. 2* v. *Edwin G. Hyde*, 104 S. Ct. 1551 (1984).

36. U.S. Department of Justice, *Vertical Restraints Guidelines* (January 23, 1985); reprinted in Bureau of National Affairs, *Antitrust and Trade Regulation Report* 48 Special Supplement (January 24, 1985): 1–12; and in *Journal of Reprints for Antitrust Law and Economics* 16 (1986): 11–57.

37. Edward H. Chamberlin, *The Theory of Monopolistic Competition* (Cambridge: Harvard University Press, 1933).

38. Joan Robinson, *The Economics of Imperfect Competition* (London: Macmillan, 1933).

39. Chamberlin, *The Theory of Monopolistic Competition*, chapter 3.

40. William Fellner, *Competition among the Few* (New York: Knopf, 1949).

41. Joe S. Bain, *Barriers to New Competition* (Cambridge: Harvard University Press, 1956).

42. See Chamberlin, *The Theory of Monopolistic Competition*.

43. For a summary of these data, see F. M. Scherer, *Industrial Market Structure and Economic Performance*, 2d ed. (Chicago: Rand McNally, 1980), chapter 3.

44. For a summary, see Scherer, *Industrial Market Structure and Economic Performance*, chapter 9; Leonard W. Weiss, "Quantitative Studies of Industrial Organization,"in *Frontiers of Quantitative Economics*, ed. Michael D. Intriligator (Amsterdam: North Holland, 1971), 362–411; and Leonard W. Weiss, "The Concentration-Profits Relationship and Antitrust," in *Industrial Concentration: The New Learning*, ed. Harvey J. Goldschmid, H. Michael Mann, and J. Fred Weston (Boston: Little, Brown and Co. 1974), 201–220.

45. See Ronald H. Coase, "Industrial Organization: A Proposal for Research," in *Policy Issues and Research Opportunities in Industrial Organization*, ed. Victor R. Fuchs, vol. 3 (New York: National Bureau of Economic Research, 1972), 59–73; and Oliver E. Williamson, "Credible Commitments: Using Hostages to Support Exchange," *American Economic Review* 73 (September 1983), 519–540.

46. And they were not helped by the contorted analyses of resale price maintenance provided in Supreme Court decisions. For critiques of these decisions, see Richard A. Posner, *Antitrust Law: An Economic Perspective* (Chicago: University of Chicago Press, 1976), chapter 7; and Robert H. Bork, *The Antitrust Paradox* (New York: Basic Books, 1978), chapter 14.

47. See, for example, the prefaces in Posner, *Antitrust Law: An Economic Perspective*, and in Bork, *The Antitrust Paradox*. See also Edmund W. Kitch, ed., "The Fire of Truth: A Remembrance of Law and Economics at Chicago, 1932–1970," *Journal of Law and Economics* 26 (April 1987): 163–234.

48. See, for example, Robert H. Bork, "Vertical Integration and the Sherman Act: The Legal History of an Economic Misconception," *University of Chicago Law Review* (Autumn 1954): 157–201; Robert H. Bork and Ward S. Bowman, Jr., "The Crisis in Antitrust," *Fortune* 68 (December 1963): 138–140, 192–201; Robert H. Bork and Ward S. Bowman, Jr., "The Crisis in Antitrust," *Columbia Law Review* 65 (March 1965): 363–376; John S. McGee, *In Defense of Industrial Concentration* (New York: Praeger, 1971); Ward S. Bowman, Jr., *Patent and Antitrust Law: A Legal and Economic Appraisal* (Chicago: University of Chicago Press, 1973); Richard A. Posner, *Antitrust Law: An Economic Perspective*; and Bork, *The Antitrust Paradox*.

49. Ward S. Bowman, Jr., "Tying Arrangements and the Leverage Problem," *Yale Law Journal* 67 (November 1957): 19–36.

50. Meyer L. Burstein, "A Theory of Full-Line Forcing," *Northwestern University Law Review* 55 (March-April 1960): 62–95.

51. Lester G. Telser, "Why Should Manufacturers Want Fair Trade?" *Journal of Law and Economics* 3 (October 1960): 86–105. See also Ward S. Bowman, Jr., "The Prerequisites and Effects of Resale Price Maintenance," *University of Chicago Law Review* 22 (Summer 1955): 825–873.

52. For any wholesale price set by the manufacturer, competition among its retailers would normally yield it more profits, since competition would keep the retail price low and the manufacturer would thereby sell more units. If the manufacturer considered the retail price to be too low, it could raise the wholesale price and thereby gain more profits for itself.

53. If a manufacturer were "bludgeoned" by a dealer cartel into adopting RPM, then the practice could have anticompetitive effects.

54. See Howard P. Marvel and Stephen McCafferty, "Resale Price Maintenance and Quality Certification," *Rand Journal of Economics* 15 (Autumn 1985): 346–359; Howard P. Marvel and Stephen McCafferty, "The Welfare Effects of Resale Price Maintenance," *Journal of Law and Economics* 28 (May 1985): 363–379; Howard P. Marvel, "How Fair Is Fair Trade?" *Contemporary Policy Issues* 3 (Spring 1985): 23–36; and G. Frank Mathewson and Ralph A. Winter, "An Economic Theory of Vertical Restraints," *Rand Journal of Economics* 15 (Spring 1984): 27–28.

55. See Lawrence J. White, "Vertical Restraints in Antitrust Law: A Coherent Model," *Antitrust Bulletin* 26 (Summer 1981): 327–345.

56. See Howard P. Marvel, "Exclusive Dealing," *Journal of Law and Economics* 25 (April 1982): 1–25.

57. See the summary by Harold Demsetz, "Two Systems of Belief about Monopoly," in Goldschmid, et al., *Industrial Concentrations: The New Learning,* 164–184.

58. John M. Vernon and Daniel A. Graham, "Profitability of Monopolization by Vertical Integration," *Journal of Political Economy* 79 (July/August 1971): 924–925.

59. George A. Hay, "An Economic Analysis of Vertical Integration," *Industrial Organization Review* 1 (1973): 188–198.

60. Richard Schmalensee, "A Note on the Theory of Vertical Integration," *Journal of Political Economy* 81 (March/April 1973): 442–449.

61. Frederick R. Warren-Boulton, "Vertical Control with Variable Proportions," *Journal of Political Economy* 82 (July/August 1974): 783–802.

62. Fred M. Westfield, "Vertical Integration: Does Product Price Rise or Fall?" *American Economics Review* 71 (June 1981): 334–346.

63. See also John S. McGee and Lowell R. Bassett, "Vertical Integration Revisited," *Journal of Law and Economics* 19 (April 1976): 17–38.

64. See Westfield, "Vertical Integration: Does Product Price Rise or Fall?"

65. Steven C. Salop and David T. Scheffman, "Raising Rivals' Costs," *American Economic Review* 73 (May 1983): 267–271.

66. For an actual application of the Salop-Scheffman paradigm to an antitrust merger that involved vertical elements, see Lawrence J. White, "Anti-

trust and Video Markets: The Merger of Showtime and The Movie Channel as a Case Study," in Eli M. Noam, ed., *Video Media Competition: Regulation, Economics, and Technology* (New York: Columbia University Press, 1985), 338–363.

67. William S. Comanor and H. E. Frech III, "The Competitive Effects of Vertical Agreements," *American Economic Review*, 75 (June 1985): 539–546.

68. William S. Comanor, "Vertical Price-Fixing, Vertical Market Restrictions, and the New Antitrust Policy," *Harvard Law Review* 98 (March 1985): 983–1002; William S. Comanor and John B. Kirkwood, "Resale Price Maintenance and Antitrust Policy," *Contemporary Policy Issues* 3 (Spring 1985): 9–16.

69. F. M. Scherer, "The Economics of Vertical Restraints," *Antitrust Law Journal* 52 (1983): 687–707.

70. A. Michael Spence, "Monopoly, Quality, and Regulation," *Bell Journal of Economics* 52 (1983): 687–707.

71. For a critique of the Comanor-Scherer position, see Lawrence J. White, "Resale Price Maintenance and the Problem of Marginal and Inframarginal Customers," *Contemporary Policy Issues* 3 (Spring 1985): 17–22.

5

Vertical Price Restraints: Per se or Rule of Reason?

Robert J. Larner

In an address at the National Institute on Antitrust Economics in September 1983, Professor F. M. Scherer compared the state of economic theory regarding vertical restraints to the state of celestial mechanics at the time of Ptolemy, before the contributions on Copernicus, Galileo, Kepler, and Tycho Brahe—everything revolved around the earth.[1] In Scherer's view, the economic theory was imperfectly developed and the law was some distance behind. While there have been subsequent advances in economics with respect to both the theory and empirical evidence regarding vertical restraints, and resale price maintenance in particular, it is still a fair assessment that considerable work remains to be done before economists develop a satisfactory understanding of these practices.

Imperfect knowledge about the motivations and effects of a business practice, however, does not warrant continued adherence to inappropriate legal treatment of the practice. This chapter is not intended to advance the economic theory or empirical evidence regarding vertical restraints, but rather to suggest how the law might incorporate recent economic learning. Specifically, the chapter proposes that the law on vertical price restraints be made consistent with the law on nonprice vertical restraints, and that the per se treatment of resale price maintenance be replaced by a rule-of-reason standard.

This chapter contains three sections. The first section summarizes the legal background of vertical price restraints and proposes a specific rule-of-reason standard for adjudicating such restraints. The second section develops the reasons why a standard of presumptive legality for resale price maintenance is more appropriate than a per se prohibition. It also reviews different economic analyses of RPM and the available empirical evidence on the intent and effects of RPM. The third section suggests guidelines for distinguishing vertical price restraints that likely contribute to efficient distribution from those restraints that are more likely to have anticompetitive effects.

A PROPOSED RULE OF REASON FOR RPM: PRESUMPTIVE LEGALITY

The Legal Background of Vertical Price Restraints

Since the *Dr. Miles* case in 1911,[2] the courts have consistently condemned agreements between a manufacturer and a dealer[3] that fix resale prices as restraints of trade. The Supreme Court in *Monsanto*[4] reaffirmed its treatment of vertical price fixing as a per se offense, despite an amicus brief from the Department of Justice urging the court to adjudicate cases involving RPM according to the rule of reason.[5]

In contrast to the per se treatment of vertical price restraints, nonprice restraints between a manufacturer and dealer have been tested under the rule of reason since the *Sylvania* case in 1977.[6] Under a per se standard, the plaintiff is not required to demonstrate the market impact or anticompetitive effects of the challenged practice. The per se standard is applied to "agreements whose nature and necessary effect are so plainly anticompetitive that no elaborate study of the industry is needed to establish their illegality."[7] Per se rules have the advantages of economizing on scarce judicial and legal resources and of providing clearer guidance to businessmen concerning the types of behavior likely to run afoul of the law.

The rule of reason, on the other hand, provides more flexibility. It is applied to practices that may promote efficiency and competition but that may also in some circumstances have anticompetitive effects. In implementing the rule-of-reason standard, the court conducts a full factual examination of the competitive effects of the challenged restraint in the case at hand. The methodology the Supreme Court adopted in *Sylvania*, for example, was to weigh the harmful effects on intrabrand competition arising from the manufacturer's restriction on the location from which a franchised dealer could sell Sylvania television receivers against the locational restriction's promotive effects on interbrand competition.[8] On remand, after evaluating and balancing the factors set out by the Supreme Court, the District Court determined

that Sylvania's location clause did not unreasonably restrain competition.[9]

While economists generally favor some type of rule-of-reason standard for nonprice vertical restraints, few would frame the test in the
Court's language in *Sylvania*, which spoke of assessing the comparative
effects on intrabrand and interbrand competition.[10] In evaluating the
possible procompetitive consequences of the restraint, economists
would instead inquire directly into its effects on the efficiency with
which the product is distributed and into the extent to which rival
manufacturers may be using methods of distribution as a means of
competition.[11] And the economic inquiry into possible anticompetitive
effects would focus not on intrabrand competition but on whether the
restraint is likely to increase the likelihood of collusion, either by
facilitating coordination on price by upstream or downstream firms or
by raising barriers to entry at the upstream level. The balancing that
is done involves weighing any increase in competition or efficiency
among upstream firms resulting from their distribution strategies
against any decrease in competition found at either the upstream or
downstream level.[12]

The Proposed Standard

The rule-of-reason standard proposed here is a middle ground between the current per se prohibition against vertical price restraints
and the standard of per se legality advocated by commentators such
as Robert Bork[13] and Richard Posner.[14] The proposal is that vertical
price restraints should be held unlawful only where the plaintiff can
demonstrate that one of the following three situations exists:

1. The vertical price restraints are used to facilitate horizontal price fixing at
   either the manufacturer level or the dealer level.
2. The challenged practices are part of a bundle of vertical restraints, including
   exclusive dealing, that are used to foreclose manufacturers from a substantial part of the dealer market.
3. The restraints, in the context of the particular industry, have led to specific
   anticompetitive effects and these effects have outweighed any associated
   efficiencies in distribution.[15]

An example of the third situation might be found where (1) the
manufacturing level is characterized by high concentration and strong
product differentiation, (2) virtually all of the leading manufacturers
practice resale price maintenance, and (3) the services provided by
dealers are of little value to consumers and merely enhance the already
strong brand images enjoyed by the leading manufacturers.

THE ADVANTAGES OF A RULE OF REASON

A review of the economic literature on vertical restraints reveals two basic considerations that make a rule-of-reason standard superior to a per se standard in the treatment of vertical price restraints and of minimum resale price maintenance in particular.[16] First, no basis exists in either economic theory or empirical evidence for the current blanket per se prohibition of RPM. The range of effects that RPM can have is too wide and the variety of market circumstances in which it may be used is too diverse to justify its universal condemnation. Second, there is no basis in either logic or public policy interests for treating vertical price restraints differently from nonprice vertical restraints, which can have the same motivation and accomplish the same effects. These considerations are developed below.

Theoretical Explanations of RPM

Special Services

In his classic 1960 article, Professor Lester Telser developed an explanation of RPM rooted in efficiency rather than anticompetitive behavior.[17] Other factors being the same, a manufacturer benefits from rigorous competition among its dealers. The manufacturer will charge its dealers a price that maximizes its profits and seek resale prices as low as possible in order to sell more units. Telser pointed out that, where demand for the product depends upon the dealer's providing special presale services specific to the product (such as instruction about its use or a demonstration), RPM can be a means of inducing dealers to provide the demand-increasing services because it protects a full-service dealer from being undersold by a discounter who has not borne the cost of providing the special services. The additional dealer selling effort induced by the protection of RPM can increase consumer demand for the product. This is illustrated in figure 5, where demand increases from D_0D_0 to D_1D_1. The retail price is higher than without RPM (P_1 is greater than P_0), but output also increases, from Q_0 to Q_1.

There are two points to note in assessing the dealer services explanation of RPM. The first is that a nonprice vertical restraint may be a substitute for RPM. For example, if the manufacturer's objective is to increase the dealer's gross margin in order to provide financing (and incentive) for the special dealer services desired, the use of territorial restrictions along with exclusive territories may achieve the same end, although not perhaps at the same cost to the manufacturer. A functional allowance may also be an alternative, although again not nec-

Figure 5
Demand-Increasing Effects of RPM

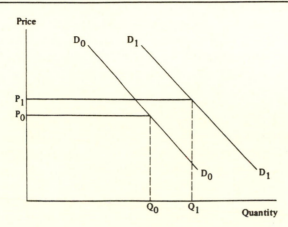

essarily at the same cost. In a competitive market, the manufacturer will adopt the particular vertical restraint that yields the largest increase in sales per dollar of cost, where cost to the manufacturer includes the transaction cost of monitoring and enforcing the restraints he adopts (or is able to convince his dealers to accept).

The nature of the product and the conditions of its sale will influence the manufacturer's choice of vertical restraints. For instance, if most sales are on a bid basis with the product made to the buyer's specifications (for example, building supplies sold to contractors), RPM is impractical. Or if the product is sold in densely located outlets (for example, grocery stores or drugstores), exclusive territories and territorial restrictions are not practical. Issues that warrant further study by economists are the comparative effectiveness and costs of different nonprice and price vertical restraints and the extent to which they are substitutes in achieving efficient distribution.

The second point about the dealer services explanation of RPM is that its scope is limited. While there clearly are examples of special, tangible presale services by dealers that are important to consumers and to the success of the manufacturer (personal computers, single lens reflex cameras, and stereo systems come quickly to mind), there are many other products that were subject to RPM or "fair trade" in the past for which tangible presale dealer services of importance to the consumer are not easily identified. Examples are Levi jeans and the many grocery, liquor, and drugstore products that were subject to RPM during the regime of fair trade laws.

If special presale dealer services and the attending free-rider problems are insufficient explanations for the wide variety of products that

at one time or another have been subject to RPM, one must search for
other explanations for the practice. Opponents of RPM offer a collusive
explanation: RPM is a means by which manufacturers or dealers can
implement or enforce a collusive arrangement on price. In this view,
RPM is merely a cover for, or an element of, a horizontal price-fixing
scheme. Before considering the collusive explanation for RPM, however, other explanations for RPM rooted in the norms of efficiency and
competition are first identified and summarized.

Other Efficiency Explanations

Another type of dealer service important to the consumer (and therefore to the manufacturer) is certification of the product's attributes.
Where the quality or style of the product is particularly important to
the consumer and the consumer regards the dealer as specially qualified to certify these product attributes, the dealer's certification will
be valuable to the manufacturer, and the manufacturer will be willing
to pay the dealer to undertake the costly search and selection process
and to carry its product. One means of protecting dealers from free-
riding discounters not incurring the costs of the search process is RPM,
although other vertical restraints may be substitutes. Professors Marvel and McCafferty have developed this "quality certification" explanation of RPM.[18]

Thomas Overstreet, building on earlier work by Professors Gould
and Preston, has developed an "outlets" explanation of RPM.[19] He
shows that manufacturers may have incentives to employ RPM when
the total demand for their product is positively related to the density
of its retail distribution. Under certain conditions, the gain to manufacturers from obtaining additional outlets through RPM-induced subsidization of relatively high-cost retailers exceeds their loss from the
negative effects on quantity demanded resulting from the protected
resale margin.[20]

In addition to these explanations that focus on inducing specific services or actions by dealers, Professor Oliver Williamson and Professors
Mathewson and Winter have developed more general explanations of
vertical restraints and RPM. Williamson, applying transaction-cost
analysis, has shown that vertical restraints can be viewed as efforts
by manufacturers to minimize the transaction costs involved in inducing desired behavior from independent dealers.[21] Transaction costs
can be significant in situations where the manufacturer and dealer
have divergent views about how the product should be marketed, where
the dealer through opportunistic behavior may seek to exploit a strategic advantage it possesses, or where the dealer's incentives conflict
with the manufacturer's.[22]

Finally, Mathewson and Winter analyze vertical restraints in the context of efficient market contracts. In a setting where dealers inform consumers and sell in spatially differentiated markets and where a manufacturer possesses some market power, there are externalities that can lead dealers to deviate from price and output decisions that would maximize combined manufacturer and dealer profits. The authors demonstrate how different types of vertical restraints, including RPM, can resolve the externalities associated with the dealer's decisions.[23] In a subsequent paper, they examine the policy question of whether vertical restrictions, including RPM, are socially efficient, and conclude that, because RPM can improve economic welfare, per se rules against it are inappropriate.[24]

In addition to the efficiency explanations described above, RPM can also be viewed as one means by which manufacturers compete among themselves for the promotional services and selling efforts that dealers can provide for their products. For instance, in some industries there may be only a slight degree of differentiation among the manufacturers' brands, and consumers may associate the product more with the dealer than with the manufacturer. An example would be where manufacturer brands enjoy little recognition or loyalty, and where the dealer provides important presale services, installs or sets up the product, and warrants its performance. In such an industry there may be intense competition for dealers among manufacturers, and a manufacturer may offer a dealer an exclusive territory and/or RPM (if lawful) to win the dealer's patronage. What the dealer promotes through its activities is not just the image of the manufacturer's brand, but a bundle of output consisting of both the manufacturer's product and the complementary services provided by the dealer. The consumer may not distinguish among the separate elements of the bundle, and his primary loyalty may be to the dealer who supplies the bundle rather than to the manufacturer whose line the dealer carries.

The review of the economic literature on vertical restraints indicates that within the context of particular markets, vertical restraints—both price and nonprice—can promote efficient distribution and enhance consumer welfare. It is also true, however, that in some contexts vertical restraints may be used not to promote efficient distribution, but for the purpose of facilitating horizontal price fixing at either the upstream or the downstream level. Distinguishing between these two uses of RPM is discussed later in the chapter.

Critique of Efficiency Explanations

Although several different efficiency explanations of RPM have been developed by economists, analyses by William Comanor and F. M.

Scherer have demonstrated that RPM can result in *reduced* economic efficiency and consumer welfare, even if output increases and there is no collusion among manufacturers or dealers.

Comanor has shown that purely vertical RPM reduces economic efficiency and consumer welfare if the benefits to marginal consumers (those whose purchases are altered) from the additional dealer services induced by RPM are less than the loss in welfare by the inframarginal consumers (those whose preference is for the product without the added dealer services but at a lower price).[25] According to Comanor and Kirkwood, this efficiency-reducing result requires four conditions: (1) the manufacturer has some degree of monopoly power, (2) marginal consumers value the services stimulated by RPM and increase purchases despite the higher price, (3) inframarginal consumers do not find the services worth the higher price, and (4) the decreased utility of inframarginal consumers exceeds the increased utility of marginal consumers.[26] Because of their doubts that a plaintiff could meet the burden of proof even where the net effects of RPM are efficiency reducing or anticompetitive, Comanor and Kirkwood urge caution in changing the rule of per se illegality for RPM, apart from a possible exception for new entrants.[27]

Scherer, agreeing with the Comanor analysis of marginal and inframarginal effects, also points out that interfirm competition could so fragment the market as a result of higher margins and expanded services (and perhaps entry of additional firms in response to high margins) that there could be a loss of scale economies or an increase in fixed costs, both absolutely and per unit.[28] His policy recommendation is that RPM be presumed legal for small upstream firms and in markets where its use is not ubiquitous; in all other situations, he would require a firm wanting to use RPM to bear the burden of proving that the net effects are not to reduce consumer welfare.[29]

Although the analyses of RPM by Scherer and Comanor are perfectly sound, neither policy prescription follows unambiguously. One reason is that their respective analyses apply not only to RPM, but to *all* promotional and differentiating activities by manufacturers.[30] As Professor Lawrence White points out, few, if any, economists or lawyers would advocate bringing all promotional efforts under the scrutiny of the antitrust laws because of concerns about the welfare of inframarginal consumers.[31] In addition, to the extent that nonprice vertical restraints are a substitute for RPM and RPM is per se unlawful, manufacturers are likely to employ more costly and less effective means of accomplishing the same ends they would seek with RPM.[32] Finally, if there is a significant group of inframarginal consumers who prefer a cheaper product without the special dealer services, a strategy of resale price maintenance by one or more established firms will invite expansion by existing rivals or entry by newcomers catering to this group by offering a "no frills" product at a lower price.[33]

Empirical Evidence Regarding RPM

There is a second set of considerations supporting a rule-of-reason standard for vertical price restraints—the empirical evidence or, perhaps more accurately, the lack thereof. A reading of the literature on RPM reveals how little agreement there is within the economics profession on the reasons for and effects of RPM *generally*. The empirical evidence published to date is at best fragmentary and mixed and offers an inadequate basis for a blanket prohibition of RPM.[34]

The historical record of RPM is extensive in time and place and contains examples of the practice with both procompetitive and anticompetitive effects.[35] According to Overstreet and Fisher, the original impetus for RPM came from manufacturers' efforts to set minimum retail prices for their trademarked products in order to safeguard their property rights in the goodwill generated by their advertising and to protect "legitimate" retailers from "loss leader" predation by "chiselers."[36]

After World War I, however, advocacy of RPM shifted to organizations of retailers and wholesalers bent on using legislation such as RPM, the Robinson-Patman Act, and chain store taxes to contain the spread of lower-cost methods of distribution. Moreover, once retailer and wholesaler groups became the dominant force behind the RPM movement, competitive abuses flourished as RPM was used for dealer interests (larger retailer profits), sometimes in contradiction to the interests of the manufacturers. For example, in its 1945 report on resale price maintenance, the Federal Trade Commission found that laws in 25 states allowed wholesalers to enter into RPM contracts with retailers *without* the prior consent of the owner of the brand or trademark and in some states apparently even against the manufacturer's will.[37] Such statutes are not easily reconciled with efficiency explanations of RPM.

Perhaps the most notorious incident involving RPM occurred in California during the mid–1930s, when the state chapter of the National Association of Retail Druggists (NARD) conducted what amounted to a group boycott against the manufacturer of Pepsodent toothpaste after Pepsodent withdrew its products from RPM in California. NARD's activities had such a strong negative effect on Pepsodent's sales that the company not only returned to RPM, but even donated $25,000 to NARD for lobbying in support of fair-trade legislation.

Overstreet and Fisher note the concentration of RPM among products sold through drugstores during the time of fair-trade laws and find the free-rider arguments less convincing than the dealer cartel explanation for the application of RPM to these products.[38]

With the development of television and the efficiency of television advertising, many manufacturers shifted their marketing strategies toward building strong brand loyalties by means of media advertising and as a corollary toward encouraging price competition among retailers. This change in marketing strategy, combined with legislation and judicial decisions that increased the enforcement costs of RPM, caused numerous manufacturers to drop RPM voluntarily prior to the repeal of the RPM-enabling legislation in 1975.[39]

Overstreet and Fisher describe the historical experience of RPM as "largely a sorry record of abuses, in sharp contrast to the contentions of RPM's missionaries."[40] The historical record is one basis for their recommendation of continuing the current standard of per se illegality for RPM, with exceptions for situations where the probability of anticompetitive effects is negligible, such as the use of RPM by small firms in in unconcentrated wholesale and retail markets, and its use by new entrants.[41]

Yet for two reasons it is likely that the written history of RPM is skewed toward instances where its intent and effects were anticompetitive, and particularly where RPM was used to facilitate collusion. First, the sources of the historical record of RPM are to a large extent antitrust cases and the 1945 FTC Report, and these sources would be expected to highlight the most flagrant anticompetitive instances of the practice. Second, RPM has been held to be a per se offense, except where protected by federal and state enabling legislation, and until the 1950s and 1960s there was no articulated efficiency explanation in the economics literature. As a consequence, the focus of the record in antitrust cases has tended to be on whether the practice existed. Whether the practice might have promoted efficient distribution of the product was not considered and data or facts pertinent to the question were not compiled or analyzed.

Professor Thomas Gilligan has recently published an interesting cross-sectional study of the competitive effects of RPM.[42] Utilizing a methodology that relies on the share price response of firms whose practice of RPM has been subject to antitrust challenge, he finds that RPM is used for a variety of reasons and produces a range of allocative and productive effects. He also finds that when RPM appears to promote efficiency in distribution, its use can become outlived and the practice can persist only because of marketing inertia. He concludes that calls for the per se legality of RPM must be based on grounds other than economic efficiency.[44]

In another recent empirical study of the welfare effects of RPM in the retail sale of distilled spirits in the United States, Ornstein and

Hanssens concluded that the efficiency arguments for RPM were not supported by the evidence. They found that RPM led to a reduction in distilled spirits consumption and a substantial transfer of wealth from consumers to owners of retail liquor stores.[44]

Maximum Resale Price Maintenance

Before considering some asymmetries in the legal treatment of RPM and other trade practices, a comment on maximum resale price maintenance is in order. Although the Supreme Court in *Albrecht* made clear that the per se prohibition of vertical price fixing applies to price ceilings as well as to price floors, the motivations for and effects of the two practices are markedly different.[45] Maximum resale price maintenance can be a tool by which a supplier disrupts a downstream cartel or curbs the pricing power of dealers enjoying a local monopoly. Work by F. R. Warren-Boulton of the Antitrust Division and by Professor George Bittlingmayer has shown that maximum RPM may be used to achieve an efficient spatial distribution of dealers while avoiding successive monopoly markups.[46]

A supplier sets maximum resale prices because of a concern that dealers will set resale prices *above* the level that maximizes the supplier's profits, while maintenance of minimum resale prices is motivated by a concern that dealers will set resale prices *below* the level that maximizes the supplier's profits. Moreover, upstream collusion cannot be an explanation for suppliers' setting maximum resale prices.

Asymmetry in Legal Treatment of Price and Nonprice Restraints

The preceding discussion of price and nonprice vertical restraints should make clear that both types of practices can have similar motivations and effects, whether competitive or anticompetitive. Illustrating this similarity, the special services, free-rider justification of nonprice vertical restraints that the Supreme Court accepted in *Sylvania* was first advanced in order to explain RPM, not nonprice vertical restraints. If the practices have similar motivations and effects, however, is it sensible as a matter of public policy to treat them by different legal standards? Should the law apply a different standard to a manufacturer which chooses to increase the gross margin of dealers by assigning each an exclusive territory and restricting sales to a designated geographical area than it does to a manufacturer which chooses to increase the gross margin of dealers by adopting resale price maintenance?

The asymmetrical legal treatment of nonprice vertical restraints and

RPM is particularly puzzling in light of the symmetrical treatment of horizontal restraints on competition: It is a per se offense for competitors to fix prices or to allocate territories. In the vertical area, on the other hand, a manufacturer that sets the resale prices of its dealers in order to increase their margins commits a per se offense, while another manufacturer, seeking to achieve the same increase in dealer margins by allocating territories through exclusive franchises and territorial restrictions, can be challenged only under the rule-of-reason standard.

Asymmetry between Horizontal and Vertical Restraints

It is instructive to contrast the debate among economists regarding resale price maintenance with the consensus within the profession regarding the per se treatment of horizontal price-fixing and agreements among competitors to restrict output or allocate markets. While many economists will concede that there may be some market conditions under which an agreement to fix prices at some level can in principle generate better economic performance than unrestrained competition, it is generally believed that these market conditions occur rather infrequently.[47] Moreover, allowing competitors to agree on price does not guarantee that they will choose to set price at the level that maximizes consumer welfare, rather than at the level that maximizes their joint profits. There is broad agreement within the economics profession that little good is foregone and much harm is avoided by a blanket prohibition of horizontal price fixing.

In contrast, the sharp debate about the causes and effects of RPM suggests that until there exists a fuller understanding of the practice and more information about the market conditions under which and the frequency with which it can be expected to result in efficient distribution on the one hand and anticompetitive consequences on the other, the appropriate public policy is a case-by-case analysis. Neither the courts nor economists know enough about vertical price restraints to follow a simple per se rule. Although more legal and judicial resources are expended under a rule-of-reason standard than under a per se standard, this case-by-case approach only reflects the complexity of the practice, the diversity of circumstances under which it can occur, and the variety of effects it can have.

Consider some of the implications of a per se rule against vertical price restraints. The current per se ban against vertical price fixing prohibits a manufacturer from setting a *maximum* resale price designed to curb the exercise of market power by dealers; a small firm from using RPM as a competitive tactic against larger, established firms in the industry; or a firm offering a new product from employing RPM to recruit dealers. In none of these three instances is competitive harm from the use of RPM evident. Indeed, the practice is likely to promote competition in each instance. Even economists who in general are opposed to RPM may find its use acceptable in one or more of these instances.[48] However, once exceptions to a per se standard are made, a de facto rule-of-reason standard is created.

Overstreet and Fisher label the rule-of-reason standard for RPM "a litigation nightmare," and contend that in cases in which both pro-competitive and anticompetitive effects are a genuine possibility, the side with the burden of proof would probably lose virtually all the time.[49] Yet the dominant type of anticompetitive effect found in RPM's historical record is its use as part of a collusive scheme, often at the dealer level. Under the rule-of-reason standard proposed here, the use of RPM to facilitate collusion would still be treated as a per se horizontal offense and could not be saved because efficiencies in distribution are also present. In relatively few cases would the anticompetitive effect be foreclosure or another outcome that would require the court to engage in a full weighing and balancing of the disparate effects of RPM. On the whole, RPM cases would consume fewer judicial and legal resources than are now consumed in cases involving nonprice vertical restraints.

GUIDELINES FOR EVALUATING VERTICAL PRICE RESTRAINTS

Advocacy of a rule-of-reason standard for vertical price restraints raises the question of how one can distinguish between RPM that promotes efficient distribution of the manufacturer's product and RPM that facilitates collusion at the manufacturer or dealer level. A rule of reason accompanied by a handful of straightforward, easily applied criteria for separating instances of procompetitive RPM from anticompetitive ones would yield some of the benefits of per se rules, such as predictability and conservation of judicial and legal resources.

Unfortunately, there is no litmus test that allows dispositive categorization. Some guidelines are proposed below, but litigating an RPM case will consume more than a trivial amount of business, legal and judicial resources.

Table 8 summarizes these guidelines. It identifies variables whose values are evidence in discriminating between RPM undertaken to promote efficient distribution of the manufacturer's product and RPM designed to facilitate collusion or achieve some other anticompetitive effect.

The first variable is the incidence of RPM within the industry. If RPM is practiced by only a few firms in the industry, it is unlikely to be a vehicle for effective collusion or to have other anticompetitive effects. Indeed, the optimal situation for the consumer is being able to

Table 8
Guidelines for Evaluating RPM

Variable	Explanation	
	Collusion or Anticompetitive Effect	Efficiency
Incidence of RPM within industry	Widespread	Limited or widespread
Nature of product	Homogeneous, few presale services	Complex, special resale services
Dealer	Unimportant	Important because of tangible services, certification, or location
Output	Down	Up (?)
Price (post-RPM)	Down	Uncertain
Market share	No change or down	Up
Dealer markup	High (dealer) Low (manufacturer)	High

choose between brands subject to RPM and brands with fewer services sold at lower prices. If RPM is a widespread practice within the industry, however, its use is harder to interpret. On the one hand, the widespread use of RPM is consistent with the collusion hypothesis; however, if RPM really is an efficient means of distribution, it should not be a surprise if most firms in the industry employ it.

The nature of the product provides important clues about the nature and effects of RPM. The special services arguments for RPM presume a complex product with important presale services provided by the dealer. Where the product is homogeneous and there are few or no presale services provided by the dealer, collusion might be suspected, although certification or density of outlets may be the explanation.

The role and markup of the dealer may also provide some clues. Where the dealer does not have an important function in selling the product, one might again suspect collusion. Where the dealer's role is important, either in the form of tangible services, certification of the quality of the product, or location, RPM can foster efficient distribution. Similarly, efficient distribution should result in high dealer markups as an incentive to incur the promotional costs the manufacturer desires.

Note, however, that high dealer markups are also consistent with collusion at the dealer level. On the other hand, if RPM is designed to facilitate collusion at the manufacturer level, dealer markups should be relatively low.

One can also learn about the reasons for RPM by examining changes in the standard economic variables of output, price, and market share. Where RPM is used to facilitate collusion, industry output should decrease. The market shares of the firms employing RPM should also decline, unless all suppliers are using the practice, in which case there is no reason for market shares to change. Also, a termination of the practice should lead to lower prices.

Where RPM is used for efficient distribution, output should increase and the market shares of firms employing RPM should increase at the expense of the market shares of other firms.[50] The effects on price of removing RPM, however, are uncertain. There will be an unequivocal rise in the total cost to the consumer, including in this cost not only the price he pays, but also the search costs for information that the consumer incurs directly. It is possible, however, that both price and output will fall, as part of the cost of acquiring information about the product and its attributes is borne by the consumer. What the consumer buys now, simply the product with fewer services, is worth less to him, so he pays a lower price. He also obtains a less-valued bundle of services along with the good.

All of these tests can provide useful information and clues to the antitrust enforcement agencies. None by itself, however, will conclusively identify the nature and effects of RPM. Unless there is a "smoking gun" in the form of direct evidence of collusion among dealers and/or manufacturers, careful analysis of the relevant evidence is required. Ultimately, the judgment about what is going on may be subjective and, perhaps, one about which reasonable people can disagree.

The case for rule-of-reason treatment for vertical price restraints rests on our limited understanding of the nature and effects of the practice in a variety of circumstances. Our current knowledge is sufficient to reject the standard of per se illegality, but insufficient to support simple rules to replace it, with the exception of per se legality for *maximum* resale price restraints and for restraints on minimum resale prices by new entrants, small firms, or firms offering new products.

NOTES

Although this paper was prepared after his death, I am greatly indebted to H. Michael Mann for spurring my interest in resale price maintenance and for the benefit of many discussions of the subject over several years. I also gratefully acknowledge the comments of Joen Greenwood, James W. Meehan, Jr., and Norman Yoerg, and the research assistance of Brenda Yeung.

1. F. M. Scherer, "The Economics of Vertical Restraints," *Antitrust Law Journal* 52 (1983): 687–707.

2. *Dr. Miles Medical Co.* v. *John D. Park & Sons Co.*, 220 U.S. 373 (1911). Although the Supreme Court in *Dr. Miles* did not explicitly hold that vertical price-fixing agreements are per se illegal, its reasoning clearly supported such a position and later decisions made it explicit. See, for example, the famous footnote 18 in *Continental T.V., Inc.* v. *GTE Sylvania*, 433 U.S. 36, 51 n. 18 (1977) and *California Retail Liquor Dealers Assn.* v. *Midcal Aluminum* 445 U.S. 97 (1980).

3. The term *dealer* here is used generically to refer, according to context, to distributors, retailers, or other firms in the chain of distribution between the manufacturer and the consumer.

4. *Monsanto Co.* v. *Spray-Rite Service Corp.*, 104 S. Ct. 1464 (1984).

5. This chapter uses vertical price restraints, vertical price fixing, and resale price maintenance as synonyms. While resale price maintenance represents the dominant kind of vertical price restraint or vertical price fixing, other kinds are possible. For example, in *Sun-drop Bottling Co., Inc. et al.* v. *Pepsi-Cola Bottling Company of Charlotte, Inc.* (Civil Action No. C-C–85–279M, U.S. District Court for the Western District of North Carolina, Charlotte Division, 1985), the plaintiffs, bottlers of 7-Up, Royal Crown, and Sun-drop soft drinks, alleged that the local Pepsi-Cola bottler was fixing the retail prices of plaintiffs' brands as well as its own brands, and also setting and maintaining a difference in retail price between plaintiffs' brands and its own. The plaintiffs characterized these alleged activities as vertical price fixing.

6. *Continental T.V., Inc.* v. *GTE Sylvania*, 433 U.S. 36 (1977). For the 10 years prior to *Sylvania*, vertical nonprice restraints (at least those applying to sales as opposed to consignment transactions) were subject to a per se prohibition under *U.S.* v. *Arnold Schwinn & Co.*, 388 U.S. 365 (1967).

7. *National Society of Professional Engineers* v. *U.S.*, 435 U.S.679 (1978).

8. 433 U.S. 36, 51 (1977).

9. 461 F. Supp. 1046 (N.D. Cal., 1978). The decision was affirmed by the Ninth Circuit. *Continental T.V., Inc.* v. *GTE Sylvania*, 694 F. 2d 1132 (9th Cir. 1982).

10. L. J.White, "Vertical Restraints in Antitrust Law: A Coherent Model," *The Antitrust Bulletin* 26 (1981): 327–345.

11. The Vertical Restraints Guidelines issued by the Department of Justice on January 23, 1985, explicitly recognize that methods of distribution are one of the ways in which suppliers can compete with one another. U.S. Department of Justice, Vertical Restraints Guidelines, reprinted in *Trade Regulation Report* 5, (Commerce Clearing House) (1985): §5,473.

12. White, "Vertical Restraints in Antitrust Law," 328.

13. R. H. Bork, *The Antitrust Paradox: A Policy at War with Itself,* (New York: Basic Books, 1978), 288.

14. R. A. Posner, "The Next Step in the Antitrust Treatment of Restricted Distribution: Per se Legality," *University of Chicago Law Review* 48 (1981): 6–26.

15. See J. W. Meehan, Jr., and R. J. Larner, "A Proposed Rule of Reason for Vertical Restraints on Competition," *The Antitrust Bulletin*, 26 (1981): 195–225, for a discussion of applying this standard to nonprice vertical restraints.

16. The antitrust treatment of agreements to maintain maximum resale prices is discussed in a later section.

17. L. G. Telser, "Why Should Manufacturers Want Fair Trade?" *Journal of Law and Economics* 3 (1960): 86–105.

18. H. P. Marvel and S. McCafferty, "Resale Price Maintenance and Quality Certification," *Rand Journal of Economics* 15 (1984): 346–359. A critique of their analysis can be found in Scherer, "The Economics of Vertical Restraints," 694.

19. This argument is elaborated in T. R. Overstreet, Jr., *Resale Price Maintenance: Economic Theories and Empirical Evidence*, Washington, D.C.: Bureau of Economics Staff Report to the Federal Trade Commission 1983, 45–49. It is derived in large part from a model discussed in J. R. Gould and L. E. Preston, "Resale Price Maintenance and Retail Outlets," *Economica* 32 (1965): 302–312.

20. See Overstreet, *Resale Price Maintenance*, 46.

21. O. E. Williamson, "Assessing Vertical Market Restrictions: Antitrust Ramifications of the Transaction Cost Approach," *University of Pennsylvania Law Review* 127, no. 953 (1979): 953–993.

22. For an application of Williamson's transaction cost approach to nonprice vertical restraints, see Meehan and Larner, "A Proposed Rule of Reason for Vertical Restraints on Competition," 202.

23. G. F. Mathewson and R. A. Winter, "An Economic Theory of Vertical Restraints," *Rand Journal of Economics* 15 (1984): 27–38.

24. G. F. Mathewson and R. A. Winter, "The Economics of Vertical Restraints in Distribution," in *New Developments in the Analysis of Market Structure*, ed. J. E. Stiglitz and G. F. Mathewson (Cambridge, Mass.: MIT Press 1986). Rey and Tirole conclude recent theoretical work on vertical restraints with the observation that, given the current state of research, the rule of reason seems to be a safer standard. See P. Rey and J. Tirole, "The Logic of Vertical Restraints," *American Economic Review* 76 (1986): 921–939.

25. W. S. Comanor, "Vertical Price Fixing, Vertical Market Restrictions, and the New Antitrust Policy," *Harvard Law Review* 98 (1985): 983–1002. W. S. Comanor and J. B. Kirkwood, "Resale Price Maintenance and Antitrust Policy," *Contemporary Policy Issues* 3 (1985): 9–16.

26. Comanor and Kirkwood, "Resale Price Maintenance and Antitrust Policy," 14.

27. Ibid., 14. The authors point out that "First, no market tests exists to measure RPM's impact on either group of consumers. Their valuations of the services and higher price induced by RPM could be assessed only through indirect evidence or subjective testimony. Second, vertically motivated RPM always benefits marginal consumers. Against this certain benefit, plaintiffs would inevitably present uncertain evidence of a negative overall impact."

28. Scherer, "The Economics of Vertical Restraints," 697.

29. Ibid., 707.

30. For a critique of the Comanor-Scherer analyses, see L. J. White, "Resale

Price Maintenance and the Problem of Marginal and Inframarginal Customers," *Contemporary Policy Issues* 3 (1985): 17–22.

31. White, "Resale Price Maintenance and the Problem of Marginal and Inframarginal Customers," 18.

32. Ibid.

33. Professor James Meehan pointed out this possibility to me.

34. The most useful empirical studies are those of the staff of the Federal Trade Commission. See R. N. Lafferty, R. H. Lande, and J. B. Kirkwood (eds.), *Impact Evaluations of Federal Trade Commission Vertical Restraint Cases* (Washington, D.C.: Bureau of Competition and Bureau of Economics of the Federal Trade Commission, 1984); Overstreet, *Resale Price Maintenance,* chapter 6; and *Report of the Federal Trade Commission on Resale Price Maintenance* (1945). An excellent summary and discussion of the empirical evidence can be found in T. R. Overstreet, Jr., and A. A. Fisher, "Resale Price Maintenance and Distributional Efficiency: Some Lessons from the Past," *Contemporary Policy Issues* 3 (1985): 43–58.

35. This section draws heavily from the paper by Overstreet and Fisher, "Resale Price Maintenance and Distributional Efficiency."

36. Overstreet and Fisher, "Resale Price Maintenance and Distributional Efficiency,"48.

37. *Report of the Federal Trade Commission on Resale Price Maintenance*, xxxviii.

38. Overstreet and Fisher, "Resale Price Maintenance and Distributional Efficiency," 50.

39. Ibid., 51.

40. Ibid., 45.

41. Ibid., 43.

42. T. W. Gilligan, "The Competitive Effects of Resale Price Maintenance," *Rand Journal of Economics* 17, no. 544 (1986): 544–556.

43. Gilligan, "The Competitive Effects of Resale Price Maintenance," 555.

44. S. I. Ornstein and D. M. Hanssens, "Resale Price Maintenance: Output Increasing or Restricting? The Case of Distilled Spirits in the United States," *The Journal of Industrial Economics* 36 (1987): 1–18.

45. *Albrecht* v. *Herald Co.*, 390 U.S. 145 (1968).

46. See F. R. Warren-Boulton, *Vertical Control of Markets* (Cambridge, Mass.: Ballinger Publishing Co., 1978); G. Bittlingmayer, "A Model of Vertical Restrictions and Equilibrium in Retailing," *Journal of Business* 56, no. 477 (1983): 477–496.

47. An example might be a buffer stock cartel operating in an industry with high overhead costs and subject to severe random or cyclical fluctuations in demand.

48. Comanor and Kirkwood, "Resale Price Maintenance and Antitrust Policy," 15.

49. Overstreet and Fisher, "Resale Price Maintenance and Distributional Efficiency," 53.

50. As discussed above, however, an inference of increased economic efficiency cannot be made on the basis of increased output alone.

6

Antitrust Law and Economics at the Political Frontier

Donald I. Baker

The core antitrust idea of competition policy enforced by law challenges all involved in the process. It challenges lawyers, legislators, and judges to craft legal rules that are both predictable enough to work in markets and sufficiently refined to produce economically rational results. It challenges economic analysts to bring order to endlessly complex reality by analyzing clearly and translating their insights into forms that can be applied by policymakers and judges who may be economic laymen. It challenges decisionmakers to be humble and yet wise: to recognize that public decisions (or decisions by default) will have to be made even when a satisfactory analytic framework has not yet been developed.

Economists have changed the face of antitrust in the quarter century since *Brown Shoe*.[1] The imprecise populism of that decision was combined with a laundry list of then economically relevant factors (for example, in defining markets), but without guidance as to how these factors were actually to be weighed and applied. Now the populism is largely gone, and our commonly accepted economic tests are a lot clearer conceptually. Today economists are right in the middle of the antitrust process—as public policymakers, as government investigators, as business advisers, as expert witnesses, and as scholarly critics.

Michael Mann exemplified this growing rule of economists, as teacher, scholar, and public official. He challenged us who were his colleagues in the government to rethink what we thought we knew, to expand our horizons, and to be vigorous when our instincts could be supported by creditable economic analysis. He did this in a style which mixed practical insights with patience and even humility. He treated a colleague as a fellow traveler on a voyage and not as a member of a lecture room audience. His spirit and wisdom dares one to think anew about practical gaps in antitrust analysis and how we can hope to narrow or fill them.

One such gap is the province of neither economists nor antitrust lawyers—and yet none of us can safely ignore it. The question is how, if at all, do we factor future politics, both at home and abroad, into any economic analysis of long-run market performance. This seems a particularly important question in analyzing mergers and joint ventures at a time when foreign competition is a hot political topic.[2].

Markets rarely exist in a political vacuum. Indeed, the more important a market is seen as being, the more likely that it will be subject to special political intervention. The line between "competition" and "politics" in the market context might be characterized as follows: Adam Smith's ideal of the "invisible hand"—with its indifference to the exact identity of winners and losers—is fundamentally at odds with the political process, which is concerned with constituency service generally and with an often "visible hand" seeking the "right" results for key constituents. What distinguishes the "highly political market" from others is that obtaining a "right" result is seen as much too important to leave to the random, rough-and-tumble of the competitive process. Such a market is generally subject to government regulation, government-sponsored (or tolerated) cartels, government ownership, special entry barriers, or other market manipulation.

As an aid to analysis, one might postulate a spectrum running from "perfect market politics" at one end to "purely political market" at the other, thus roughly paralleling the economics textbook model, running from "perfect competition" to "pure monopoly." Some of the main points on the "political" spectrum would be as follows:

- *"Perfect market politics"*: a market in which prices are significantly influenced by political decisions (for example, on monetary or defense procurement policy), and yet the government has not sought to manipulate the market in any way. Such a concept is even further from the real world than "perfect competition" ever was.

- *"Rational market politics"*: the government does not intervene in the market process unless it it necessary to protect consumers against market imperfections or to protect economic public goods or to protect the public against generally accepted and clearly articulated public evils to which the market process does not provide correction (for example, natural monopoly, fraud, or clearly unsafe products).

- *"Workable market politics"*: periodic, perhaps random, government interventions in the market process more motivated by constituency service than any refined principles. Such interventions are not so frequent that they have become the rule rather than the exception.

- *"Pure market politics"*: pervasive government involvement to ensure specific constituency goals, such as low prices for consumer-constituents, high prices for employer-constituents and farmer-constituents, and job security at high wages for worker-constituents.

Each of the foregoing "political market" categories may be clearly seen in the currency foreign exchange markets of different countries at various times. Foreign exchange rates tend to reflect political facts and concerns, as well as a nation's underlying economic strength; and they are influenced by government monetary policy and by central bank trading activities. Such rates have often been fixed by governments for political reasons and they are sometimes the object of government exchange control regulation.

There are numerous instances in antitrust enforcement when it is seriously relevant to be able to predict whether a market is likely to be "workably competitive," "workably political," or even "purely political."

The issue arises most frequently in the merger enforcement area, particularly (but not exclusively) in connection with evaluating the impact of foreign competition. Both Clayton Act section 7 and common sense call for a long-term predictive judgment in each case: Will the market be substantially less competitive—that is, more prone to collusion—over the long term as a result of this merger? If the answer is "yes," then the merger should normally be blocked. If the answer is "no," it should definitely be allowed to go forward.

The Justice Department's 1982 and 1984 *Merger Guidelines* give us a rational set of economic tools with which to analyze a proposed merger of two competitors. Broadly, they ask us to consider the impact of a postmerger 5 to 10 percent price increase: Would consumers turn to different substantive products or go to more distant geographic sources? Would new producers enter the market or existing producers expand capacity? Where the answers to these questions are generally "yes," the market either is not properly defined or it is not a market in which collusion is likely to be successful. The problem is, of course, that we have to make these predictions within a relatively short period (for example, the *Merger Guidelines* set up a one-year period for shifts to substitute products and a two-year period for new entry). Thus, the *Guidelines* do not, and probably cannot, provide all the answers in the long-term predictive judgment.

The 1984 *Merger Guidelines* makes some effort to deal with political factors in the foreign trade context.[3] Section 2.34 explains that,

Although voluntary or involuntary quotas may prevent foreign competitors from increasing imports into the United States in response to a domestic price increase, the Department will not exclude foreign competitors from the relevant market solely on the basis of quotas.

Quite properly, the department notes that, "it frequently is difficult to determine and measure the effectiveness and longevity of a particular quota and any offsetting supply response from firms in countries not subject to quotas." Meanwhile, section 3.23 ("Special Factors Affecting Foreign Firms") elaborates on the point in some detail but without any precise conclusion. It simply notes that quotas may cause current import sales data to overstate a foreign firm's competitive significance, especially where they are located in "countries subject to binding quotas." This section also mentions "other types of trade restraints and changes in exchange rates" as "less significant, but still important factors." The department does not give any further specificity on how it will go about making these determinations, it simply seems to be saying that *it* will discount importers' market shares where *it* believes such shares overstate the competitive significance of foreign firms. The actual details of such shading have never become clear in practice, largely because the Justice Department has not come close to applying the actual percentage (Herfindahl-Hirschman Index) tests stated in the *Guidelines* during the 1984–1987 period.

MARKET SITUATIONS INVITING POLITICAL ANALYSIS

At least three types of market situations invite us to try to make a careful political appraisal in analyzing a merger or joint venture. The first concerns a market subject to recurring current (and perhaps short run) political distortions, as would often be the case in many agricultural and foreign exchange markets. The second involves a politically precarious competitive market—a situation classically illustrated by increasing foreign competition to major domestic employers. The third category would be the politically precarious regulated industry—the entry- or price-protected industry facing increasing public pressure for partial or complete deregulation.

Markets Subject to Current Political Distortion

Governments love to manipulate markets. Indeed, political distortion is probably the rule rather than the exception in many markets for agricultural products, energy, and foreign exchange. To the extent that this process continues to be reasonably predictable, it probably gets factored to current antitrust analysis as part of the "base case" assumption. The situation may be a little different where the particular market is subject to some special short-run distortion. Foreign exchange markets would seem a good example here. Finance ministers and central bankers certainly try to influence this market by public statements and open market trading activities. Thus, for example, the U.S. government purports to have been trying, directly and through cooperation with other leading industrial countries, to push the exchange rate for the dollar downward vis-à-vis leading trading currencies in Europe and the Far East during 1985–1987. Whether such intervention is likely to be successful over even the medium term is, I am sure, an open question.

What is less open to question is that foreign exchange rates are a key factor in analyzing mergers and markets (even if such rates get but scant reference in the Department of Justice *Merger Guidelines*). Exchange rates translate directly into pricing. An aberrant but favorable exchange rate may make an importer highly competitive within the United States in one year, while it remains largely noncompetitive in another year. Some inquiry ought to be made by antitrust enforcers and courts as to whether a current exchange rate is "unusual" because of certain factors and, if so, whether a future return to more "normal" exchange rates would be likely to increase or decrease the competitiveness of exporters from a particular country. If the answer is that such an event would make them a lot less competitive in the United States, then their current market shares should be discounted.

Politically Precarious Competitive Markets

Paul McCracken has recently noted the obvious: "Those producing [any] increased imports do not vote, those experiencing a shrinkage of export markets do and the generalized advantage to consumers is not usually a political force."[4] Domestic employers and workers rarely welcome foreign competition into their markets and *increasing* foreign competition naturally heightens their anxiety in a very special way because it tends to threaten *existing* plant investment and jobs.

The problem is particularly acute in mature industries with heavily unionized employment, for here the imports—like domestic production by nonunionized competitors—threaten the often above-market deal between the union and employers pursuant to the National Labor Relations Act. This naturally leads the unions and their employers toward a "hot cargo" approach to imports: prohibit or restrict them or a least raise their prices with heavy tariffs and penalties. They argue strongly that the menacing foreign competition is "unfair" or is "subsidized"or is based on "sweat shop labor." While this situation may be most acute in heavily unionized old industries, it is certainly not confined to these, and indeed, we have now seen the areas of dispute move from the old "rustbelt" industries to Silicon Valley, with its clean, nonunionized plants.[5]

Where significant numbers of domestic jobs in politically important constituencies are being lost to this process, Congress is very likely to try to shut down or slow down or penalize the domestically disruptive imports. This political reality is very much a fact of life in the United States in the mid–1980s;[6] and the risk of import restraint in any particular market is enhanced today by a more general "mood of populism, isolationism and protectionism in the United States."[7] Such a political overhang may cause a variety of different trade restraints, ranging from legislative quotas at one extreme to "voluntary" export restraints imposed by a foreign government for fear of such American legislation. It becomes less important for antitrust purposes to predict *exactly what* will happen than that *something restrictive* will happen in a particular market. In these circumstances, the antitrust enforcers and courts should discount the current market shares of foreign importers in evaluating a merger between two major domestic competitors. It may also be an appropriate reason to discount the import market share of a foreign competitor seeking to enter the U.S. market directly by buying a substantial U.S. producer. The reason in both cases would be the same: The importer may well not be here tomorrow as an effective choice.

Politically Precarious Regulated Markets

The core ideas of economic regulation—namely, restriction on entry and/or pricing—are of course fundamentally at odds with antitrust policy. However, antitrust enforcers and courts have not for this reason simply abandoned regulated markets as an area of antitrust concern, except where Congress has explicitly ousted antitrust jurisdiction.[8] In fact, the antitrust courts have used the entry limitations built into various regulatory schemes to pronounce quite strict rules as to mergers within a regulated market. This has been especially true in commercial banking, where entry has been restricted in many instances and pricing restricted in a few instances, while leaving other areas of activity open to competition. In its seminal *Philadelphia National Bank* decision, the Supreme Court in fact used the legally permitted area of branching activity as the relevant geographic market and broadly opined, "The fact that banking is a highly regulated industry critical to the Nation's welfare makes the play of competition not less important but more so."[9] The Court stressed the risks of "the businessman [being] denied credit because his banking alternatives had been eliminated by mergers" and "the costs of banking services and credit [being] allowed to become excessive by the absence of competitive pressures."[10] Because of entry restrictions, the Justice Department and the courts applied the bank merger rules to horizontal mergers among direct competitors in very small markets, in which the capital costs for entry would not be large.[11]

Today the banking industry is undergoing substantial deregulation, admittedly complex and rather ad hoc, but deregulation nonetheless. Leading states are liberalizing their restrictions against branch banking within the state and the historic barriers against interstate expansion are coming down very rapidly, mostly through state legislative action. Had antitrust enforces foreseen these developments, and they were not too distant, the Justice Department would have been justified in applying somewhat less stringent rules to bank mergers than they did in the post-*Philadelphia* cases. Indeed, it may be just such thinking that explains the 1986 departure by the Department of Justice and the Federal Reserve Board from their traditional antitrust standards in approving the $16.2 *billion* merger (measured in domestic deposits) between Wells Fargo Bank and Crocker National Bank in California— a merger that increased concentration in the San Francisco metropolitan area far beyond anything that was apparently allowed under the Department of Justice *Merger Guidelines*. Similar issues may be raised in large horizontal bank holding company mergers now being proposed in such states as Texas.

The same general point could be made in the context of the airline industry. Historically, the Justice Department opposed airline mergers before the CAB (Civil Aeronautics Board) (which could exempt them) where the carriers competed directly on at least a few major city-pair routes. Prior to 1978, airline routes had to be granted by the CAB, and an important route proceeding tended to be uncertain in result and drawn out in practice. Accordingly, this "route specific" approach to mergers in the airline industry was entirely appropriate in, say, the early 1970s. [12] However, had the enforcers been able to foresee the complete route and pricing freedom that was to emerge from the Airline Deregulation Act of 1978, they clearly could have afforded a much more permissive approach to mergers.[13]

The same general point could also be made in the context of a domestic product market that we would not ordinarily think of as a "regulated" industry but that was subject to government-enforced restrictions on imports into the market. If it seems highly likely that existing restraints on imports are likely to be lifted in the foreseeable future, this form of potential "deregulation" is as relevant to merger analysis as traditional deregulation of banks or airlines.

It is one thing to say that we ought to consider the economic consequences of reasonably foreseeable political action. It is a much more difficult question to see exactly how we ought to do it. Merger analysis is probably already too complex and involves many hard-to-predict variables in any difficult case. Yet the political dimension seems sufficiently important to some merger situations that we should not ignore it simply because it would incrementally complicate the basic problem of structuring workable antitrust rules for analyzing mergers and joint ventures.

The problem is least serious where the political factor would cause the government to take a more permissive view of a merger than would otherwise be the case. This would clearly occur in some "politically precarious regulated industry," as discussed above. Here, probable political change simply becomes a *prosecutorial discretion* item. The Justice Department and the Federal Trade Commission are very much in the middle of the domestic political process and hence really could make their own judgments as to probable political change. Even in the international environment, they (or at least the Justice Department) would probably have access to some projections by other government agencies (the Departments of State, Commerce, Defense, and so on) as to the likelihood of certain political events happening abroad. In any event, it would be sufficient for the government to conclude that existing entry rules or quotas are likely to be liberalized and hence current import sales statistics understate long-term competition; and therefore section 7 case would not be justified even though the current market share statistics would indicate a clear *Merger Guidelines* violation.

The situation is entirely different where prospective political change would cause the government to apply a stricter antitrust test than current market shares and sales would imply—as typically would be the case in "politically precarious competitive industry." In this instance, the matter is not entirely discretionary. Some workable rule of law would have to be developed to govern how these transactions were to be handled in court. The Justice Department has struck at least a glancing blow at this issue in section 3.23 of the 1984 *Merger Guidelines*, where it indicated that *existing* government trade restraints may cause "actual import sales and shipment data . . . to overstate the competitive significance of firms in countries subject to binding quotas." But I am taking it a step further from *existing* trade restraints and applying the idea to *reasonably foreseeable* future restraints. In the case of the existing restraint, the government could present an economic expert witness who would explain why the existing trade restraints prevent the foreign firm from increasing supply into the U.S. market and thus may greatly reduce its effectiveness as a competitive check on future price increases. My approach might require that the government first put on a political scientist as expert witness, for the purpose of establishing that some form of political restraint on imports was reasonably probable in the present circumstances; and then the government could put on the economic expert to testify as to what the likely effects of such restraints would be. This would surely complicate merger investigations and cases to some degree.

An alternative approach would in essence be to create some form of legal presumption. This might allow the judge to take judicial notice from published data, newspaper reports, editorials, and others that there exists some practical risk of trade restraints.[14] Having done this, the judge might then be permitted to discount the present shares of import competitors in assessing a particular merger. Broadly speaking, such an approach would be analogous to the *Philadelphia National Bank* rule, which allowed courts to infer adverse market effects from certain market shares, without necessary proof in a particular case.

Clearly, one does not wish to see every merger or joint venture case or investigation complicated by an extensive "probable political change" inquiry. What we should be trying to do is to isolate cases in which political overhangs are reasonably foreseeable and would have substantial potential effect on future market performance. This is too well illustrated by the American political situation in 1987, when the pressure for job protection at home is creating momentum not only for import restraints in specific sectors, but also for more broadly based import restrictions related to balance of payment considerations. It would be folly at this time to assume that the market position of foreign importers into a critical U.S. market in mid–1988 is going to look about the same as it did in mid–1986, regardless of whether the market is computer chips or automobiles or sheet steel. A cautious and pragmatic enforcement program would at least try to take this reality into account and be somewhat more conservative in approving horizontal mergers in markets that now depend on importers (or other political outsiders) to ensure competitive results.

NOTES

1. *Brown Shoe Co.* v. *United States*, 370 U.S. 294 (1962).
2. This issue would also arise in Sherman Act section 2 enforcement aimed at structural relief, for here too decisions should be based on probable long-

term market effect. See Donald I. Baker, "Government Enforcement of Section Two," *Notre Dame Law Review* 61 (1986): 898.

3. U.S. Department of Justice Merger Guidelines, 49 Fed. Rev. 26,823 (June 29, 1984); and see generally, Donald I. Baker and William Blumenthal "The Revised Merger Guidelines: One Step Forward, Two Steps Back." *National Law Journal*, July 9, 1984, 39.

4. Paul W. McCracken, "Toward World Economic Disintegration," *Wall Street Journal*, February 9, 1987, 18.

5. See, for example, "Chips Fight—Reagan's Tariff Move May Be Turning Point in Japanese Relations," *Wall Street Journal*, March 30, 1987, 1.

6. See McCracken, "Toward World Economic Disintegration"; and Leonard Silk, "United States and the World Economy," *Foreign Affairs* 65 (1987): 458.

7. Silk, "United States and the World Economy," 468.

8. See, for example, *Pan American World Airways Inc.* v. *United States*, 371 U.S. 296 (1963) and *Hughes Tool Co.* v. *Trans World Airlines, Inc.*, 409 U.S. 363 (1973), broadly construing the exemption powers of the Civil Aeronautics Board under section 408 of the Federal Aviation Act of 1958, 49 U.S.C. S1378.

9. *United States* v. *Philadelphia National Bank*, 374 U.S. 321, 372 (1963).

10. *United States* v. *Philadelphia National Bank* at 372.

11. See, for example, *United States* v. *Phillipsburg National Bank & Trust Co.*, 399 U.S. 350 (1970) (invalidating a merger of two of three banks in a county closed to outside entry by state law; the merging parties had $25.3 *million* in deposits).

12. See, for example, Justice Department opposition to the proposed American Airlines–Western Airlines merger, which was ultimately abandoned by the parties.

13. P. L.95–504.

14. For example, McCracken, "Toward World Economic Disintegration," and Silk, "United States and the World Economy."

7

Antitrust Law and Policy: Rule of Law or Economic Assumptions?

Timothy J. Waters

The vigorous and intense debate about the scope, purpose, and objectives of the antitrust laws, sparked most recently by the Reagan administration's legislative proposals to amend those laws, in particular section 7 of the Clayton Act, frames the subject for this chapter.[1] The issue is whether the existing antitrust statutes, as refined and shaped through case law, have failed to keep pace with new developments in economic learning concerning industrial organization behavior and its consequences. The proposed amendments to section 7 of the Clayton Act squarely present the question as to whether the existing statutory framework must be reoriented in a manner consistent with contemporary economic thought.[2]

Many distinguished lawyers and some economists argue that there should be no serious debate; the Sherman and Clayton Acts, and the legal precedent developed thereunder, represent the proper and defined scope of the statutes constituting our antitrust laws.[3] Under this view, the present statutory framework has worked for almost 100 years, and substantive modification is neither necessary nor appropriate.

Other lawyers, including former Assistant Attorney General William Baxter, and perhaps most economists argue that the exclusive purpose and justification for the antitrust laws is economic efficiency. Under this view, the existing body of law inappropriately allows non-economic considerations to be taken into account in the enforcement or interpretation of the antitrust statutes.[4] Accordingly, statutory modification is necessary to eliminate the effects of outmoded precedent and to enable the courts to give immediate recognition to the pressing economic concerns of today.[5]

Having accepted the assignment to submit a chapter as part of an appropriate memorial for Mike Mann, I decided to research the answer I would have expected from Mike. I concluded that the ever-diplomatic Mike would have sought to find a compromise. His instinct would have had merit. Despite the periodic economic and political debates, the existing antitrust statutes have in fact accommodated changing economic theories and goals, as well as contemporary industrial and business concerns. The rule of law that has developed (and continues to develop) through the thousands of cases decided by the courts fundamentally has served our nation well.

The debate with respect to antitrust enforcement policy, of course, is not properly a dispute between the role of the rule of law and the role of various economic models. The antitrust laws were not conceived, either in 1890 or 1914, as statutes for general economic planning.[6] Indeed, the Sherman Act is a criminal statute whose origins can be traced to common law, various state statutes, and state constitutional provisions that predate the Sherman Act.[7] After almost 100 years of enforcement actions and judicial decisions, however, there is little doubt that antitrust law has so absorbed economic learning and methods that it is difficult to distinguish between what is "economic" and what is "law."[8]

In many respects, reference to the perceived differences between law and economics as a "debate" is a misnomer. The various arguments are framed more to support particular philosophical outcomes and policy directions than they are intended to define the proper scope and the purpose of the antitrust laws.[9] The so-called intellectual war in antitrust[10] is not truly between law and economics.[11] Terms such as *monopoly* and *restraint of trade* find their genesis in economics. Terms such as *fair* or *unfair* are rooted in common law legal concepts, not economic theory. The legislative history and judicial decisions are filled with terms such as *fair competition, economic justice,* and *free and open competition,* which merge, if not confuse, economic learning and legal canons. Fundamentally, the aim of law is "justice, not truth,"[12] just as economic science is not "a body of concrete truth, but an engine for the discovery of concrete truth."[13] Antitrust *policy* is the proper blending of the rule of law and of the appropriate economic principles in the context of a *factual* evaluation (or litigation) as to the *legality* of specific business conduct.

Frequently, the courts have failed to recognize these distinct predicates of antitrust law and economic policy and have permitted the case law to drift for a period of time under one economic premise to the apparent exclusion of others. The statutes themselves are neutral and, by design, are sufficiently broad to address all forms of business conduct that "restrain trade." What is remarkable, however, and often overlooked in the present debate is that the Sherman Act and the Clayton Act have in fact accommodated the different and various economic and legal points of view.

For example, the antitrust law section of the American Bar Association already has expressed opposition to the "significant probability" standard against which the reasonableness of the likelihood of the anticompetitive effect is to be judged. According to the antitrust law section, the use of the word *significant* suggests an inflexible quantitative standard.[14] This concern with adequately flexible standards for antitrust enforcement is what the antitrust laws and the present debate are all about.

This chapter attempts to underscore the importance and value of the existing statutory framework of the antitrust laws. Congress enacted the antitrust laws with the specific objective of crafting flexible language that could adapt to changing political, social, and economic conditions, and learning, in the nation.[15] The Sherman Act was intentionally drafted with the "generality and adaptability" of a constitution.[16] Thus, the antitrust laws, as opposed to antitrust policy, were not developed from the perspective of the so-called Harvard "oligopoly" school, the Chicago "efficiency" school, or any other economic model of competitive performance.[17] Based upon this premise, it is as erroneous to argue that the antitrust laws were designed solely to achieve "allocative efficiency" as it is to argue that those laws condemn "bigness as bad."

The very intensity of recent debate, and the continuing evolution of antitrust policy, suggests that the proposed amendments to the substantive provisions of the antitrust laws be undertaken with great caution. The history of antitrust judicial decisions, as outlined below, demonstrates that the antitrust laws are sufficiently broad to evaluate legal challenges to specific business conduct in the context of the various present, and evolving, economic theories. Efforts to reduce or eliminate that flexibility may prove to be counterproductive, as new economic theories are developed or as past or present legal and economic assumptions prove invalid or unsupportable.

While President Reagan's legislative proposals properly will be the catalyst for reevaluation of our present antitrust laws and policy, neither the debate nor the criticism is new. Nor is it the result of any clear consensus on a particular economic model.[18] The debate is a political process no different from that occurring in 1890, 1914, and 1950.[19] In the end, Congress can be expected to conclude that the present statutory framework serves the national competitive policy well, and the present amendments to section 7 of the Clayton Act are no

more appropriate than the proposed industrial reorganization amendments of the late 1960s.

LEGISLATIVE HISTORY OF THE SHERMAN ACT
REFLECTS BROAD PURPOSES TO ELIMINATE
RESTRICTIVE BUSINESS CONDUCT

A variety of important goals were reflected in the enactment of the
Sherman Act; some were economic, others were not. As first reflected
in the Declaration of Independence, Americans have always placed a
high value upon individual freedom and, conversely, have been suspicious of concentration of economic or political power.[20] The Sherman
Act, and later the Clayton Act, reinforced this fundamental belief in
individual liberty by seeking to promote competition and to prohibit
unfair business conduct, as well as to prevent the accumulation of
potentially dangerous economic power.[21] Modern economic (or legal)
theories cannot mask the political and social conditions giving rise to
the Sherman Act. This should not be any more surprising than the
fact that the present political climate, as well as the national and
international competitive environment, is the primary catalyst for the
current debate about the need and the rationale for antitrust policy.[22]

The last half of the nineteenth century represented a turbulent industrial age. The nation was witnessing its transformation from a local
and regional agrarian economy into a rapidly expanding industrial
country. The lightning rod for the legislation, however, was not industrial change in and of itself. Large and politically powerful seg-
ments of the business and consuming public, including farmers, labor,
and small businesses, felt threatened and abused by the spread of
financial and industrial organizations controlled by newly formed
trusts.[23] These contemporary concerns were highlighted in President
Cleveland's 1888 State of the Union Address wherein he deplored the
growth of

trusts, combinations, and monopolies, while the citizen is struggling far in the
rear or is trampled to death beneath an iron heel. Corporations, which should
be the carefully restrained creatures of the law and the servants of the people,
are fast becoming the people's master. [Rowe, "The Decline of Antitrust and
the Delusions of Models," p. 1515]

The new business combinations of the day were viewed by these
groups as artificial devices to control the market, to restrict competition, and to exploit the public.[24] Organizations such as the Standard
Oil Trust were seen as a "menace to republican institutions themselves" and "made it impossible for other persons to engage in fair

competition."[25] The sponsors of antitrust legislation, however, were not hostile to mere size or to market power.[26] Their purpose was not to prevent business from triumphing but "to preserve the competitive process and to channel it along socially productive lines."[27] As designed by Congress and implemented by the courts, the antitrust mission was to foster a "wider dispersal of power and opportunity."[28]

Thus, the Sherman Act reflected the political and social judgments that the economy should be controlled by broad "rules of trade," as a means of restricting economic power and preserving the competitive process for the economic and political well-being of the nation as a whole.[29] In adopting a general and flexible statutory standard, Congress intentionally delegated to the courts the central role and duty of giving "shape and content" to this legal standard in the ever-changing business and economic conditions of the times.[30]

The Clayton Act, passed in 1914, reinforced the Sherman Act's diverse concerns. It constituted a response to the Supreme Court's interpretation of the Sherman Act in general, and the announcement of the rule of reason in particular, and sought to proscribe particular conduct, including the merger movement at the turn of the century.[31] Along with the Federal Trade Commission Act, the Clayton Act was designed to provide a vehicle to challenge "incipient" Sherman Act conduct.[32] Both the Robinson-Patman Act in 1936 and the Celler-Kefauver amendments to section 7 in 1950 underscored these basic tenets of individual freedom and preservation of the competitive process in the antitrust laws.[33]

In sum, the legislative history of the antitrust laws reflects a clear congressional distrust of the accumulation of the economic power by American industry, even in spite of the possible economic costs. By maintaining the freedom of economic opportunity, the antitrust laws sought to ensure that individual self-interest would control the success or failure of business enterprises.[34] Judicial decisions, as discussed in the following section, have adhered to this broad legislative intent. As intended, the courts have sought (and sometimes struggled) to shape the contours of the antitrust proscriptions to contemporary industrial conditions. Because these Acts were wisely and carefully crafted, they have accommodated the changing economic and political trends of the twentieth century and will continue to accommodate future economic models seeking to inform and to persuade government enforcement policies and judicial decisions.[35]

ANTITRUST DECISIONS REFLECT CONTEMPORARY VALUES

While the antitrust laws and enforcement policies have generated political and economic debates, they have withstood the test of time.

Current Supreme Court decisions provide ample support for this proposition. As political, social, and economic philosophies have evolved
throughout the century, the antitrust laws have remained a strategic
tool for the political and economic policies of virtually every administration, at least since Franklin D. Roosevelt.

The history of antitrust decisions can be broadly broken down into
five discernible periods of legislative activity: (1) the formulative era
beginning with the Sherman Act and leading to the Clayton Act, (2)
the period following the Clayton and FTC Acts, (3) the Great Depression and the period leading up to and following the Robinson-Patman
Act, (4) the period following the Celler-Kefauver amendments, and (5)
the current period wherein various amendments have been proposed
by both liberals and conservatives, particularly with reference to the
appropriate merger standards under section 7 of the Clayton Act.[36]

These same periods have represented vastly different economic and
political climates that typically can be discerned in the statements by
the antitrust enforcement officials as well as the decisions of the courts.
When viewed in this historical context, it is not surprising that the
decisions of the Supreme Court have shifted from decade to decade.

The Formulative Era (1890–1914)

The initial decisions of the Supreme Court dealt with classic "trusts"
or combinations that today would be classified as cartels or horizontal
agreements among competitors to eliminate competition and restrict
output. The restraints reviewed by the Court were much more direct
and obvious than those presented in such recent decisions finding antitrust violations as *National Soc'y of Prof'l Eng's* v. *United States*, 435
U.S. 679 (1978) and *Federal Trade Commission* v. *Indiana Federation
of Dentists*, 476 U.S. 447 (1986). It is likely that any of the cases in
which violations were found to exist during this period also would be
held unlawful by the present Court. Moreover, the Court's review of
the exceedingly detailed records on the nature and effect of the various
arrangements presented to the Court are the cornerstone of the past
and present antitrust law and policy with respect to such practices as
price fixing, boycotts, and market allocating schemes.

Despite the prior common law and judicial history with respect to
restraints of trade,[37] and the various state constitutions and statutory
provisions essentially identical to the Sherman Act, the Supreme Court
initially approached the Sherman Act literally and cautiously.[38] In the
first Supreme Court decision under the Sherman Act, *United States* v.
E. C. Knight Co., 156 U.S. 1 (1895), the Court held that a combination
that had acquired control of 98 percent of all sugar manufactured in
the United States was not a monopoly in violation of the Sherman Act.

According to the Court, the manufacture of a product was not commerce, and the fact that a manufactured article may be intended for interstate transportation did not make the manufacturing process itself part of interstate commerce. (Although this case has never been expressly overruled, the principle announced has been superseded.)

Two years later, in *United States* v. *Trans-Missouri Freight Association*, 166 U.S. 290 (1897), the Court concluded that the Sherman Act prohibited *all* combinations in restraint of trade, not merely those that were deemed unreasonable. Noting the great industrial changes occurring in the country, the Court ruled that an agreement between railroads entered into for the purpose of mutual protection by maintaining "reasonable" rates, to be set by an association and to be binding on all members of the association, was an agreement in restraint of trade and illegal (166 U.S. at 319, 323). As with almost every case during this period, price fixing was the vice deemed unlawful and anticompetitive. When the Court failed to detect efforts by the business combination to affect prices or to otherwise control competition, however, the agreements were found to be valid and proper and not in restraint of trade. For example, *Anderson* v. *United States*, 171 U.S. 604 (1898) (agreements for the bona fide purpose of reasonably regulating the conduct of competitors not found to be in restraint of trade); *Chicago Board of Trade* v. *Christie G. & S. Co.*, 198 U.S. 236 (1905) (contracts to limit distribution of quotations of grain prices to those who meet certain conditions not in restraint of trade).

Thus, the law was initially applied narrowly and only with respect to clearly anticompetitive conduct by industrial organizations such as railroads, meat packers, cotton exchanges, as well as against labor unions participating in boycotts against the products of manufacturers.[39] By 1911, the Court found that practices such as price fixing were unlawful under both the common law and the Sherman Act (*Dr. Miles Medical Co.* v. *John D. Park & Sons*, 220 U.S. 373 [1911]).

Twenty years of experience with business conduct under the Sherman Act, however, also brought a reevaluation by the Court of the wisdom of its literal application of the Act. Thus, in *Standard Oil Co.* v. *United States*, 221 U.S. 1 (1911), the Court concluded that inasmuch as the Sherman Act was general in its terms, it could be applied only by the use of reason; therefore, the Act was interpreted to prohibit only "unreasonable" restraints of trade. It should be noted that in articulating the rule of reason, the Court took very aggressive positions with respect to the specific conduct challenged by the government as well as the relief required to redress the unlawful conduct found to exist. The Court ordered dissolution of the combinations of both Standard Oil and American Tobacco.[40]

While the Court continued to apply the Sherman Act against all combinations resulting in boycotts, allocation of markets, and price fixing, the rule of reason standard engrafted upon the Sherman Act precipitated a major political debate and culminated in the enactment of the Clayton Act and the FTC Act in 1914.[41]

The Clayton Act Era (1914–1936)

The Supreme Court remained impervious to political platforms demanding more vigorous enforcement of the Sherman Act in the election of 1912 and to the congressional debates over the Clayton Act and the FTC Act. The Court continued to issue a series of cases narrowly construing the Sherman Act, and dismissing charges that did not fall within one of the previously defined areas of unlawful competition.

Thus, despite the adverse congressional reaction to the courts' interpretation of the newly enacted statutes, the economic climate, spanning the boom times of the roaring twenties and the onset of the Great Depression, was not antagonistic toward business. The antitrust decisions in this period reflected the era of business cooperation and, eventually, concern with the turbulent economic climate. In contrast to the almost automatic condemnation of the great industrial trusts that were presented to the Supreme Court in the first two decades of the Sherman Act era, this period produced several landmark decisions delineating the parameters of the Sherman Act that remain controlling today (and survived the Warren Court era) and provided formal sanction for cooperative business conduct that promoted, rather than suppressed competition.

Thus, in *Board of Trade* v. *United States*, 246 U.S. 231 (1918), the hours-of-trading rule of the grain exchange was found to be reasonable and one that promoted competition. Similarly, in *United States* v. *United Shoe Machinery Co.*, 247 U.S. 32 (1918), a combination of corporations that formerly had been engaged in distinct phases of shoe machinery manufacturing was not found in violation of the antitrust laws since the companies had not been engaged in direct competition with one another but in complementary phases of the industry. In *Buckeye Powder Co.* v. *DuPont Powder Co.*, 248 U.S. 55 (1918), the Court concluded that the mere existence of a dominant power in an industry was not unlawful, absent proof of some oppressive use of that power against the plaintiff. During this period, the Court also announced the right of companies to select the persons with whom they will do business, as well as the right to refuse to do business with others (*United States* v. *Colgate and Co.*, 250 U.S. 300 [1919]).

The Supreme Court also held that neither the size of a corporation nor the possession of economic power, when achieved by lawful and proper means, is, in itself, contrary to the antitrust laws (*United States* v. *U.S. Steel Corp.*, 251 U.S. 417 [1920]; see also *United States* v.

International Harvester Co., 274 U.S. 693 [1927]). Finally, in 1933, the Court held that a cooperative group of independent producers in a common selling agency, organized to mitigate and to eliminate abuses in a highly competitive industry, was not illegal merely because it eliminated competition between its members where such an organization had no monopolistic tendency in view of other potential competing producers (*Appalachian Coals* v. *United States*, 288 U.S. 344 [1933]).

While the Court sanctioned a wide range of business conduct, it continued to find violations where the challenged conduct reflected outright agreements or combinations to eliminate competition. Thus, in *United States* v. *Reading Co.*, 253 U.S. 26 (1920), the Court held that the formation of a holding company was unlawful where control was obtained not by normal business expansion to meet the demands of growth, but resulted from the deliberate decision to secure control in order to dominate the supply of coal and to influence the price to consumers in the market. Similarly, in *United States* v. *Southern Pacific Co.*, 259 U.S. 214 (1922), the Court dissolved a combination of railroads formed to establish common control of otherwise competitive railroads. Finally, to the extent that there is doubt that the Court was not led by any particular economic model during this period, the Court determined that price fixing was inherently unreasonable "despite whatever differences of opinion there may be among economists" (*United States* v. *Trenton Potteries Co.*, 273 U.S. 392, 397 [1927]). This attitude toward price fixing has persisted even in the face of modern economic theory. For example, *Monsanto* v. *Spray-Rite*, 465 U.S. 752 (1984).

Trade associations of independent competitors, in contrast to restrictive trusts or pools, also began to flourish during this period. The Supreme Court's initial decisions did not discourage their development. The activities of such organizations, which were sanctioned, included the gathering and the dissemination of information concerning prices, production costs, and other economic information, even though such activity might have resulted in uniformity in price (*Maple Flooring Mfrs. Ass'n.* v. *United States*, 268 U.S. 563 [1925]; *Cement Mfrs. Protective Ass'n.* v. *United States*, 268 U.S. 588 [1925]). However, when an association sought to secure adherence to announced prices and to terms of sale by its members, the practices were struck down as unlawful (*Sugar Institute* v. *United States*, 297 U.S. 553 [1936]; *American Column & Lumber Co.* v. *United States*, 257 U.S. 377 [1921]).

The Robinson-Patman Era Act (1936–1950)

Although the Robinson-Patman Act is beyond the scope of this chapter, it is referenced here to underscore continued congressional concern with the impact of the enforcement of antitrust laws upon small businesses and its coincidence with the Great Depression. Industry performance, or lack of performance, during the Depression rekindled the undercurrents of political hostility against big business, and precipitated an era of confrontation with industry.[42] Congress, not the courts, once again reflected its distrust of market forces and, in particular, the perceived unfair advantages large corporations held over small business. "Competition was out of favor as the regulator of the economy."[43]

This period also reflected the intensified political and academic interest in the impact of economic concentration and resulted in a recommendation in 1941 by the Temporary National Economic Committee (TNEC) that new legislation be adopted to slow the pace of mergers.[44] During this period industrial organization economics had its first clear impact upon the philosophy and the enforcement policies of the antitrust laws and corresponded to the New Deal era of government "intervention to make markets work."[45]

Between the enactment of the Robinson-Patman Act of 1936 and the Celler-Kefauver amendments of 1950, a number of significant decisions were issued by the Supreme Court, many of which were precipitated by the enforcement policies of Thurman Arnold, the assistant attorney general responsible for antitrust policy under President Roosevelt. The Court was faced with questions regarding the application of the antitrust law in such diverse areas as (in addition to the Robinson-Patman Act), government administrative regulations, state action, fair trade laws, labor issues, ancillary patent restraints, exclusive dealing arrangements, treble damage criteria, and further refinements on the range of permissible price-related activites and joint business conduct.[46] Moreover, a single merger decision by the Supreme Court during this period may have been the catalyst that ensured adoption of the Celler-Kefauver amendment to section 7 of the Clayton Act and the resulting expansive Supreme Court merger decisions of the 1960s. See *United States* v. *Columbia Steel Co.*, 334 U.S. 495 (1948).

The Court's decisions during this period fundamentally are issue specific. While many of the results reflected in these decisions may be different under modern economic analysis, overall the cases stand for a clear, albeit gradual, evolution of the antitrust rules to the changing economic climate of increasing government regulation of commercial conduct and the evolving corporate structural and business arrangements of American industry.[47]

The Celler-Kefauver Act Era

The 1950s may have been tranquil politically and economically, but a number of major antitrust issues were argued before the Supreme

Court during this period. Most of these decisions suggest that the Court was influenced by the contemporary economic debate concerning the impact of concentrated markets and, most importantly, the legislative intent reflected in the Celler-Kefauver amendments.[48] Significantly, all of the justices sitting on the Court had witnessed the upheaval of the Depression and of World War II and were pressed with a wide array of important national political issues, ranging from civil liberties to criminal rights. Following the regulatory initiatives of the executive branch during the late thirties and forties, the Supreme Court became the activist branch of government in the 1950s and 1960s regarding a vast array of national issues that, invariably, had an impact on antitrust. While there were a number of major antitrust decisions during this period, the Court's merger decisions, as reflected in current efforts to amend section 7 of the Clayton Act, precipitated some of the greatest controversy.

Despite the large number of corporate consolidations toward the end of the nineteenth century, mergers were all but neglected until the passage of the Clayton Act in 1914.[49] The Sherman Act, although not passed with mergers in mind, was not unable to address them. *In Northern Securities Company* v. *United States*, 193 U.S. 197 (1904), the Supreme Court struck down the "combination" of the Great Northern and Northern Pacific Railroads on the ground that it facially violated section 1. As noted, this interpretation was short lived and, in part, resulted in the development of the rule of reason announced in *Standard Oil Co.* v. *United States*, 221 U.S. 1 (1911). While the Sherman Act was effectively used in a number of railroad cases even after 1911,[50] the major mergers in mining and in manufacturing were untouched by the Act.[51]

With both the Sherman Act and the Clayton Act (because asset acquisitions were omitted) effectively unable to deal with corporate mergers and acquisitions as a result of Supreme Court decisions, the Celler-Kefauver amendments were born of the confluence of the New Deal, increasing federal regulatory initiatives, and growing public concern with industrial concentration.[52] The governmental and legislative debate surrounding the Celler-Kefauver Act of 1950 reflected that concern.[53] Not surprisingly, therefore, much of the Court's antitrust and economic philosophy was articulated by the Court in the context of mergers or acquisitions reviewed by the Court during this period.[54]

The first enforcement action under the Celler-Kefauver amendments considered by the Supreme Court was *Brown Shoe Co.* v. *United States*, 370 U.S. 294 (1962). The Court was obviously influenced by the congressional concern with the "rising tide of economic concentration in the American economy" as well as "the threat to other values a trend toward concentration was thought to pose" (370 U.S. at 315–316). Seeking to define the now disputed factors relevant to market definition, the Court relied upon contemporary economic models and sought to identify the "reasonable interchangability of use or the cross elasticity of demand between the product itself and substitutes for it" (370 U.S. at 325). In evaluating the probable effects of the merger upon the particular markets affected by the transaction, the Court concluded that it must also "consider its probable effects upon the economic way of life sought to be preserved by Congress" (370 U.S. at 333).

In the Court's view, when an industry is found to consist of numerous independent units, the legislative history of the Celler-Kefauver Act required the Court to preserve that industry structure.[55] The Court's analysis expressly sought to follow the extensive legislative history of the Celler-Kefauver Act and was viewed at the time as consistent with prevailing economic study.[56]

Only one year later, in *United States* v. *Philadelphia National Bank*, 374 U.S. 321 (1963), the Court concluded that in a merger whose size makes it "inherently suspect," evidence of an undue percentage share of the market, or of a significant increase in concentration of firms, would be enough to prove a violation of section 7.[57]

Between the period of 1964 and 1968 a series of conglomerate mergers also reached the Supreme Court. In each case, the Court barred the acquisition, at least in part, on new and unconventional grounds that appeared to some to provide a basis for general attack on conglomerate acquisitions. These new bases were the reciprocity and potential competition theories. See, for example, *FTC* v. *Consolidated Food Corp.*, 380 U.S. 592 (1965); *FTC* v. *Procter & Gamble Co.*, 386 U.S. 568 (1967).

The explosion in the number and size of conglomerate acquisitions during this period was widely observed with alarm in government and congressional circles.[58] In part, it resulted in the issuance of the first set of *Merger Guidelines* in May of 1968 and two presidential task force reports on antitrust policy.[59]

Ironically, it was under the Nixon administration that the most aggressive antimerger policy under the Clayton Act was advanced.[60] During this period the Department of Justice initiated five conglomerate test cases including LTV's acquisition of Jones and Laughlin Steel, Northwest Industries' attempt to acquire BF Goodrich, and ITT's acquisitions of Grinnell Corporation, Canteen, and Hartford Life Insurance. Despite the political climate, the influence of the Harvard school and the oligopoly model, and the breadth of the Supreme Court merger decisions, the Department of Justice cases failed to achieve any substantial results.[61]

In *Northwest Industries*, for example, the government argued that the merger of two of the largest nonfinancial corporations constituted a violation, without more, of section 7.[62] The district court disagreed: "The law as it now stands, however, makes the adverse effect on competition the test of validity and until Congress broadens the criteria, the Court must judge proposed transactions on that standard" (*Northwest Industries*, 301 F. Supp. at 1096). The suits against LTV were settled, and the government lost in its effort to obtain preliminary injunctions in the ITT cases. *United States* v. *ITT*, (Grinnell) 306 F. Supp. 766, 796–97 (D. Conn. 1969) (If "the standard [of lessened competition] is to be changed, . . . that determination [must] be made by the Congress and not by the courts"). *United States* v. *ITT*, (Canteen), 1971 Trade Cases, #73,619 (N.D. Ill. 1971); *United States* v. *ITT*, (Hartford), 1971 Trade Cases, #73,666 (D. Conn. 1971).

Thus, even before the political and the economic conditions began to change in the 1970s, the courts began to adjust their analysis of the appropriate parameters of the Clayton Act. It also should be noted that despite the vigorous enforcement of the merger laws and the broad decisions by the Court during this period, the country experienced a great wave of mergers. Moreover, the extraordinary number and size of recent mergers and acquisitions fails to support the proposition that the Supreme Court's merger decisions of the 1960s inhibited business consolidations in the 1970s and 1980s.[63]

The Post–Celler-Kefauver Era (1975–Present)

The interventionist approach of the government arising out of the New Deal ultimately produced the political, as well as economic, counterreaction of the 1970s. With increasing economic and scholarly commentary challenging past assumptions about the effect of concentration and presumed adverse effects of mergers and acquisitions, the judicial decisions of the 1970s marked the beginning of what is now viewed as a fundamental change in merger and antitrust enforcement policy.[64] As the country became more cognizant of the impact of international competitive forces on domestic jobs and national economic growth, the antitrust laws became the target of increasing criticism.[65] Instead of presumptions against mergers, the enforcement policy of the 1980s was marked by "economic" assumptions in favor of business consolidations and marketing arrangements. Guided by economic studies that hold that most mergers are efficiency enhancing, the Court's decisions, without the benefit of (or need for) congressional intervention, began to reflect a concern for productive efficiency and consumer welfare.[66]

The Court's decision in *United States* v. *General Dynamics Corp.*, 415 U.S. 486 (1974), was the first major signal of a retrenchment from policies articulated by the Court in the 1960s. There, the Court determined that the most accurate measure of a coal producer's competitive power was the amount of its uncommitted reserves, not present market shares. Because the combined corporation's reserves were relatively small, the acquisition was not viewed as a threat to competition. The Court held that the combined market shares of the companies and industry concentration were significant but were not conclusive indicators of anticompetitive effects.

In *Continental T.V.* v. *GTE Sylvania, Inc.*, 433 U.S. 36 (1977), the Court formally substituted the "rule of reason" for the "per se" rule utilized in the 1960s for nonprice vertical restraints. In reversing the *Schwinn* decision issued 10 years earlier, the Court looked to "market impact," and assessed that impact in terms of efficiency. Relying upon contemporary economic analysis, the Court determined that there was "no persuasive support for expanding the per se rule" (433 U.S. at 57). In *Broadcast Music Inc.* v. *CBS*, 441 U.S. 1, 19–20 (1979), the Court described whether conduct should be characterized as per se:

Our inquiry must focus on whether . . . the practice facially appears to be one that would always or almost always tend to restrict competition and decrease output . . . or instead one designed to "increase economic efficiency and render markets more, rather than less, competitive."

The focus upon efficiency implications of business conduct clearly has dominated recent Supreme Court analyses. In *Matsushita Electric Industrial Co.* v. *Zenith Radio Corp.*, 475 U.S. 574 (1986), American electronic firms alleged a predatory pricing conspiracy by certain Japanese manufacturers. The Court found no probative evidence that Japanese companies had entered into an agreement or acted in concert with respect to exports in any way that could have injured the American firms. Relying on classic economic theory, the Court found no "plausible motive" for the Japanese companies to engage in such "irrational" business behavior. Further examples of the Court's promotion of consumer welfare analysis is evident in *Copperweld Corp.* v. *Independence Tube Corp.*, 467 U.S. 752 (1984) (intraenterprise conduct not subject to Sherman Act) and *Northwest Wholesale Stationers Inc.* v. *Pacific Stationery & Printing Co.*, 105 S. Ct. 2613 (1985) (procedures excluding members from an association not relevant to legality of exclusion).

While the Court's recent decisions undoubtedly reflect contemporary political and economic insights, recent decisions do not reflect abdication of the flexible approach followed by the Court over the past 97 years nor a predilection to abandon legal standards developed over years of judicial experience. Thus, in *Monsanto* v. *Spray-Rite*, 465 U.S. 752 (1984), despite the urging of the Department of Justice, the Court refused to overturn the per se rule with respect to resale price maintenance. Similarly, in *Jefferson Parish Hospital* v. *Hyde*, 466 U.S. 22 (1984), the Court declined to abandon the per se legal standard for tying arrangements. Despite lack of support from the Department of Justice and the Chicago school orthodoxy, the Court also held that horizontal agreements to fix maximum prices are as unlawful as agreements to fix minimum prices (*Arizona* v. *Maricopa County Medical Society*, 457 U.S. 332 [1982]).

Finally, the Court also declined to adopt a per se rule against standing by competitors to challenge acquisitions (*Cargill Inc.* v. *Monfort of Colo., Inc.*, 107 S. Ct. 484 [1987]). See also *Catalano* v. *Target Sales*, 446 U.S. 643 (1980) (agreements with regard to credit terms per se unlawful as price fixing); *Aspen Skiing Co.* v. *Aspen Highlands Skiing Co.*, 472 U.S. 585 (1985) (monopolist's refusal to deal with competitor with exclusionary effect or purpose is unlawful). These cases suggest that any firmly established rule of law is not likely to be reversed simply on the basis of a contemporary economic theory.

Another example of the convergence of the rule of law and modern economic learning is reflected in *Federal Trade Commission* v. *Indiana Federation of Dentists*, 476 U.S. 447 (1986). The Court held that the federation's practice of withholding x-rays from dental insurers was a restraint of trade that impeded the consumer choice and the give and take of the marketplace. The Court ruled that, as a matter of law, neither proof of market power, definition of a relevant market, nor evidence of increased prices to consumers is required to condemn a naked restraint on price or output. According to the Court, proof of detrimental market effects can "obviate the need for inquiry into market power, which is but a surrogate for detrimental effects" (476 U.S. at 461). The Court dismissed arguments that concerns for quality of health care were adequate under the rule of reason to justify the challenged restraints. The decision reinforced the Court's decision in *Professional Engineers*, to the effect that a self-serving claim that a restraint serves the public is insufficient as a matter of law.

In a 1988 antitrust decision, the Supreme Court concluded that an agreement by a supplier to terminate a discounter because of its pricing policies at the request of a competing retailer does not constitute an agreement to fix prices or otherwise enforce an unlawful price fixing scheme. *Business Electronics Corp.* v. *Sharp Electronics Corp.*, 485 U.S. —— (May 2, 1988) and 99 L. E. D. 2nd 808. Relying on classic economic theory and "plausible" purposes for supplier restrictions upon distributors (none of which was before the Court as justification for the termination in this case), six justices of the Supreme Court, over a vigorous dissent by Justice Stevens (joined by Justice White), held that a vertical price fixing arrangement requires a specific agreement on "price or price levels." While adhering to the rule of law that vertical agreements on resale prices are illegal *per se*, the Court clearly narrowed what facts will constitute an agreement to fix prices.

The decision represents a significant advancement beyond the Court's recent consideration of the quality and nature of evidence deemed sufficient to justify an inference of an unlawful vertical price fixing in *Monsanto Co.* v. *Spray-Rite Service Corp.*, 465 U.S. 752 (1984). Now, under the Court's analysis, apparently no amount of evidence can justify a vertical price fixing allegation absent an agreement on specific prices or price levels.

In *Sharp*, the undisputed jury finding of an agreement to terminate a "price cutter" was held inadequate to rebut the presumption in favor of a "rule of reason" standard. The Court further emphasized that interbrand competition (*i.e.*, between manufacturers, as opposed to their distributors) is the "primary concern of the antitrust laws" and that any departure from the rule of reason standard enunciated in *Continental T.V., Inc.* v. *GTE Sylvania, Inc.*, 433 U.S. 36 (1977) must be justified by "demonstrable economic effect." Thus, the Court concluded that there "has been no showing here than an agreement between a manufacturer and a dealer to terminate a 'price cutter,' without a further agreement on the price or price levels to be charged by the remaining dealer, almost always tends to restrict competition and reduce output."

The specific holding of the Court with respect to the legal standard for vertical price fixing is important in and of itself. But the fact that the decision obtained a six-justice majority, including Justices Brennan and Marshall, is more noteworthy. (Justice Kennedy did not participate.) Most importantly, it suggests that regardless of the party or policies of the next administration, the antitrust enforcement policies of the Reagan administration are now firmly entrenched in this Court, without any prior need for a legislative initiative.

FRAMEWORK AND HISTORY THAT FORMED THE ORIGINAL UNDERPINNINGS OF ANTITRUST LAWS SHOULD NOT BE ABANDONED WITHOUT BROAD CONSENSUS AND CAREFUL STUDY

The recent decisions by the Court can be interpreted or presented as support for both sides of the debate on the scope and the purpose of the antitrust laws. This fact in and of itself suggests that the antitrust laws have accomplished the original congressional objective by providing an effective statutory standard against which the courts can evaluate specific factual allegations in terms of evolving legal and economic theories. While one can disagree with any particular result, the statutory scheme has worked.

There remain, of course, various and competing points of view as to appropriate improvements and refinements of the antitrust laws and policy. This debate has existed since enactment of the Sherman Act. There continues to be a serious disagreement, however, as to whether today's allocative efficiency model is or should be the sole and exclusive predicate for antitrust law and policy.[67] While this debate has forged a strong consensus that the antitrust laws should not be used in ways that interfere with productive efficiency, there remains a wide disagreement on how to measure, quantify, predict, or establish such efficiency. Despite the fact that these political and economic debates continue, the courts must deal with actual disputes in a constantly changing business and commercial environment.

In antitrust, as elsewhere in the law, we must be careful about unqualified absolutes.[68] Resolution of factual disputes almost invariably will turn on estimates and judgments about commercial reality, about which economists' opinions are divided, or which judges also are qualified to decide. Moreover, legal issues may also turn on matters of statutory interpretation, characteristics of the legal system, or other matters of policy on which "economic science" has little to contribute.[69]

The present debate is more relevant to antitrust policy and economic assumptions than the validity and viability of the antitrust statutes. As intended, the courts have construed the antitrust laws to accommodate past and present economic theories.[70] There is no reason to conclude that the present laws will not also accommodate tomorrow's economic learning. To pursue statutory changes in favor of today's economic assumptions would only serve to restrict the present statutory flexibility and limit the courts' ability to reflect the economic policy changes that can be expected to evolve in the years to come. As Joel Dirlam and Alfred Kahn inquired 30 years ago, "Can one, on purely economic grounds, draw the [legal] line between power enough and power too much, or between its reasonable and excessive exercise?"[71]

If case law teaches us anything over the past decades, it is that anticompetitive conduct will defeat any post hoc economic model attempting to justify market restricting conduct.[72] It is equally clear that novel legal theories can be defeated by cohnerent economic theory and evidence of market-enhancing effects.[73]

History demonstrates that human behavior is unpredictable. History also confirms that business managers do not always act rationally. The antitrust laws are designed to address and provide the limits and contours for the unpredictability and irrationality of human business behavior. On the whole, the statutes have accomplished that objective. To the extent the excesses occurred, whether by businessmen, judges, or law enforcers, we should not "assume" that the solution is a revision of the statutes in the likeness of any currently acceptable economic model. The neutrality of the antitrust laws, over the long term, has served the antitrust policy well.

Today's statutory solutions can be tomorrow's regulatory impediments. The Chicago school proponents have informed and influenced the antitrust enforcement agencies as well as the courts during the past decade. The force of their convictions should not be permitted to impede further debate. The allocative efficiency model can prevail on its merits in any particular antitrust proceeding without sacrificing the very statutory text that has provided it with the opportunity to influence the course of antitrust policy. The efforts to legislate the oligopoly model were premature in the past, and the efforts to legislate the efficiency model are premature at present. Let us not fix a system that "ain't broke."

NOTES

1. The "Trade, Employment, and Productivity Act of 1987" proposes to amend, *inter alia*, section 7 of the Clayton Act, to distinguish more clearly between procompetitive, efficiency-enhancing mergers and mergers that are likely to increase prices to consumers. The legislation would amend section 7 of the Clayton Act in three ways. First, a merger would be prohibited only if a "significant probability" that the merger would be anticompetitive could be demonstrated. Second, the legislation would seek to identify the specific anticompetitive harm with which section 7 is concerned, the exercise of market power (defined in the bill as "the ability of one or more firms profitably to maintain prices above competitive levels for a significant period of time"). This language would replace the current text: "may be to lessen competition or to tend to create a monopoly." Finally, the bill sets forth six specific factors that courts should consider in evaluating a merger or an acquisition: "(i) the number and size distribution of firms and the effect of the acquisition thereon; (ii) the ease or difficulty of entry by foreign or domestic firms; (iii) the ability of smaller firms in the market to increase production in response to an attempt to exercise market power; (iv) the nature of the product and terms of sale; (v) the conduct of firms in the market; (vi) efficiencies deriving from the acquisition; and (vii) any other evidence indicating whether the acquisition will or will not substantially increase the ability, unilaterally or collectively, to exercise market power." *Antitrust and Trade Regulation Report* no. 1303 (February 19, 1987): 348, 352.

2. American Bar Association, Section of Antitrust Law, "Report to the House of Delegates on Proposed Amendments to Section 7 of the Clayton Act," *Antitrust Law Journal* 55 (October 1986): 673.

3. See, for example, "Comments of Milton Handler, Professor Emeritus of Columbia University's School of Law," *Antitrust and Trade Regulation Report* no. 1317 (May 28, 1987): 969 ("theories behind antitrust laws are based on

'legal and not economic principles' "). See also F. Rowe, "The Decline of Antitrust and the Delusions of Models: The Faustian Pact of Law and Economics," *Georgetown Law Journal* 72 (1984): 1511; E. Fox, "The Modernization of Antitrust: A New Equilibrium," *Cornell Law Review* 66 (1981): 1140; E. Fox, "The 1982 Merger Guidelines: When Economists Are Kings?" *California Law Review* 71 (1983): 281; "National Institute on Antitrust and Economics," *Antitrust Law Journal* 52 (1983): 515; E. Fox and J. Halverson, *Antitrust Policy in Transition: The Convergence of Law and Economics* (Chicago: American Bar Association Press, 1984).

4. According to former Assistant Attorney General Baxter, the meaning of the Sherman Act must be found in the particular set of words contained in the statute. Mr. Baxter concludes: "There is nothing in the language of the antitrust laws that suggest that small business, [the] freedom principle, or something else, should somehow be force-fed into the enforcement process. It is not in the language." W. Baxter, "Vertical Practices—Half Slave, Half Free," *Antitrust Law Journal* 52 (1983): 743, 753. See also, Robert Bork, *The Antitrust Paradox: A Policy at War with Itself* (New York: Basic Publishing, 1978); Richard A. Posner, *Antitrust Law: An Economic Perspective* (Chicago: University of Chicago Press 1976); Frank H. Easterbrook, "Is There a Ratchet in Antitrust Law?" *Texas Law Review* 60 (1982): 705.

5. American Bar Association, Section of Antitrust Law, "Report to the House of Delegates on Proposed Amendments to Section 7 of the Clayton Act," 686. The antitrust law section of the ABA, however, would change the threshold of likely anticompetitive effect from a "significant" probability to a "reasonable" probability, the current legal standard, *Brown Shoe Co.* v. *United States*, 370 U.S. 294, 323 (1962). Ibid, 682.

6. J. Dirlam and A. Kahn, *Fair Competition, the Law and Economics of Antitrust Policy* (Westport, Conn.: Greenwood Press, 1984), 15.

7. J. May, "Antitrust Practice and Procedure in the Formative Era: The Constitutional and Conceptual Reach of State Antitrust Law, 1880–1918," *University of Pennsylvania Law Review* 135 (March 1987): 495, 497–502; see also *Standard Oil Co.* v. *United States*, 221 U.S. 1, 61–66 (1911); *Chicago Board of Trade* v. *U.S.*, 246 U.S. 231, 238 (1918).

8. P. Areeda, "Introduction to Antitrust Economics," *Antitrust Law Journal* 52 (1983): 523, 532; see also Dirlam and Kahn, *Fair Competition, the Law and Economics of Antitrust Policy*, 18.

9. The Antitrust Law Section of the American Bar Association has noted "Any effort to develop a single, regularly applied standard from the decided cases seems fruitless. Different schools of economics tend to support different results." ABA, *Merger Standards under U.S. Antitrust Laws* (Chicago: University of Chicago Press, 1981), 1, 87. Thomas Campbell, former director of the FTC's bureau of competition defines the debate as one over the proper burden of proof. T. Campbell, "Has Economics Rationalized Antitrust?" *Antitrust Law Journal* 52 (September 1986): 607, 615.

10. Robert H. Bork in E. Fox, and J. Halverson, *Antitrust Policy in Transition: The Convergence of Law and Economics*, 7.

11. Stephen G. Breyer in E. Fox, and J. Halverson, *Antitrust Policy in Transition: The Convergence of Law and Economics*, 9.

12. Ibid., 10.

13. F. Rowe, "The Decline of Antitrust and the Delusions of Models: The Faustian Pact of Law and Economics," *Georgetown Law Journal* 72 (1984): 1552 (quoting A. Marshall).

14. ABA, Section of Antitrust Law, "Report to the House of Delegates on Proposed Amendments to Section 7 of the Clayton Act," 682. The antitrust law section did endorse the new test of anticompetitive effect ("will substantially increase the ability to exercise market power") contained in the Reagan administration's proposed amendment to section 7. This test, however, is tied to an elusive definition of market power ("the ability of one or more firms profitably to maintain prices above competitive levels for a significant period of time"). This test appears inappropriate. As Phillip Areeda noted, "our estimates of market power are never very rigorous." P. Areeda, "The Rule of Reason—A Catechism on Competition," *Antitrust Law Journal* 55 (October 1986): 571, 578.

15. *National Soc'y of Prof'l Eng'rs* v. *United States*, 435 U.S. 679, 687–688 (1978); *United States* v. *U.S. Gypsum Co.*, 438 U.S. 422, 438 n. 14 (1978); F. Rowe, The Decline of Antitrust and the Delusions of Models," 1553.

16. *Appalachian Coal, Inc.* v. *United States*, 288 U.S. 344, 359–60 (1933). See also, T. Vakerics, *Antitrust Basics*, §1.01 (New York: New York Law Publishing Co. 1985).

17. While nineteenth-century economic philosophy has been somewhat overlooked in the current antitrust debate, there appears to be little basis upon which to conclude that contemporary economic attitudes did not play an important role in the drafting of the legislation and in the original interpretation of the Sherman Act by the courts. It is almost impossible to review the legislative history of the Sherman Act without concluding that the Act reflects many political, economic, and other contemporary values. See May, "Antitrust Practice and Procedure in the Formative Era, 495. See also E. Fox, "The Modernization of Antitrust: A New Equilibrium," *Cornell Law Review* 66 (1981): 1147–1149; Rowe, "The Decline of Antitrust and the Delusions of Models," 1513–1518; S. Axinn, "A Lawyer's Response," *Antitrust Law Journal* 52 (September 1983): 643–645. G. Spivack, "The Chicago School Approach to Single Firm Exercises of Monopoly Power: A Response," *Antitrust Law Journal* 52 (September 1983): 651, 653.

18. The articles by Rowe, "The Decline of Antitrust and the Delusions of Models," 1547–1553 and Fox, "The Modernization of Antitrust," 1176–1179, provide the most comprehensive summary and reference source for the continuing debate. See also M. Boudin, "Forensic Economics," *Harvard Law Review* 97 (1984): 834; R. Lande, "Wealth Transfer as the Original and Primary Concerns of Antitrust: The Efficiency Interpretation Challenged," *Hastings Law Journal* 34 (1982): 65; A. Fisher and R. Lande, "Efficiency Considerations in Merger Enforcement," *California Law Review* 171 (1983): 1580; T. Calvani and J. Siegfried, *Economic Analysis and Antitrust Law: Selections on Industrial Organization Economics* (Boston: Little, Brown and Co., 1979).

19. In 1954, Alfred Kahn wrote with respect to the then "vociferous criticism" of the antitrust laws that "a paucity of evidence has been offered to show that antitrust decisions have actually had or even threatened to have the awful

economic consequences that they predict so freely." Dirlam and Kahn, *Fair Competition, the Law and Economics of Antitrust Policy*, 260 (note 2).

20. "[Nothing] is more threatening than the inequality of condition, of wealth, and opportunity that has grown within a single generation out of the concentration of capital into vast combinations to control production and trade and to break down competition." *Congressional Record* 21 (1890): 2460 (remarks of Senator Sherman). See also Fox, "The Modernization of Antitrust," 1149; P. Areeda, "Introduction to Antitrust Economics," 534–537; G. Spivack, "The Chicago School Approach to Single Firm Exercises of Monopoly Power," 652–654.

21. "They [antitrust statutes] were intended only to prevent the unfair exertion of bargaining power and to strike at gigantic monopolistic consolidations," Dirlam and Kahn, *Fair Competition, the Law and Economics of Antitrust Policy*, 15; see also Rowe, "The Decline of Antitrust and the Delusions of Models," 1513.

22. See, for example, Lester C. Thurow, *The Zero-Sum Society* (New York: Basic Books, 1980).

23. See *Standard Oil Co.* v. *U.S.*, 221 U.S. 1, 50 (1911); *United States* v. *Addyston Pipe & Steel Co.*, 85 F. 271, 280, 254, 288 (6th Cir. 1898), *modified and aff'd*, 175 U.S. 211 (1899). See also, Rowe, "The Decline of Antitrust and the Delusions of Models," 1513–16; Fox, "The Modernization of Antitrust," 1147–1148; May, "Antitrust Practice and Procedure in the Formative Era," 569.

24. *Congressional Record* 21 (1890): 2460.

25. Ibid., 3152.

26. Ibid., 3151–3152.

27. Dirlam and Kahn, *Fair Competition, the Law and Economics of Antitrust Policy*, 16–17; see also Fox, "The Modernization of Antitrust," 1146–1147, 1152–1155.

28. See *U.S.* v. *AT&T*, 552 F. Supp 131, 164 (D.D.C. 1982), *aff'd per curiam sub. nom.*; *Maryland* v. *U.S.*, 460 U.S. 1001 (1983) ("The antitrust laws seek to diffuse economic power in order to promote the proper functioning of both our economic and our political systems."); *Northern Pacific R. Co.* v. *United States*, 356 U.S. 1, 4–6 (1958). See also E. Rostow, "The New Sherman Act: A Positive Instrument of Progress," *Chicago Law Review* 1411 (1947): 567–569–570.

29. "The Sherman Act was designed to be a comprehensive charter of economic liberty aimed at preserving free and unfettered competition as the rule of trade. It rests on the premise that the unrestrained interaction of competitive forces will yield the best allocation of our economic resources, the lowest prices, the highest quality and the greatest material progress, while at the same time providing an environment conducive to the preservation of our democratic political and social institutions." *Northern Pacific R. Co.* v. *United States*, 356 U.S. 1, 4 (1958); see also *United States* v. *Topco Associates Inc.*, 405 U.S. 596, 610 (1972) (the antitrust laws "are as important to the preservation of economic freedom and our free enterprise system as the Bill of Rights is to the protection of our fundamental personal freedoms"). See also Rowe, "The Decline of Antitrust and the Delusions of Models," 1516; Fox, "The Modernization of Antitrust," 1152–1155.

30. See, for example, *United States* v. *U.S. Gypsum Co.* 438 U.S. at 438 n. 14; *United States* v. *Associated Press*, 52 F. Supp. 362, 370 (SDNY 1943), *aff'd* 326 U.S. 1 (1945); see also, *National Soc'y of Prof'l Eng'rs*, 435 U.S. at 679, 687–688, *Jefferson County Pharm. Assn'n* v. *Abbott Laboratories*, 460 U.S. 150 (1983).

31. As originally enacted, however, section 7 did not apply to asset acquisitions. The loophole was quickly recognized and widely utilized. It was not removed until the 1950 Celler-Kefauver amendments to the Clayton Act. See P. Steiner, *Mergers: Motives, Effects, Policies* (Ann Arbor: University of Michigan Press, 1975), 152–157.

32. S. Rep. No. 698, 63rd Cong. 2d Sess. (1914).

33. "The Robinson-Patman Act Revisited in Its 50th Year," *Antitrust Law Journal* 55 (April 1986): 133; S. Rep. No. 1775, 81st Cong. 2d Sess. (1950); Fox, "The Modernization of Antitrust," 1150–1151; Fisher and Lande, "Efficiency Considerations in Merger Enforcement," 1588–1592.

34. R. Pitofsky, "The Political Content of Antitrust," *University of Pennsylvania Law Review* 127 (1979): 1051, 1053–1054. Compare Senator Reed's comments in 1914:

We wrote it into our creed, that all men were created free and equal, and that all are entitled to life, liberty, and the pursuit of happiness. We construed "liberty" to mean not merely the right to walk upon the streets of cities...but liberty...to engage in commerce, to solve for one's self the problem of one's own happiness and success. So we began enacting legislation calculated to produce a condition which would leave open for all men, big and little, the opportunity to engage in the affairs of life.

Congressional Record 51 (1914): 15867 and Representative Celler's comments in 1949:

I want to point out the danger of this trend toward more and bigger combines. I read from a report filed with [the former secretary of war] as to the history of the cartelization and concentration of industry in Germany: "Germany under the Nazi set-up built up a great series of industrial monopolies...[that] soon got control of Germany, brought Hitler to power and forced virtually the whole world into war." I do not want to see my country go the way of Japan or the way of Italy or the way of Germany or even the way of England. Small, independent, decentralized business of the kind that built up our country,...is fast disappearing, and second, is being made dependent upon monster concentration. It is very difficult now for small business to compete against the financial, purchasing, and advertising power of the mammoth corporations. Do not make that competition even more difficult by failing to plug this loophole in the Clayton Act.

Congressional Record 95 (1949): 11486.

35. Rowe describes three distinct economic models that have significantly informed and affected antitrust policies and court decisions as the (1) oligopoly model, (2) efficiency model, and (3) experience curve model. Rowe, "The Decline of Antitrust and the Delusions of Models," 1540–1559.

36. One commentator has categorized these as periods of (1) antitrust genesis, (2) antitrust demise, (3) antitrust revival, and (4) antitrust reformation. See Rowe, "The Decline of Antitrust and the Delusions of Models," 1513.

37. More than 15 years prior to the enactment of the Sherman Act, the Supreme Court concluded:

It is a well settled rule of law than an agreement in general restraint of trade is illegal and void; but an agreement which operates merely in partial restraint of trade is good, provided it be not unreasonable and there be consideration to support it. . . . In order that it may not be unreasonable, the restraint imposed must not be larger than is required for the necessary protection of the party with whom the contract is made.

Oregon Steam Nav. Co. v. *Winsor*, 87 U.S. 64, 66–67 (1874).

38. See May, "Antitrust Practice and Procedure in the Formative Era," 497–507.

39. *Addyston Pipe & Steel Co.* v. *United States*, 175 U.S. 211 (1899) (pipe); *Northern Securities Co.* v. *United States*, 193 U.S. 197 (1904) (railroads); *Swift & Co.* v. *United States*, 196 U.S. 375 (1905) (meat packers); *Southern Cotton Oil Co.* v. *Texas*, 197 U.S. 115 (1905) (cotton); *Loewe* v. *Lawlor*, 208 U.S. 274 (1908) (labor).

40. *Standard Oil Co.* v. *United States*, 221 U.S. 1 (1911); *United States* v. *American Tobacco Co.*, 221 U.S. 106 (1911).

41. See, for example, *Standard Sanitary Mfg. Co.* v. *United States*, 226 U.S. 20 (1912) (price fixing); *United States* v. *Patten*, 226 U.S. 525 (1913) (market allocation); *Straus* v. *American Publishers' Assoc.*, 231 U.S. 222 (1913) (market allocation, price fixing); *Eastern States Retail Lumber Dealers Assoc.* v. *United States*, 234 U.S. 600 (1914) (boycott).

42. President Roosevelt advised Congress in a 1938 message: "The liberty of Democracy is not safe if the people tolerate the growth of private power to the point where it becomes stronger than their democratic state itself. . . . Among us today a concentration of private power without equal is growing." *Congressional Record* 83 (1938): 5992.

43. The Robinson-Patman Act Revisited in Its 50th Year," 133–137. See also "Report of the Antitrust Section to the ABA House of Delegates on Amendments to the Robinson-Patman Act," *Antitrust Law Journal* 55 (October 1986): 629.

44. Rowe, "The Decline of Antitrust and the Delusions of Models," 1521.

45. Ibid., 1541.

46. See, for example, *Interstate Circuit* v. *United States*, 306 U.S. 208 (1939) (price-fixing agreement could be inferred); *United States* v. *Borden Co.*, 308 U.S. 188 (1936) (Capper Volstead Act and Department of Agriculture marketing agreements provided only limited antitrust immunity); *United States* v. *Socony-Vacuum Oil Co.*, 310 U.S. 150 (1940) (price fixing per se illegal); *Apex Hoisery Co.* v. *Leader*, 310 U.S. 469 (1940) (labor strike not restraint of trade); *Fashion Orginators Guild* v. *Federal Trade Commission*, 312 U.S. 457 (1941) (unlawful boycott); *United States* v. *Cooper Corp.*, 312 U.S. 600 (1941) (U.S. government not a "person" entitled to maintain a treble damage action); *Georgia* v. *Evans*, 316 U.S. 159 (1942) (state cannot maintain treble damage action); *National Broadcasting Co.* v. *United States*, 319 U.S. 199 (1943) (FCC may consider policy of antitrust laws in granting licenses); *Parker* v. *Brown*, 317 U.S. 341 (1943) (antitrust laws not intended to restrain official state action); *American Medical Association* v. *United States*, 317 U.S. 519 (1943) (boycott of HMO unlawful); *McLean Trucking* v. *United States*, 321 U.S. 67 (1944) (ICC may approve mergers otherwise in violation of antitrust laws); *United States* v. *Bausch and Lomb Optical Co.*, 321 U.S. 707 (1944) (Miller-

Tydings Act provided only limited antitrust exemption); *Hartford Empire Co. v. United States*, 323 U.S. 386 (1945) (abuse of patent protection to suppress competition); *United States* v. *Frankfort Distillers*, 324 U.S. 293 (1945) (resale price maintenance agreements per se unlawful); *Allen Bradley Co.* v. *Local Union No. Three*, 325 U.S. 797 (1945) (combination by labor unions with non-labor groups to restrain trade violates the Sherman Act); *Associated Press* v. *United States*, 326 U.S. 1 (1945) (use of a cooperative association to impose onerous conditions upon membership in order to discourage competition unlawful); *Bigelow* v. *RKO Radio Pictures*, 327 U.S. 251 (1946) (computation of damages); *American Tobacco Co.* v. *United States*, 328 U.S. 781 (1946) (actual exclusion of competitors not necessary to establish unlawful monopoly); *United States* v. *National Lead Co.*, 332 U.S. 319 (1947) (use of patents to control competition unlawful); *United States* v. *Yellow Cab Co.*, 332 U.S. 218 (1947) affiliated corporations may conspire); *International Salt Co.* v. *United States*, 332 U.S. 392 (1947) (use of patents as tying devices unlawful); *United States* v. *U.S. Gypsum Co.*, 333 U.S. 364 (1948) (patents utilized to unlawfully monopolize market); *United States* v. *Griffith*, 334 U.S. 100 (1948) (use of combined buying power to obtain competitive advantages held to be monopolization); *Mandeville Island Farms* v. *The American Bristol Sugar Co.*, 334 U.S. 219 (1948) (antitrust laws forbid a price-fixing combination among purchasers as well as among sellers); *Standard Oil Co. of California* v. *United States*, 337 US 293 (1949) (exclusive dealing arrangements unlawful even though company did not dominate the market); *United States* v. *National Association of Real Estate Boards*, 339 U.S. 485 (1950) (price fixing per se unreasonable regardless of motives or objectives).

47. This period precipitated perhaps the first major political and economic debate regarding the "uninformed" enforcement policies of Thurman Arnold and the failure of the Court to apply the rule of reason more carefully. Dirlam and Kahn, *Fair Competition, the Law and Economics of Antitrust Policy*, 10–15, 268–280.

48. Fox, "The Modernization of Antitrust," 1149–1151.

49. P. Steiner's text on the history of merger enforcement notes that George Stigler, in his 1950 study, minimized any economies from the merger wave at the turn of the century and stressed the monopolization effects. In contrast, Joe Bain argued that the mergers were significantly motivated by attempts to achieve the economies of large-scale production and distribution. G. Stigler, "Monopoly and Oligopoly by Merger," *American Economic Review, Papers and Proceedings* (May 1950), 23–34. J. S. Bain, "Monopoly and Oligopoly by Merger," *American Economic Review, Papers and Proceedings* (May 1950), 64–66. See Steiner, *Mergers: Motives, Effects, Policies*, 50.

50. See *United States* v. *Union and Pacific Railroad*, 226 U.S. 61 (1912) and *United States* v. *Southern Pacific Co.*, 259 U.S. 214 (1922); Steiner, *Mergers: Motives, Effects, Policies*, 152–153 (note 5).

51. In 1920, the Supreme Court held that U.S. Steel's acquisition of 180 former competitors did not violate section 1 of the Sherman Act because U.S. Steel had not achieved a monopoly. *United States* v. *United Steel Corp.*, 251 U.S. 417 (1920).

52. See, for example, *Aluminum Co. of America* v. *United States*, 148 F.2d 416 (2d Cir. 1945).

53. See FTC, *Report On The Merger Movement: A Summary Report* (Wash-

ignton, D.C.: U.S. Government Printing Office, 1948); see also, Rowe, The Decline of Antitrust and the Delusions of Models," 1523; Fox, "The Modernization of Antitrust," 1150–1151; Fisher and Lande, "Efficiency Considerations in Merger Enforcement," 1588–1592.

54. There were, of course, significant nonmerger decisions issued by the Court during this period. See, for example, *United States* v. *DuPont*, 351 U.S. 377 (1956) (relevant market in monopolization case includes products "reasonably interchangeable"); *Northern Pacific R. Co.* v. *United States*, 356 U.S. 586 (1958) (tying arrangements per se unlawful); *Klors, Inc.* v. *Broadway-Hale Stores, Inc.*, 359 U.S. 207 (1959) (group boycotts per se unlawful); *United States* v. *Parke Davis & Co.*, 362 U.S. 29 (1960) (refusal to deal cannot be used as vehicle to enforce resale price maintenance); *Eastern Railroad President Conference* v. *Noerr Motor Freight, Inc.*, 365 U.S. 127 (1961) (Sherman Act does not apply to efforts to influence legislation even if anticompetitive); *Tampa Electric Co.* v. *Nashville Coal Co.*, 365 U.S. 320 (1961) (exclusive dealing and requirements contracts not illegal per se); *White Motor Co.* v. *United States*, 372 U.S. 253 (1963) (vertical territory restrictions not per se unlawful); *Silver* v. *New York Stock Exchange*, 373 U.S. 341 (1963) (exclusion of members from regulated exchange requires "fair procedures"); *United States* v. *Grinnell Corp.*, 384 U.S. 463 (1966) (no distinction between "line" of commerce in section 7 and "part" of commerce under Sherman Act); *United States* v. *Arnold Schwinn & Co.*, 388 U.S. 365 (1967) (nonprice vertical restraints may be per se unlawful); *Albrecht* v. *Herald Co.*, 390 U.S. 145 (1968) (agreements to fix maximum prices per se unlawful); *Perma Life Mufflers, Inc.* v. *International Parts Corp.*, 392 U.S. 134 (1968) (unclean hands no defense to treble damage action); *United States* v. *Container Corp.*, 393 U.S. 333 (1969) (exchange of price information held part of unlawful price-fixing scheme); *Fortner Enterprises* v. *United States Steel*, 394 U.S. 495 (1969) (tying per se unlawful); *United States* v. *Topco*, 405 U.S. 596 (1972) (allocation of territories by competitors per se unlawful despite small market share); *Goldfarb* v. *Virginia State Bar*, 421 U.S. 773 (1974) (no learned profession exemption from the antitrust laws).

55. *Brown Shoe Co.* v. *United States*, 370 U.S., at 333.

56. See American Bar Association, Report to the House of Delegates on Proposed Amendments to Section 7 of the Clayton Act, 676–677, 683–685; see also Rowe, "The Decline of Antitrust and the Delusions of Models," 1524.

57. This approach was taken to the most obvious extreme in *Von's Grocery Co.*, 384 U.S. 270 (1966). In that case, the two companies combined held only 7.5 percent of the market; the merger nevertheless was held illegal. See also *United States* v. *Aluminum Co. of America*, 377 U.S. 27 (1964) (increase of only 1.3 percent on relevant market sufficient for section 7 violation). Generally, the decisions of the Supreme Court subsequent to the 1950 amendments reflect an effort to address the perceived fear by Congress of increasing concentration in American industry. The cases are diverse, but in each case the Court delineates tests that seek to balance the actual competition as already existed by the potential competition that might develop in defining relevant markets and the potential of competitive injury in a "noncompetitive" market structure. See *United States* v. *El Paso Natural Gas*, 376 U.S. 651 (1964); *United States* v. *Aluminum Co. of America*, 377 U.S. 271 (1964); *United States* v. *Continental Can Co.*, 378 U.S. 441 (1964); *United States* v. *Penn Olin Chemical*

Co., 378 U.S. 158 (1964); *FTC* v. *Procter & Gamble Co.*, 386 U.S. 568 (1967); *Ford Motor Co.* v. *United States*, 405 U.S. 562 (1972). This approach is not totally at odds with the current *Merger Guidelines'* focus upon potential competition in defining relevant markets.

58. See, for example, FTC, *Economic Report on Mergers* (Washington, D.C.: U.S. Government Printing Office, 1969); see also, Steiner, *Mergers: Motives, Effects, Policies*, 156–158.

59. The Neal Task Force, appointed by President Johnson, proposed an expansion of section 7 of the Clayton Act and prohibition of certain large firm mergers, *White House Task Force Report on Antitrust Policy* (Neal Report) (Washington, D.C.: U.S. Government Printing Office, July 5, 1968). (The legislation would have forbidden mergers between large firms, with sales in excess of $500 million or assets in excess of $250 million or by leading firms with market share of 10 percent or more in an industry with four-firm concentration of assets of 50 percent). The *Stigler Task Force Report on Productivity and Competition*, submitted in January 1969 at the request of President-elect Nixon, argued against further amendments to the Clayton Act and urged further study and analysis (Washington, D.C.: U.S. Government Printing Office, January 1969).

60. The 1972 platforms of both the Democratic and Republican parties expressed substantial concern with the conglomerate merger movement and perceived increased economic concentration. John Mitchell, then attorney general of the United States (and not known for populist views) noted the danger that increasing concentration poses to the economic, political, and social structure of the country. Steiner, *Mergers: Motives, Effects, Policies*, 288.

61. By 1972, the FTC's bureau of economics, after review of nine corporations which had engaged in substantial conglomerate acquisitions, concluded that the effects of such acquisitions were competitively neutral. The bureau could discern no substantial evidence of synergism, efficiencies, or any evidence of anticompetitive effect. FTC, *Economic Report on Conglomerate Merger Performance: An Empirical Analysis of Nine Corporations* (Washington, D.C.: U.S. Government Printing Office, 1972).

62. *United States* v. *Northwest Industries, Inc.*, 301 F. Supp. 1066 (N.D. Ill. 1969).

63. See Testimony of John D. Ong, chief executive officer of B. F. Goodrich Company, before the Antitrust Subcommittee, Committee of the Judiciary, U.S. Senate (March 11, 1987). See also American Bar Association, "Report to the House of Delegates on Proposed Amendments to Section 7 of the Clayton Act," 673.

64. The contemporary political climate in the United States cannot be overlooked in evaluating the shifting judicial approach to merger challenges and other antitrust proceedings. See Fox, "The 1982 Merger Guidelines," 297 (note 106) (new merger policy is not driven by new learning in economics but a triumph of political conservatism).

65. Ibid., 282. Any disadvantage U.S. companies face from foreign competition, however, may be more the result of government subsidies provided foreign competitors then U.S. antitrust policy. For example, 29 of the largest European industrial companies are totally or partially owned by the state and

are operated for the national interest rather than profit maximization. Speech by Dwayne O. Andreas, CEO, Archer-Daniel-Midland Company (January 26, 1986).

66. Fox, "The 1982 Merger Guidelines," 282. See also American Bar Association, "Report to the House of Delegates on Proposed Amendments to Section 7 of the Clayton Act," 683–686.

67. "The isolation of efficiency as the sole goal of antitrust requires a conscious rejection of equally dominant values that underlie the antitrust statutes." Fox, "The Modernization of Antitrust," 1146. Like the Harvard school before it, the Chicago school has had an important impact upon the economic and legal underpinnings of antitrust analysis and enforcement. While some view the Chicago school as the sole, controlling, and most rationally developed theory of antitrust and economic policy, new theories already are emerging. Rowe, "The Decline of Antitrust and the Delusions of Models," 1533. Even Judge Posner has acknowledged that the Chicago school has benefited from the debate regarding basic assumptions underlying certain of the Chicago school's premises, such as predatory pricing. R. Posner, "The Chicago School of Antitrust Analysis," *University of Pennsylvania Law Review* 127 (1979): 925, 940.

68. Areeda, "Introduction to Antitrust Economics," 437. See also Rowe, "The Decline of Antitrust and the Delusions of Models," 1561.

69. Areeda, "Introduction to Antitrust Economics," 533. As one noted commentator concluded over 30 years ago during a similar debate:

It is not the traditional Sherman Act that needs changing; that would be unthinkable. It is only the excessively doctrinaire, legalistic, economically naive interpretations recently originated by the enforcement agencies that have been unnecessary and require reconsideration in the light of new economic conceptions of workable competition.

Dirlam and Kahn, *Fair Competition, the Law and Economics of Antitrust Policy*, 10.

70. FTC Chairman Daniel Oliver has articulated precisely the reason statutory charges based on present economic learning should be undertaken only after careful study. According to Chairman Oliver, section 7 must be amended because the court's past decisions relied upon then "prevailing economic theories." Apparently Chairman Oliver cannot foresee any valid future economic study that might further inform antitrust policy. Address by Daniel Oliver, FTC chairman, before the Senate Judiciary Committee (May 21, 1986).

71. Dirlam and Kahn, *Fair Competition, the Law and Economics of Antitrust Policy*, 14.

72. See, for example, *Professional Engineering*, 435 U.S. 679 (1978), and *Indiana Federation of Dentists*, 476 U.S. 447 (1986).

73. Rowe, "The Decline of Antitrust and the Delusions of Models," 1535.

8

The Structural School, Its Critics, and Its Progeny: An Assessment

James W. Meehan, Jr.
and
Robert J. Larner

Michael Mann believed that individuals and ideas make a difference. This belief influenced every aspect of his life. As a teacher, he challenged students to think for themselves and to take risks by exploring new approaches to old problems. In his role as an economic adviser and expert witness, he worked to move antitrust policy in a direction consistent with the goal of maximizing societal welfare. As a scholar, he realized the importance of moving beyond a superficial understanding of how markets work. Near the end of his life, he became convinced from his work as a scholar, government official, and consultant and witness in antitrust cases that an adequate understanding of markets could be achieved only by focusing on detailed, empirical studies of industries and the practices of firms.

Mike's scholarly writings and activity as an antitrust practitioner clearly put him in the "structuralist" school. It is inaccurate and unfair, however, to characterize him narrowly, as Richard Posner has done, as a "diehard" industrial organizationist.[1] Mike's views on antitrust were strongly influenced by his terms at the Department of Justice and the Federal Trade Commission and also by his experience as an expert witness in a number of antitrust cases. His thinking was never stagnant, but evolved as a result of his scholarly research and his work in antitrust cases. At the end of his life, Mike still held the view that the structure of an industry significantly influences its behavior and performance, but he also believed that it is important to understand firm conduct and its effects on competition if economists are to provide useful guidance for antitrust policy. It is the effort to understand firm conduct and its competitive consequences that has been the stimulus for this volume.

This chapter provides an overview of the development of the economic thinking and research related to the issues discussed in the other papers in this volume. It also assesses the contribution of the structuralist school to economists' understanding of markets and to antitrust policy. The theme is that the intellectual endeavors of economists—in the form of research and analysis—have had an impact on antitrust policy and that their influence is likely to continue. We begin by evaluating the structure-conduct-performance paradigm and its influence on antitrust policy. Next, we turn to the contributions of the "Chicago school," the "transaction-cost" approach, and finally to the "new industrial organization" literature. We also critically evaluate what economists have learned about antitrust issues in the last three decades and assess the changes in antitrust policy during the last decade.

THE STRUCTURE-CONDUCT-PERFORMANCE PARADIGM

The structure-conduct-performance paradigm had its origins in the writings of Professor Edward S. Mason[2] of Harvard, but it was the work of one of Mason's students, Joe S. Bain, that nurtured the paradigm to full maturity.[3] Mike Mann was one of several scholars who contributed significantly to the development of the structuralist view. In 1966 he published an article, "Seller Concentration, Barriers to Entry, and Rates of Return in Thirty Industries, 1950–1960," which is frequently cited, along with Bain's work, as one of the early empirical studies supporting the structuralist paradigm.[4] Although Mike authored or coauthored a number of other articles in the structuralist vein, his greatest influence as a proponent of the structuralist position came during his career in government, especially at the Federal Trade Commission.[5] Before turning to the influence of the structuralist paradigm on antitrust policy, and Mike's role in implementing it, however, we discuss the theory and the evidence underlying it.

The Theory

The structuralist approach to markets is based upon the proposition that economic theory predicts that the key structural elements of a market determine market conduct and especially market performance. At the heart of the paradigm is the competitive equilibrium model, which is used as the framework for evaluating the performance of firms and industries. The competitive model defines the conditions for allocative and technical efficiency in long-run equilibrium: Allocative efficiency is achieved when price is equal to long-run marginal cost, and technical efficiency occurs when price is equal to the minimum point *1st part.* on the firm's long-run average cost curve; that is, when all of the industry's output is produced in plants of optimal scale and there is neither a shortage nor a surplus of productive capacity. In the competitive model, allocative and productive efficiency result from two structural conditions—a large number of buyers and sellers and easy entry.

The paradigm also uses oligopoly models to predict the ways in which the various elements of market structure influence market conduct and market performance. In general, the models predict that as the number of firms in an industry decline and barriers to entry increase, there will be a greater opportunity for the coordination of behavior among firms and an increase in the probability that price will be greater than long-run marginal and average costs. Although other hypotheses have been derived from the paradigm, this one has received the most empirical attention and has had the greatest impact on public policy.[6]

The Evidence

The structuralist paradigm was employed by Mason and his followers as the framework for in-depth case studies of highly concentrated industries.[7] In addition, Bain recognized that the model could be generalized and applied to a cross section of firms and industries. He reasoned that if the various elements of structure, conduct, and performance could be identified and measured, it would be possible to test the structuralist paradigm across a sample of industries. In 1951, Bain published his first study of the relationship between structure and performance for a sample of 42 industries for the period 1936 to 1940.[8] As a measure of market structure, he used the four-firm concentration ratios published by the U.S. Bureau of the Census, and as a measure of market performance he used the average accounting rate of return as a percentage of stockholders' equity. He found a weak, but positive and statistically significant, relationship between concentration and profit rates.

Five years later, Bain published his second, and most ambitious, empirical study of the relationship between market structure and market performance.[9] In this study, he painstakingly measured the extent of the barriers to entry for 20 manufacturing industries and tested the relationship between barriers to entry and profit rates for this sample of industries for the periods 1936 to 1940 and 1947 to 1951. Again, the study found a weak, but positive, relationship between concentration and profit rates. More importantly, Bain also found that the average rate of return was significantly higher in the industries classified as having very high barriers to entry than in the industries classified as having either substantial or moderate-to-low barriers to entry.

The next study to test these hypotheses was Mike Mann's 1966 article.[10] His study was significant for two reasons: He expanded the sample of industries studied to 30, and he examined a period (1950 to 1960) that included neither the Great Depression nor the years of rapid postwar inflation. His results confirmed Bain's findings. Since 1966 there have been a large number of cross-sectional studies, most of which have confirmed the weak, but positive explanatory power of such structural measures as concentration, market share, and barriers to entry.[11]

It is worth noting that the empirical tests of the paradigm never attempted to measure directly the influence of firm conduct on performance. Bain defined conduct as the patterns of behavior that sellers follow in adapting or adjusting to the markets in which they deal, and described conduct as a "link between the structural situation in which sellers find themselves and the end results or performance they produce...."[12]

Bain offered two explanations for downplaying the conduct link. First, he argued that there are "no valid a priori generalizations concerning fixed relationships of patterns of interseller coordination to pricing principles or market performance [that] can be advanced."[13] According to Bain, each of the more common devices for interseller coordination (for example, simple price collusion, price leadership, or tacit collusion) is consistent with practically the full range of both price-calculating principles and market outcomes.[14] In addition, he noted that even if theory provided the a priori generalizations, it is difficult, if not impossible, to determine from the available data the effective principles of price-output determination followed in the industry. The principle (or principles) can at best be inferred from the evidence regarding the market performance that emerged from the sellers' conduct.[15]

Mike Mann accepted this reasoning. He believed that conduct was not central to the paradigm and this belief colored his view of antitrust policy. In two speeches, given while he was director of the Bureau of Economics at the Federal Trade Commission, he lamented the courts' obsession with conduct cases.[16] However, this inability of the structuralists to link conduct directly to structure and performance limited the influence that the paradigm had on the enforcement of antitrust policy.

Influence of the Paradigm on Antitrust Policy

To structuralists, the implication of their work was clear: antitrust policy should be less concerned with firm conduct and more concerned with market structure. In their view, the emphasis on conduct was misplaced for at least two reasons. First, behavior aimed at facilitating overt collusion or excluding competitors—the focus of much antitrust activity—is more likely to occur in unconcentrated industries than in concentrated industries where market power is a more serious problem. In the words of Mike Mann:

Antitrust violations turn upon tactics designed to thwart the competitive process: trade boycotts, price conspiracies, allocation of markets, exclusive dealing arrangements, and the like. These practices are apt to be found in unconcentrated markets where concerted efforts are necessary to hinder competition, but when . . . it is unlikely that they would succeed. Oligopolies, on the other hand, can usually rely upon tacit understandings to preserve a stable arrangement with respect to the permissible bounds of competitive behavior. The result . . . is persistent noncompetitive pricing, largely unchallenged by the law.[17]

Second, structuralists maintained that antitrust relief designed to modify firm behavior is ineffective because the ultimate source of market power is market structure. Consequently, "unless the underlying market structure is altered, superficial conduct may often be readily altered to comply with specific prohibitions without really altering the effective aims of price-output determination or the performance outcome."[18]

Although the structuralists were never completely successful in shifting the emphasis in antitrust from conduct to market structure, their work did have a substantial impact on antitrust policy, especially during the period from the late 1950s to the early 1970s. Our discussion will focus on the contribution of the structuralists to three areas of antitrust policy: monopolization cases, mergers, and the selection of cases by the antitrust agencies.

Monopolization Cases

The early monopolization cases were primarily concerned with practices that the Supreme Court (and the American public) considered inherently unfair or abusive; they were not based on the economic concept of monopoly power. After World War II the Court shifted to a standard of liability that required proof of the willful acquisition or maintenance of monopoly power.[19] This standard eventually evolved into a two-part test: (1) a demonstration that monopoly power exists and (2) a showing that the monopoly power was acquired or maintained by the use of predatory or exclusionary conduct.[20]

The Court's adoption of the two-pronged test made economic analysis an integral part of monopolization cases. First, the courts needed practical indices that could be used to identify the presence of monopoly power. In addition, they needed an analytical framework that could be used to determine the market conditions under which various business practices (for example, tying arrangements, long-term leases, exclusive dealing arrangements, and expansion of capacity in anticipation of demand) reduce competition.[21] The structuralist paradigm, which gained acceptance in the late 1950s and early 1960s, strongly influenced the Court's interpretation of both parts of this test.

The first element in the monopolization test is the existence of monopoly power. As the chapter by Kenneth G. Elzinga indicates, diagnosing monopoly is a complex task.[22] The structuralist approach to the problem emphasizes market share, industry concentration, and barriers to entry. The analysis begins with the definition of the relevant market and proceeds to an examination of the evidence on market structure. Since the structuralists believe that economic theory and empirical evidence support the conclusion that high concentration and high barriers to entry lead to monopoly profits, the analysis of market power is commonly completed by examining the profit rates of the alleged monopolist. For the structuralist, market power exists if the market is highly concentrated, barriers to entry are significant, and the profit rates of the leading firms are significantly above the average for all manufacturing corporations for a sufficiently long period of time.

Although the courts never formally accepted the broad outlines of the structural approach to determining market power in monopolization cases, it soon became a standard practice for economists to testify regarding the relevant market and the existence of market power. The witnesses for the plaintiff were usually economists of the structuralist view, who determined market power by reference to the evidence on market structure and profit rates. While thoughtful structuralists recognized the limitations of their measures of market power, they maintained that these measures provided a useful way to begin the analysis of market power. It was left for the defendant's expert economists to demonstrate that the high concentration and high profit rates could be explained by causes consistent with economic efficiency. If they could not, the presumption was that market power was the underlying cause.[23]

This line of defense leads into the second issue for examination under the two-pronged test: whether predatory or exclusionary practices have been used to acquire or maintain monopoly power. Here again, economic analysis is necessary to determine when, if at all, these practices are likely to have an anticompetitive effect.

The structuralists find behavior to be predatory or exclusionary when it results in high concentration or raises the barriers to entry.[24] As a general proposition, this line of analysis is sensible; if business practices strategically eliminate rivals or make their entry into the market more difficult, market power is potentially increased. The practical application of the standard is more controversial, however, because almost all business practices of antitrust concern have some exclusionary effect, at least in the sense of taking business away from rivals. Therefore, to support a conclusion of anticompetitive effects, it is necessary to show that the practice not only excludes rivals, but that it also substantially increases monopoly power.

A few structuralists did look at the effects of firm behavior on competition. They investigated a variety of practices that were the focus of contemporary antitrust cases; in each instance they found that the practices had an anticompetitive effect because they raised the barriers to entry.[25] These studies were important because they provided an economic rationale for what Donald Turner called the inhospitality tradition of antitrust, a tradition that was the ruling doctrine in monopolization cases for nearly three decades, until its influence began to wane in the late 1970s.[26]

Although the structuralists framed the question correctly, they never rigorously demonstrated *how* the various kinds of exclusionary practices raise barriers to entry or create monopoly power. This was unfortunate because the courts, which had to evaluate firm behavior without the benefit of specific economic advice, filled the vacuum by adopting the position that a firm is guilty of monopolizing a market if it possesses monopoly power and it uses practices that have the effects of excluding rivals. As a consequence, the courts tended not to examine the effect of business behavior on competition, but rather to look at the effect on competitors.[27]

Merger Policy

The implications of the structuralist paradigm for merger policy are also clear. If high market shares and high barriers to entry are the cause of anticompetitive performance, policy should be designed to prevent mergers that increase the level of concentration and raise barriers to entry. Horizontal mergers are the prime target because they have a direct effect on market share, but vertical mergers and conglomerate mergers are also suspect if they eliminate a potential entrant, make entry into a concentrated industry more difficult, or entrench a leading established firm.

In a series of decisions in the late 1950s and early 1960s, the Supreme Court developed a legal standard for mergers that was consistent with the structuralist arguments in at least two ways. First, the Court used structural criteria to identify the mergers that were objectionable. For horizontal mergers, the Court considered the market shares of the merging firms, the level of industry concentration, the trend in concentration, and the effect of the merger on concentration.[28]

Similar criteria were also used to evaluate vertical and conglomerate mergers. As with horizontal mergers, the Court began its analysis by looking at the size distribution of firms. In addition, it examined the effect of the vertical and conglomerate merger on barriers to entry. In *Brown Shoe* a vertical merger was found to be anticompetitive because it foreclosed entry into a concentrated market.[29] The Court also held that a conglomerate merger was anticompetitive if a significant potential entrant into a concentrated market was eliminated (*Falstaff*)[30] or if the merger raised a barrier to entry (*Clorox*).[31]

Secondly, the Court supported a tough antimerger policy that blocked almost all mergers resulting in even marginal increases in concentration or barriers to entry. In *Brown Shoe*, the Court found a horizontal merger between two firms with a combined share of 5 percent in an unconcentrated market to be illegal, and in *Von's Grocery*, it found a horizontal merger between two firms with a combined share of less than 8 percent to be illegal.[32] Vertical and conglomerate mergers in fragmented markets were also subject to vigorous attack. Again, in *Brown Shoe* the Court was concerned about a small amount of foreclosure in an unconcentrated market, and in *Clorox* and *Falstaff* the Court took an equally hard stand against conglomerate mergers.

Although the Court used the principles of the structural paradigm, economists from the structural school did not endorse every aspect of the Court's merger doctrine. Few of them would agree with the Court's acceptance of an arbitrary definition of the relevant market, nor would many accept the Court's argument in *Brown Shoe* and that economies that result from a merger can be grounds for finding the merger anticompetitive. Finally, there was not widespread agreement with the Court's position that a deconcentrated market is an end in and of itself, regardless of the effect on economic efficiency. In fact, many structuralists would probably agree with Professor Scherer that a large number of the mergers that were successfully challenged were trivial in their effects on competition.[33]

The influence of the structural school on merger policy reached its peak with the issuance of the Department of Justice's (DOJ) first set of *Merger Guidelines* in 1968.[34] The purpose of the *Guidelines* was to translate the antimerger precedents of the Supreme Court into a set of quantitative structural rules for horizontal, vertical, and conglomerate mergers. In each case, the DOJ adopted a purely structural approach. For horizontal mergers, the *Guidelines* focused on the level of market concentration and the shares of the market held by the acquiring and the acquired company. In the case of vertical mergers, the DOJ focused on the effect of the merger on foreclosure and barriers to entry, and for conglomerate mergers, the *Guidelines* emphasized the elimination of potential competition. The *Guidelines* also explicitly excluded the possibility of using an efficiency defense.

The impact of the *Guidelines* on merger policy was significant. For almost a decade after their adoption, the DOJ and the Federal Trade Commission used the *Guidelines* as the basis for selecting mergers for scrutiny and challenge. In addition, the courts generally accepted the *Guidelines* as a basis for their decisions (especially for horizontal mergers), partly because they were consistent with Supreme Court decisions. As a result of the vigorous enforcement of the *Guidelines*, horizontal mergers significantly decreased in importance. For example, Professor Scherer reports that horizontal mergers accounted for only 12 percent of all large mergers during the period from 1963 to 1972 and 15 percent during the period from 1973 to 1977, compared with almost 37 percent during the period from 1948 to 1953.[35]

Case Selection

The structuralists also had an influence on other kinds of cases that the DOJ and the FTC brought. During their zenith, structuralist views were held by many of the lawyers and economists who led and staffed the enforcement agencies. The most prominent example is Donald Turner, who was one of the leading proponents of the structural school at the time he was appointed assistant attorney general in charge of the Antitrust Division in 1962.[36] Early in his tenure, he created the Office of Special Assistant for Economics, and each of the first four economists to hold that position (William S. Comanor, William G. Shepherd, Leonard W. Weiss, and H. Michael Mann) was clearly identified with the structural school. The people who served as chairman and commissioners of the FTC during this time cannot be classified as easily, but at least two of the directors of the Bureau of Economics during this period (Willard F. Mueller and H. Michael Mann) held strong structuralist views.

The policies pursued by these people clearly reflect their views. As noted above, their enforcement of merger policy, especially against horizontal mergers, was particularly vigorous. Perhaps even more significant was their attempt to redirect the enforcement efforts toward concentrated industries that were dominated by one or a few large firms. The DOJ's monopolization cases against IBM and AT&T and the FTC's cases against Xerox and the leading ready-to-eat cereal companies all were filed during the late 1960s and early 1970s.

THE CRITICS

At about the time that the influence of the structural school reached its peak, a number of scholars began to direct a frontal attack on the theoretical and empirical foundations that supported the school's policy prescriptions. These attacks came from a variety of sources, but the most vocal ones came from the Chicago school. We focus on three aspects of their criticism. Critics from the Chicago school argued that the structural paradigm is flawed because it is based on the model of perfect competition. They also held that the evidence of a correlation between concentration and profit rates (or between barriers to entry and profit rates) did not demonstrate the existence of market power. Finally, they used the tools of microeconomic theory to demonstrate that various forms of conduct, such as selling below cost, vertical restraints, and product differentiation, rarely, if ever, restrict competition by raising barriers to entry. Instead, the critics contended that these forms of behavior will usually lead to increased efficiency. Below is a brief summary of each of their criticisms.

The Chicago school faulted the structuralists for seeking monopoly explanations when the structure of an industry departs from the structural conditions of perfect competition. Rather, members of the school contended, that high concentration does not imply monopoly power as long as entry into the market is open and expansion of output by established firms is possible (that is, there are no governmentally imposed restrictions on competitive activities).[37] To understand the dispute between the two schools, it is necessary to examine how each has thought about barriers to entry.

Joe Bain defined a barrier to entry as "the extent to which, in the long run, established firms can elevate their selling prices above the minimal average costs ... without inducing potential entrants to enter the industry."[38] The Chicago economists defined barriers to entry quite differently. George Stigler suggested that barriers exist when the entering firms incur costs that the established firms do (or did) not have to bear.[39] Harold Demsetz argued that barriers to entry exist only when socially desirable entry is prevented.[40] In his view, as long as the supply curves for inputs are upward sloping, entry will be more costly for new firms than it was for established firms. For Demsetz, however, these higher costs do not represent a barrier to entry in the sense of protecting firms that are exploiting monopoly power. In his view, entry is not socially desirable as long as no attempt is made to artificially restrict output. If the established firms do attempt to restrict output and raise prices artificially, entry will be desirable and it will take place.

The differences in the definitions lead to different conclusions about what constitutes specific structural barriers to entry. Bain believed that the specific barriers to entry are economies of scale, product differentiation, and absolute cost advantages that occur when the established firms have control of superior resources or have access to capital funds on terms more favorable than do potential entrants. For the Chicago economists, none of these is a barrier to entry. Economies of scale are not a barrier if the potential entrants can produce along the same long-run average cost curve as the established firms. Advertising expenditures are not a barrier to entry because information is costly and advertising is a low-cost source of information. Finally, the cost of capital is not a barrier to entry because the lower cost of loanable funds for the established firms reflects a risk differential.[41]

If true barriers to entry do not exist, what explains the observed statistical relationship between concentration and profit rates and the relationship between various measures of the structural barriers to entry and profit rates? Some have argued that the relationship is merely a statistical artifact; if profit rates are adjusted for risk, and if advertising and R&D expenditures are treated as an investment and capitalized, the statistical relationship will disappear.[42] Others have argued that the observed relationship is a short-term disequilibrium phenomenon, explained by growth in demand or decreases in costs. As the industries move toward long-run equilibrium, the relationship dissipates.[43]

The most compelling criticism of the structuralists' empirical work came from Demsetz, who argued that the statistical relationship between concentration and profit rates is explained by economic efficiency and not the exploitation of monopoly power.[44] In a competitive market without barriers to entry, concentration will increase as the efficient firms grow and the inefficient firms shrink in size. Concentration will be positively related to profit rates because the rate of return of the efficient firms will also increase as they grow in size. The higher profit rates found in concentrated industries are not monopoly profits, but simply rents to the scarce factors that create the differential advantages related to firm size. Demsetz presented evidence to support his explanation of the correlation between concentration and profit rates, but, as Scherer points out, more work needs to be done before we can completely unravel the relationships between concentration and profit rates.[45]

Another branch of the Chicago school, led by Aaron Director and his colleagues, has focused on conduct that the courts have found to be objectionable. Their work is based on the premise that the primary goal of antitrust is economic efficiency, and they evaluate firm conduct on the basis of whether it promotes this goal. They have been particularly critical of the courts for being more concerned with protecting competitors than with protecting competition. They point out that competitive behavior—and especially the kind that enhances economic efficiency—will by its very nature injure rivals. Therefore, the appropriate test under the antitrust laws is not whether conduct injures competitors or excludes rivals, but whether it enhances the ability of the firm to restrict output and increase price above the competitive level in the long run.

The findings of Director and his disciples suggest that tie-ins, vertical integration, restricted distribution, predatory pricing, and other assorted practices rarely, if ever, lead to an increase in monopoly.[46] Using the tools of neoclassic microeconomics, they demonstrate that if these practices are used to enhance or extend monopoly power, they generally lead to lower profits. Therefore, they conclude that the motive for these practices cannot be the extension of monopoly power.[47]

The Chicago analysis of firm behavior shifted the focus from market power to economic efficiency. In this view, tying arrangements are justified on the grounds that they allow the firm to protect its good will. Vertical integration is justified because it leads to lower production costs, and vertical restraints are justified because they can protect the firm from the possibility that rivals will free ride on the information or services that it provides jointly with the sale of the product.

The work of other economists, who are not a part of the Chicago school, has also contributed to our understanding of how various business practices improve economic efficiency. The most important has been that of Oliver Williamson and those who advance the proposition that business practices can be explained by a firm's effort to economize on transaction costs.[48] In a world of uncertainty and imperfect information, parties to a transaction may try to increase their profits by acting opportunistically. To protect itself against opportunistic behavior, a party will invest time and resources in the process of negotiating, monitoring, and enforcing agreements. Consequently, there will be transaction costs (that is, the costs of negotiating, monitoring, and enforcing agreements) associated with market exchange. When these costs are high, the buyer and the seller will seek ways to minimize them. Viewed in this light, vertical integration, tying arrangements, and other restraints on distribution can be explained as the means by which both buyers and sellers can organize the exchange of goods and services to economize on transaction costs.

The first real hint that the Supreme Court was ready to accept efficiency explanations for existing market structures and firm conduct came in the *Sylvania* case.[49] In its decision, the Court recognized that nonprice vertical restraints can enhance economic efficiency as well as reduce competition. As a result, the Court announced that it would no longer treat these restraints as per se illegal, but instead evaluate them under a rule-of-reason analysis. This trend was expanded in succeeding cases. The per se treatment of tie-ins, vertical price fixing, agreements not to compete, and some horizontal agreements on price also has been narrowed and, at least in some circumstances, these practices are being analyzed under a rule of reason.[50]

The Court's position on monopoly cases is less clear. In the *Berkey* case, the Supreme Court turned down the opportunity to review an

Appeals Court decision that a dominant firm is not liable under section 2 as long as it does not engage in practices that specifically reduce competition.[51] In the *Aspen Ski* case, on the other hand, the Court held that dominant firms are liable if they use practices that are exclusionary.[52]

If the Court's position on monopoly cases is unclear, the position of the enforcement agencies—which are led and staffed by lawyers and economists schooled in the Chicago tradition—is not. Both DOJ and the FTC have abandoned the large structural cases of the kind they initiated during the ascendancy of the structuralist school. The DOJ dropped its suit against IBM[53] and settled its suit against AT&T,[54] although AT&T was required to undertake substantial vertical divestiture.[55] In addition, the FTC dismissed its complaints against the largest cereal companies and also against DuPont, which was accused of monopolizing the market for titanium dioxide.[56]

The final area in which the Chicago school has had an impact is merger policy. The DOJ revised its *Merger Guidelines* in 1982 and again in 1984.[57] The revisions are significant in a number of ways. First, they use economic principles to provide a rational basis for defining the product and geographic dimensions of markets. Second, they measure concentration using the Herfindahl-Hirschman Index instead of the four-firm concentration ratio. Third, they raise the concentration levels that are used to identify potentially harmful mergers. Fourth, barriers to entry are explicitly included in the analysis of the merger and are a necessary condition for a conclusion that there is likely to be an anticompetitive effect. Finally, the 1984 *Guidelines* explicitly require the DOJ to weigh efficiency gains against potential anticompetitive effects when deciding whether to challenge a merger.

The enforcement of the new *Merger Guidelines* has had an effect on the number and mix of cases. Professor Scherer reports that the FTC became less aggressive in challenging mergers during the period 1981 to 1985.[58] Another study by two DOJ economists found that "... about one of every five cases filed before the 1982 *Merger Guidelines* took effect involved markets with concentration levels and changes below the minimum standards of the 1982 *Guidelines*."[59] In addition, they reported that the mix of merger cases investigated by the DOJ shifted from primarily vertical cases to horizontal ones.[60]

NEW SCHOOL OF INDUSTRIAL ECONOMICS

Just as the courts began to accept the Chicago position that many business practices can be explained by economic efficiency, a new school of industrial economics began to analyze strategic behavior that under certain circumstances can reduce competition. This new school emerged, at least partially, in response to the Chicago School's denial of the possibility that business practices can be used strategically to reduce competition. Since one of the chapters in this volume analyzes the work of this school in detail, we limit our discussion here to the way in which their work compares and contrasts with that of the structural school and the Chicago school.[61] In addition, we will assess the influence of the new school on antitrust policy.

Oliver Williamson has suggested that the new school can be divided into three branches.[62] One branch argues that dominant firms can strategically deter entry by making credible threats to impose losses on firms attempting entry. This is accomplished by having the dominant firm precommit to investments that involve sunk costs.[63] A second branch emphasizes the postentry response: A dominant firm can deter entry in the future if it acquires the reputation of acting tough after entry takes place.[64] The third branch takes the position that entry can be deterred by engaging in activity that raises rivals' costs.[65]

The structural school was skeptical of business practices used by dominant firms, and the new school of industrial economics shares this skepticism. The new school differs from the earlier tradition in that it uses formal economic theory to model how various practices deter entry and restrict competition, instead of relying on a loose interpretation of oligopoly theory. As Richard Schmalensee points out, in this respect the new school is similar to the Chicago school.[66] It differs from the latter in that its members believe that markets are imperfect and strategic behavior is profitable under certain circumstances.

The development of the theory of strategic behavior is still in its infancy, and therefore it is premature to undertake a formal evaluation of the influence of this school on antitrust policy. To our knowledge, only two cases have relied on some version of the theories of the new school. In one case, the FTC charged the three largest cereal companies with strategically foreclosing competition by using such practices as brand proliferation, product promotion, and the allocation of shelf space.[67] In that case, Richard Schmalensee was retained by the staff of the commission to analyze the effects of brand proliferation on entry. His work was central to the staff's case, and it also led to the publication of a scholarly article that has contributed to the development of the new school.[68] The hearing examiner and the commission, however, were not convinced that practices such as brand proliferation inhibited entry in a socially undesirable way and the complaint was dismissed.[69]

The other case that relied on the theories of the new school was also an FTC case. In that case, the commission staff argued that DuPont preempted entry into the titanium dioxide market by investing in excess capacity. Here again, the commission did not find that the facts of the case supported the argument that DuPont's behavior strategically reduced competition.[70] Although neither case was successful, it is premature to claim that the views of the new school will not have an impact in the future.

WHAT HAS BEEN LEARNED AND THE IMPLICATIONS FOR ANTITRUST POLICY

During the past few years, economists in the field of industrial organization have reached a consensus on a number of important issues. The impact of this emerging consensus on antitrust policy has been significant; however, there are still many unresolved issues. In this section, we examine the areas of agreement and disagreement and evaluate the implications for antitrust policy. We conclude by assessing the needs for future research.

Areas of Agreement and Disagreement

In his chapter in this volume, Professor Elzinga argues persuasively that there is no convenient, unambiguous measure of monopoly power. For example, most economists would probably be unwilling to conclude that a firm has monopoly power simply because it has a dominant share of the market and earns persistently high accounting rates of return. These facts may be symptomatic of monopoly power, but they may also indicate that the firm has been more efficient than its rivals.

In the absence of unambiguous summary measures of monopoly power, there is no substitute for a full investigation of the market. The investigation usually involves an analysis of market structure, recent changes in market structure, firm conduct, and market performance. If the industry has been dominated by a single firm (or a few firms) over a period of time, the investigator must determine if there are any barriers to entry, and this determination will almost certainly involve an in-depth examination of firm conduct. There is no unique method for conducting these investigations, but Professor Elzinga cites examples of the kind of analysis that needs to be done.[71]

Although there appears to be no easy way to identify monopoly power, there is still some debate over the role that market share plays in determining market performance. Attacks by the Chicago school on the empirical studies of the relationship between concentration and profit rates have been telling, but economists from the structural school still maintain that market share and concentration are important determinants of market power. In an effort to avoid some of the problems of the earlier studies, they are reexamining the relationship between market structure and market performance using price instead of profit rates as the dependent variable.[72] These studies are not without their own problems, but they do suggest that market share and concentration still have a role to play in identifying monopoly power.[73] One study of the airline industry found that, after controlling for a number of economic variables, "carriers in concentrated markets have the ability to price above cost."[74] Another recent study found that resale price maintenance is more likely to have an anticompetitive effect in markets that are highly concentrated.[75] In short, there is evidence to suggest that high market share and high concentration are at least necessary conditions for market power.

There is still a dispute over how to identify barriers to entry. This controversy is important because identifying and evaluating barriers to entry is the key to identifying monopoly power. If entry to a market is easy, there cannot be persistent monopoly power.

Defining barriers to entry is critical to identifying barriers that are socially undesirable. Disagreement about the definition of barriers to entry is reflected in the disagreement over what constitutes a barrier to entry. Most of the definitions focus on the advantages of the incumbent firms versus the potential entrants, and the debate centers on whether the differential cost of entering is the result of socially desirable or undesirable activities.[76]

The new industrial organization economists have attempted to provide an answer to this question. In their chapter in this volume, Charles Holt and David Scheffman discuss the kind of conduct that can be used strategically to disadvantage rivals and potential entrants. As they point out, however, this literature has not developed to the point of yielding forceful or straightforward policy implications.

Most of the practices that can strategically deter entry also can be efficiency enhancing. None of the literature, however, explains satisfactorily how economists or antitrust enforcers can discriminate between the competing explanations of anticompetitive behavior and efficiency-enhancing conduct. Consequently, the practical implications of this literature at present are severely limited. Before this work can be useful to judges or antitrust officials, the new breed of industrial organization economists will have to develop operational rules that identify when business practices are more likely to be anticompetitive than efficiency enhancing.

There is nearly universal agreement that "naked" horizontal restraints are anticompetitive.[77] However, a number of scholars have argued that some horizontal restraints, ancillary to pooling agreements, can be motivated by economic efficiency.[78] An example of such restraints would be the blanket licensing agreements used by performing-rights organizations such as ASCAP (American Society of Composers, Authors, and Publishers) and BMI (Broadcast Music, Inc.).

These nonexclusive agreements allow the user to buy the rights to the music of the entire membership for a single price. Although these licenses restrict the members of the organizations from competing among themselves in selling the right to use their music, they also reduce the transaction costs to the user of negotiating with individual copyright holders.[79]

Perhaps the most significant revolution in economics has occurred in the way economists now think about single-firm conduct and, in particular, vertical restraints. There is general agreement that there are efficiency explanations for a broad range of single-firm conduct. In fact, vertical restraints and tie-ins, which were once presumed to be inherently anticompetitive, are now regarded as more likely than not to be efficiency enhancing unless the vertical restraints are part of a collusive scheme or the tying arrangement is being used by a dominant firm to exploit its market power. The changes in economists' thinking about vertical restraints are discussed by Professor White in this volume.[80]

There is, however, still some disagreement as to the importance of single-firm conduct as a source of monopoly power. Members of the Chicago school believe that this kind of conduct is rarely, if ever, anticompetitive.[81] Other economists from the new school of industrial organization believe that the anticompetitive effects occur more frequently. William S. Comanor[82] and F. M. Scherer,[83] for example, argue that vertical restraints can have an anticompetitive effect, even if they result in an increase in output, if the benefits to the marginal consumers from increased output are outweighed by the losses to inframarginal consumers from higher prices.[84] Others have shown that single-firm conduct can be anticompetitive when it raises rivals' costs.[85]

The arguments of the new school suggest that single-firm conduct may not be as benign as the Chicago school has argued. Once again, however, there is no clear-cut way of separating the cases in which the conduct is primarily anticompetitive from those in which it is efficiency enhancing. One point of agreement between the Chicago school and the new school is that single-firm conduct is not likely to restrict competition unless there is preexisting monopoly power.[86]

A consensus has also emerged on the effects of mergers. The presumption with regard to both vertical and conglomerate mergers is that they are efficiency enhancing and that they will have an anticompetitive effect only infrequently. Conglomerate mergers are only a concern in highly concentrated markets where there are substantial barriers to entry and a significant potential entrant is eliminated. Vertical mergers present a problem only when they raise the barriers to entry or facilitate collusion in highly concentrated industries with substantial barriers to entry. Horizontal mergers, on the other hand, are viewed more skeptically, but most economists accept that efficiency considerations can also motivate these mergers.

Implications for Antitrust Policy

A full explanation of the underlying reasons for the revolution in antitrust is beyond the scope of this chapter. Part of the explanation is, of course, the change in political climate and the resulting changes in appointments to the federal courts and to the top positions in the antitrust agencies. Another important reason is the emerging consensus on the key economic issues relating to antitrust policy. In this section, we discuss some of the significant changes in antitrust policy that have taken place over this period and evaluate their impact on economic efficiency.

It is unlikely that the federal antitrust agencies will file major monopoly or oligopoly cases in the near future. During the late 1960s and early 1970s, the antitrust agencies were searching for cases in highly concentrated industries. Influenced by the work of the structural school, agencies filed cases against IBM, AT&T, Xerox, the leading cereal manufacturers, and the major oil companies.

Today economists have a better understanding of how markets work. No longer is there a general presumption that monopoly power exists because the industry is highly concentrated and entry is slow to occur. As Professor Scherer has pointed out, a "good" monopolization case now requires that three criteria be met: "... (i) monopoly power exists and has been demonstrably exercised; (ii) the possession or retention of that power is attributable to something more than superior products, service, or business acumen; and (iii) one can identify remedies likely to benefit the consumer."[87]

Each of these conditions presents the plaintiff with a difficult burden of proof. Meeting Scherer's first condition is more difficult now than it was 10 years ago, because monopoly power can no longer be assumed when an industry is concentrated and the leading firms earn profit rates significantly above the average for all manufacturing corporations. Demonstrating the existence and exercise of monopoly power will require a detailed study of the industry and in particular a careful analysis and evaluation of conduct.

Establishing the second condition is also a difficult burden. Much of the conduct that economists once considered exclusionary is now viewed as efficiency enhancing, or at least potentially so. And although recent literature has reestablished the fact that single-firm conduct can have anticompetitive effects, there is no simple method for determining which effect is dominant in individual cases.

Finding relief that will benefit consumers is no simple task either. Structural relief and injunctions against conduct may promote competition, but they may also inhibit economic efficiency. Consequently, before such relief is imposed upon an industry, there must be sufficient reason to believe that it will improve competition without a greater reduction in efficiency.

Placing such a heavy burden on the plaintiffs can be justified on at least two grounds. First, economic research during the past few years has raised serious doubts about the wisdom of pursuing a policy directed against concentrated industries solely on the basis of their structure and claims that competition has been harmed because rivals have been injured. Second, the error costs of restructuring industries that are efficiently organized and of preventing efficiency-enhancing conduct can be greater than the error costs of not intervening to check monopoly power. The reasoning behind the second point is that once an efficient structure is altered, or efficient conduct is prevented, the benefits are lost forever. On the other hand, once monopoly power is exploited, the costs may be short lived because there is a strong incentive for existing rivals and new entrants to erode the market power. In sum, it is probably a good policy to be more conservative on monopoly cases.[88]

Recent changes in merger policy also reflect a growing consensus among economists. During the past few years, the enforcement agencies have moved away from the mechanistic application of structural rules and substituted a set of rules more consistent with current economic thinking. As noted above, the 1982 and 1984 *Merger Guidelines* improve upon the 1968 *Merger Guidelines* in several ways.

The Supreme Court still treats "naked" horizontal restraints as per se illegal but recently has expressed some willingness to consider ancillary restraints under a rule of reason.[89] This distinction is consistent with current economic thinking, because the former almost always reduce competition, while the latter at least have the potential of improving efficiency.

The influence of the new learning on antitrust policy has been greatest in the area of exclusionary single-firm conduct. Economists generally agree that such conduct can both enhance efficiency and reduce at least some forms of competition. In fact, much of the economic literature suggests that single-firm conduct will be anticompetitive only in narrow circumstances. If this conclusion is correct, the courts should evaluate single-firm conduct under a rule of reason and not a per se rule.[90]

Beginning with *GTE Sylvania*, the Supreme Court began to accept the new economic learning and reassess its per se treatment of various types of single-firm conduct. In this decision, the Court recognized that nonprice vertical restraints, such as territorial restrictions and location clauses, can have efficiency justifications; consequently, it ruled that these restraints should be judged under a rule-of-reason analysis. In a series of recent decisions (*Monsanto*,[91] *Hyde*,[92] *Northwest Stationers*,[93] and *Aspen Ski*), the Court demonstrated that it is not yet willing to abandon its per se treatment of exclusionary practices such as vertical price fixing, tie-ins, and refusals to deal. However, in each of these decisions the Court also indicated that it was still wrestling with the issue and that in the future it would judge these practices by their effect on competition and not their effects on competitors.[94]

The enforcement agencies have been even more willing to adopt the new learning. Neither agency has initiated a vertical restraint case or a tying case in the past several years. Furthermore, the DOJ's guidelines on vertical restraints suggest that it will challenge these practices only when there is clear evidence of market power and evidence that these practices have the potential to facilitate collusion or exclude rivals.[95] The DOJ has also intervened in the *Monsanto* and *Hyde* cases to argue that both vertical price fixing and tying arrangements should be adjudicated under the rule of reason instead of a per se rule.

Although the Court did not agree with the DOJ's arguments in *Monsanto* and *Hyde*, we believe that it is only a matter of time until vertical price fixing, tying arrangements, and refusals to deal are treated under a rule of reason. Ten or 15 years ago it was easy for the Court to condemn these practices, because they were seen to exclude competitors and economists did not fully understand how they could improve efficiency. Today, there is a strong consensus among economists that these practices can enhance efficiency as well as reduce competition. Consequently, it will be increasingly difficult for the Court to continue to resist the logic of deciding cases involving these practices under a rule of reason.

Need for Further Research

In this section we highlight some of the areas where further research is necessary. The list recites only some of the important unresolved issues and is by no means exhaustive.

Given the lack of success in the past, it is not clear that economists can devise a simple and reliable measure of monopoly power. Since the identification of market power is crucial to the outcome in so many antitrust cases, we would encourage the search for a more reliable way to measure it. Perhaps there is no substitute for the in-depth analysis of the market, but even if that is the case, economists should provide the courts with some guidelines on the factors to include in the study and how to evaluate those factors.

Because of the severe measurement problems, the questionable basis for inferring monopoly profits from accounting rates of return, and the difficulties of demonstrating causal relationships, we do not think that further empirical tests of the concentration-accounting profits relationship are useful.[96] Although the recent studies that use either price or Tobin's q as the dependent variable also suffer from some of the same problems, this line of research has some promise.[97]

The concept of barriers to entry needs to be clarified. Recent work by Harold Demsetz[98] and Christian von Weizsacker[99] has helped to clarify the concept, but there is still disagreement over whether and when advertising and other promotional efforts, excess capacity, and various vertical restraints are barriers to entry. The work of the new industrial organization economists has demonstrated that, under certain conditions, some business practices can be used strategically to deter entry or disadvantage rivals. However, it is not enough to simply prove that this outcome is a theoretical possibility: The proponents of this position must also identify the market conditions under which the anticompetitive use of strategic behavior is likely to occur. Moreover, because these practices can be both anticompetitive and efficiency enhancing, it is desirable to provide the courts with a means of determining which of these effects predominate in individual cases.

The presumption that most single-firm conduct is efficiency enhancing has not been adequately tested. Most of the empirical studies of the effects of single-firm conduct have been case studies.[100] While these studies provide some insights into various forms of firm behavior, they do not always provide conclusive evidence of the effects of that behavior, sometimes even in the particular case that is being studied.

A recent cross-sectional study of the effects of resale price maintenance shows more promise.[101] Thomas Gilligan's study uses stock market data to determine the primary effects of resale price maintenance. The author finds evidence that is consistent with both the efficiency-enhancing and anticompetitive explanations. Another interesting finding is that measures of market structure are helpful in identifying the cases in which the anticompetitive effects are prevalent. Additional research along these lines is needed to determine if the results are robust and if they apply to other types of single-firm conduct.

As a number of scholars have pointed out, the courts are not particularly well equipped to carry out the kind of balancing of the costs and benefits of firm behavior that a rule-of-reason analysis requires.[102] Some have suggested that the way to manage these types of inquiries is to develop a two-part test for evaluating the particular business practice.[103] The first part of the test involves a set of guidelines for screening out those cases in which the practice is more likely to be anticompetitive from those in which it is more likely to be efficiency enhancing. The second part of the test is an in-depth analysis of these cases. The kind of filters that have been suggested differ from author to author, but it is interesting to note that all of the proposals include some form of structural condition.

We believe that this approach is a fruitful one; however, more research needs to be done before economists can arrive at a concensus on the filters that should be used. The new industrial organization economists need to specify more precisely the market characteristics that make exclusionary practices a viable business strategy. Again, more empirical research needs to be done in order to identify more narrowly the conditions under which various types of business practices result in anticompetitive effects.

CONCLUSION

Both the analytical power of the structural view of competition and its attractiveness as a policy norm lie in its simplicity. This view explains market conduct and particularly market performance by reference to market structure, principally seller concentration and barriers to entry. The belief pervading the structural school has been that market structure differs significantly across industries and that structural differences are likely to be associated with significant differences in market performance.[104]

The primary theoretical origin for the structural view was Professor Edward H. Chamberlin's *Theory of Monopolistic Competition*.[105] In this work, Chamberlin sought to advance economics beyond the traditional polar cases of perfect competition and pure monopoly by introducing concepts such as product differentiation and recognition of mutual interdependence in order to reflect the richness and complexity of the industrial economy of the United States. Chamberlin's insights, along with later refinements by Professors Edward Mason and Joe Bain, spawned a large number of detailed industry studies, and later interindustry econometric analyses with the purpose of testing hypotheses about the suggested structure-performance links. The impetus for this work was the notion that the existence of structure-performance links could be demonstrated or contradicted empirically by comparing observable structural characteristics of markets with observed performance, without having to learn much about intrafirm or interfirm behavior.

With hindsight, it can be seen that the flaw in the structural view of markets was in its excessive simplification of its fundamental relationships. In its extreme form, the structural view maintained that structure alone was important in shaping conduct and performance in markets, and among the dimensions of market structure, the preponderant emphasis was on concentration. On the performance side, the critical dimension was profitability, a proxy for the efficiency with which resources were allocated to and within the industry. Hence the plethora of concentration-profit studies. The principal generalization that emerged from the empirical studies was the positive relationship between concentration and accounting rates of return.

Barriers to entry were included as an important structural variable, but because of the difficulty in determining and quantifying their level, they were given less weight than concentration or market share in the econometric studies. Indeed, there was a lengthy debate in the literature about whether advertising as a source of product differentiation was a barrier to entry or a means of entry. In practice, where high concentration persisted over time, the corollary existence of barriers to entry was inferred.

Associated with the structural school was a tradition of inhospitality towards business practices that were not readily understood. In 1972, Professor Ronald Coase observed that

One important result of this preoccupation with the monopoly problem is that if an economist finds something—a business practice of one sort or other—that he does not understand, he looks for a monopoly explanation. And as in this field we are very ignorant, the number of ununderstandable practices tends to be rather large, and the reliance on the monopoly explanation, frequent.[106]

Viewed with particular suspicion were vertical mergers and contracting restrictions, and also conglomerate mergers because of the perceived risks of leverage and reciprocity.

Despite the criticisms of the structural school discussed earlier in the chapter, the school has made an important contribution to economists' understanding of competition and antitrust issues. While structure alone is insufficient for understanding and explaining conduct and performance in markets, it is a necessary element of the analysis. Economists today are less prone to find barriers to entry, or to conclude that business practices and vertical restraints erect man-made barriers to entry, but it is generally accepted that without barriers to entry there can be no persisting monopoly power. And while behavior is now subject to closer scrutiny and analysis than in the structural view, concentration is still an early and important component in any competitive analysis. The 1984 *Merger Guidelines*, for example, clearly manifest their structural origins. After the market is defined, the first variable to be examined is concentration. Possible barriers to entry are also examined, as well as other factors related to the ease with which collusion can occur or to its profitability. Among the second-tier factors contributing to market structure are the degree of product homogeneity; the extent of information about transactions prices; the frequency, regularity, and magnitude of sales; and the capacity of fringe firms.

Structure alone is clearly an inadequate basis for assessing competition or monopoly. Without a careful examination of market structure, however, no economist would render such an assessment today. If, as we believe, economics is an evolutionary science, all economists in the fields of industrial organization and antitrust are structuralists in a fundamental sense of the word.

NOTES

Edward A. Snyder provided helpful comments on an earlier draft of this chapter.

1. Richard A. Posner, "The Chicago School of Antitrust Analysis," *University of Pennsylvania Law Review* 127 (April 1979): 925–948, n. 68.

2. See Edward S. Mason, *Economic Concentration and the Monopoly Problem* (New York: Atheneum, 1964), for a collection of Mason's early work.

3. See Joe S. Bain, *Essays on Price Theory and Industrial Organization* (Boston: Little, Brown and Co., 1972), for a collection of his early work, and idem, *Barriers to New Competition* (Cambridge: Harvard University Press, 1956). His textbook, *Industrial Organization* (New York: John Wiley & Sons), was first published in 1959. The second edition was published in 1968.

4. H. Michael Mann, "Seller Concentration, Barriers to Entry, and Rates of Return in Thirty Industries, 1950–1960," *Review of Economics and Statistics* 48 (August 1966): 296–307.

5. A complete bibliography of Michael Mann's publications and expert testimony appears at the end of this volume.

6. Other hypotheses have related variables such as advertising expenditures, capacity utilization, and R & D outlays to concentration.

7. Examples of these case studies are: Jesse W. Markham, *Competition in the Rayon Industry* (Cambridge: Harvard University Press, 1952); James M. McKie, *Tin Cans and Tin Plate: A Study in Two Related Markets* (Cambridge: Harvard University Press, 1959); Samuel M. Loescher, *Imperfect Collusion in the Cement Industry* (Cambridge: Harvard University Press, 1959); and Merton J. Peck, *Competition in the Aluminum Industry, 1945–1958* (Cambridge: Harvard University Press, 1961).

8. Joe S. Bain, "Relation of Profit Rate to Industry Concentration: American Manufacturing, 1936–1940," *Quarterly Journal of Economics* 65 (August 1951): 293–324.

9. Bain, *Barriers to New Competition.*

10. Mann, "Seller Concentration, Barriers to Entry, and Rates of Return."

11. Although it is somewhat dated, the best review of this literature can be found in Leonard W. Weiss, "The Concentration-Profits Relationship and Antitrust," in *Industrial Concentration: The New Learning*, ed. Harvey J. Goldschmid, H. Michael Mann, and J. Fred Weston (Boston: Little, Brown and Co., 1974).

12. Joe S. Bain, "Price Leaders, Barometers, and Kinks," *Journal of Business* 33 (July 1960): 193–203, reprinted in Bain, *Essays on Price Theory and Industrial Organization*, 146–157.

13. Ibid., 149.

14. Ibid., 148.

15. Ibid., 150.

16. H. Michael Mann, "Antitrust and the Consumer: The Policy and Its Constituency," speech given before the Association of Massachusetts Consumers, Inc., April 22, 1972; and H. Michael Mann, "A Structuralist Direction for Antitrust: The View of a Policy Advisor," speech given before the Midwest Conference on What's Happening in Antitrust, Consumer Protection, and Trade Regulation, April 28, 1973.

17. Mann, "A Structuralist Direction for Antitrust."

18. Joe S. Bain, *Industrial Organization*, 2d ed. (New York: John Wiley & Sons, 1968), 507.

19. For a brief, but excellent, discussion of the historical development of monopolization law, see Lawrence A. Sullivan, "Monopolization: Corporate Strategy, the IBM Cases, and the Transformation of the Law," *Texas Law Review* 60 (April 1982): 587–647.

20. *U.S.* v. *United Shoe Machinery Corp.*, 110 F. Supp. 295 (1953), affirmed by the Supreme Court in 347 U.S. 521 (1954); *U.S.* v. *Griffith Amusement Co.*, 334 U.S. 100 (1948).

21. For examples, see *U.S.* v. *United Shoe Machinery Corp.*, 110 F. Supp. 295 (1953) and *U.S.* v. *Aluminum Company of America et al.*, 91 F. Supp. 333 (1950).

22. Kenneth G. Elzinga, "Unmasking Monopoly: Four Types of Economic Evidence," in this volume.

23. See, for example, the testimony of Michael Mann in *Berkey Photo, Inc.* v. *Eastman Kodak Co.*, 457 F. Supp. 404 (S.D.N.Y., 1978). Mann found that continuing success at innovation was not a sufficient explanation for Kodak's persistently high market share and profit rates in the photographic markets in which it operated.

24. See Bain, *Industrial Organization*, 2d ed., 508, and William L. Baldwin, "The Feedback Effect of Business Conduct on Industry Structure," *Journal of Law and Economics* 12 (April 1969): 123–153.

25. See Donald F. Turner, "The Validity of Tying Arrangements under the Antitrust Laws," *Harvard Law Review* 72 (1958): 50–75; Baldwin, "The Feedback Effect on Business Conduct on Industry Structures" and William S. Comanor, "Vertical Territorial and Consumer Restrictions: White Motor and Its Aftermath," *Harvard Law Review* 81 (May 1968): 1419–1438.

26. Williamson attributes the origin of this term to Donald Turner. See Oliver E. Williamson, "Antitrust Enforcement: Where Has It Been; Where Is It Going," in *Industrial Organization, Antitrust, and Public Policy*, ed. John V. Craven (Boston: Kluwer-Nijhoff Publishing, 1983), 41–68.

27. For a critical view of two monopoly cases (*U.S.* v. *Aluminum Company of America et al.*, 148 F. 2d 416 [1945] and *U.S.* v. *United Shoe Machinery Corp.*, 110 F. Supp. 295 [1953]) that emphasized exclusionary practices, see

Robert H. Bork, *The Antitrust Paradox* (New York: Basic Books, 1978), 164–175.

28. The horizontal merger case that formulated the clearest set of structural rules is *U.S.* v. *Philadelphia National Bank*, 374 U.S. 321 (1963).

29. *Brown Shoe* v. *U.S.*, 370 U.S. 294 (1962).

30. *U.S.* v. *Falstaff Brewing Corp. et al.*, 410 U.S. 526 (1973).

31. *Federal Trade Commission* v. *Procter & Gamble Co.*, 386 U.S. 568 (1967).

32. *U.S.* v. *Von's Grocery Co.*, 384 U.S. 270 (1966).

33. F. M. Scherer, "Merger Policy in the 1970s and 1980s," in this volume.

34. U.S. Department of Justice, *Merger Guidelines*, May 30, 1968.

35. F. M. Scherer, *Industrial Market Structure and Economic Performance*, 2d ed. (Chicago: Rand McNally Publishing Co., 1980), 124, table 4.11.

36. Turner is a coauthor of the influential book that translated the structuralist positions into legal doctrine. See Carl Kaysen and Donald F. Turner, *Antitrust Policy* (Cambridge: Harvard University Press, 1959).

37. Harold Demsetz, "Two Systems of Belief about Monopoly," in Goldschmid, Mann, and Weston, *Industrial Concentration*, 164–184.

38. Bain, *Industrial Organization*, 2d ed., 252.

39. George J. Stigler, *The Organization of Industry* (Homewood, Ill.: Richard D. Irwin, 1968), 67–70.

40. Harold Demsetz, "Barriers to Entry," *American Economic Review* 72 (March 1982): 47–57.

41. Harold Demsetz gives the most concise explanation of these points. Ibid., 47–52.

42. This point has been made by a number of authors. See Yale Brozen, "Significance of Profit Data for Antitrust Policy," in *Public Policy Toward Mergers*, ed. J. Fred Weston and Sam Peltzman (Pacific Palisades, Calif.: Goodyear Publishing Company, 1969), 110–127; Harry Block, "Advertising and Profitability: A Reappraisal," *Journal of Political Economy* 82 (1974): 267–286; and Harold Demsetz, "Accounting for Advertising as a Barrier to Entry," *Journal of Business* 55 (1977): 345–360.

43. Yale Brozen, "Bain's Concentration and Rates of Return Revisited," *Journal of Law and Economics* 14 (October 1971): 351–369.

44. Harold Demsetz, "Industry Structure, Market Rivalry, and Public Policy," *Journal of Law and Economics* 16 (April 1973): 1–9; and Demsetz, "Two Systems of Belief about Monopoly."

45. Scherer, "Merger Policy in the 1970s and 1980s," 7–10.

46. See Robert H. Bork, *The Antitrust Paradox*, Ward S. Bowman, "Tying Arrangements and the Leverage Problem," *Yale Law Journal* 67 (November 1957): 19–36; John McGee, "Predatory Price Cutting: The Standard Oil (N.J.) Case," *Journal of Law and Economics* 1 (October 1958): 137–169; and Richard A. Posner, *Antitrust Law* (Chicago, Ill.: University of Chicago Press, 1976).

47. In its extreme form, the Chicago school holds that these practices will never create any additional monopoly power. Richard Posner, a prominent member of the Chicago school, argues that a number of these practices can increase monopoly power under some narrow circumstances. See Posner, "The Chicago School of Antitrust Analysis," 933–944.

48. See Oliver E. Williamson, "Assessing Vertical Market Restrictions: Antitrust Ramifications of the Transaction Cost Approach," *University of Pennsylvania Law Review* 127 (April 1979): 953–993; Oliver E. Williamson, *Markets and Hierarchies: Analysis of Antitrust Implications* (New York: Free Press, 1975); Williamson, "Antitrust Enforcement: Where Has It Been; Where Is It Going," and Benjamin Klein, Robert G. Crawford, and Armen A. Alchian, "Vertical Integration, Appropriable Rents, and the Competitive Contracting Process," *Journal of Law and Economics* 21 (October 1978): 297–326.

49. *Continental T.V. Inc. et al.* v. *GTE Sylvania Inc.* 433 U.S. 36 (1977).

50. See Thomas J. Campbell, "The Antitrust Record of the First Reagan Administration," *Texas Law Review* 64 (October 1985): 353–369; and Peter M. Gerhart, "The Supreme Court and Antitrust Analysis: The (Near) Triumph of the Chicago School," *Supreme Court Review* 102 (1982): 319–349.

51. *Berkey Photo, Inc.* v. *Eastman Kodak Co.*, 457 F. Supp 404 (S.D.N.Y. 1978), reviewed and remanded, 603 F. 2d 262 (2d Cir. 1979), cert. denied, 444 U.S. 1093 (1980).

52. *Aspen Skiing Co.* v. *Aspen Highlands Skiing Corp.*, 105 S. Ct. 2847.

53. *U.S.* v. *IBM*, (S.D.N.Y. 1982) (dismissed by stipulation).

54. *U.S.* v. *AT&T*, 552 F. Supp. 131 (1982) ("Modification of Final Judgment").

55. It is interesting to note that the settlement with AT&T included a substantial amount of structural relief. For a description of the relief and the Department of Justice's view of the impact of that relief on competition, see *U.S.* v. *Western Electric Company, Inc., and American Telephone and Telegraph Company*, Competitive Impact Statement in Connection with Proposed Modification of Final Judgment, *Federal Register* 47 (February 17, 1982): 7170–7184.

56. *In the Matter of Kellogg et al.*, 99 Federal Trade Commission Reports 269 (1982), and *In the Matter of E. I. DuPont de Nemours & Co.*, 96 Federal Trade Commission Reports 653 (1980).

57. U.S. Department of Justice, *Merger Guidelines*, June 14, 1982; and U.S. Department of Justice, *Merger Guidelines*, June 14, 1984.

58. Scherer, "Merger Policy in the 1970s and 1980s," 3.

59. Richard L. Johnson and David D. Smith, "Antitrust Division Merger Procedures and Policy, 1968–1984," Economic Analysis Group, Antitrust Division, U.S. Department of Justice discussion paper (June 9, 1986), 19–20.

60. Ibid., 16.

61. Charles A. Holt and David T. Scheffman, "Strategic Business Behavior and Antitrust," in this volume.

62. Williamson, "Antitrust Enforcement: Where Has It Been; Where Is It Going," 53.

63. For example, see Michael Spence, "Entry, Investment and Oligopolistic Pricing," *Bell Journal of Economics* 8 (Autumn 1977): 534–544 (excess capacity); and Richard Schmalensee, "Entry Deterrence in the Ready-to-Eat Breakfast Cereal Industry," *Bell Journal of Economics* 9 (Autumn 1976): 305–327 (brand proliferation).

64. Christian von Weizsacker, *Barriers to Entry* (New York: Springer-Verlag, 1981), 72–73; and D. M. Kreps and R. Wilson, "On the Chain-Store Paradox

and Predation: Reputation for Toughness," GSB Research Paper no. 551 (June 1980), Stanford, California. Cited in Williamson, "Antitrust Enforcement: Where Has It Been; Where Is It Going," 55.

65. Steven C. Salop and David T. Scheffman, "Raising Rivals' Costs," *American Economic Review* 73 (May 1983): 267–271; and Thomas G. Krattenmaker and Steven C. Salop, "Antitrust Analysis and Anticompetitive Exclusion: Raising Rivals' Costs to Achieve Power over Price," *Yale Law Journal* 96 (November 1986): 209–295.

66. Richard Schmalensee, "Antitrust and the New Industrial Economics," *American Economic Review* 72 (May 1982): 24–28.

67. *In the Matter of Kellogg et al.*

68. Schmalensee, "Entry Deterrence in the Ready-to-Eat Breakfast Cereal Industry."

69. *In the Matter of Kellogg et al.*

70. *In the Matter of E. I. DuPont de Nemours & Co..*

71. See John A. Stuckey, *Vertical Integration and Joint Ventures in the Aluminum Industry* (Cambridge: Harvard University Press, 1983); and Franklin M. Fisher, John J. McGowan, and Joen E. Greenwood, *Folded, Spindled, and Mutilated: Economic Analysis and U.S. v. IBM* (Cambridge: MIT Press, 1983).

72. Leonard W. Weiss, "Concentration and Price—A Possible Way Out of a Box," in *Industry Structure and Performance*, ed. Joachim Schwalbach (Berlin: Edition Sigma Rainer Bohn Verlag), 85–111; and Leonard W. Weiss, "Concentration and Price—*Not* Concentration and Profits," unpublished manuscript, August 1986.

73. Elzinga, "Unmasking Monopoly," 23–24.

74. Elizabeth E. Bailey, David R. Graham, and Daniel P. Kaplan, *Deregulating the Airlines* (Cambridge: MIT Press, 1985), 171.

75. Thomas W. Gilligan, "The Competitive Effects of Resale Price Maintenance," *Rand Journal of Economics* 17 (Winter 1986): 544–556.

76. Demsetz, "Barriers to Entry."

77. However, see Donald Dewey, "Information, Entry, and Welfare: The Case for Collusion," *American Economic Review*, 69 (September 1979) 588–593; Dominick T. Armentano, *Antitrust and Monopoly: Anatomy of a Policy Failure* (New York: John Wiley & Sons, 1982); and George Bittlingmayer, "Decreasing Average Cost and Competition: A New Look at the Addyston Pipe Case," *Journal of Law & Economics* 25 (October 1982): 201–229.

78. See, for example, Gerhart, "The Supreme Court and Antitrust Analysis," and Frank H. Easterbrook, "The Limits of Antitrust," *Texas Law Review* 63 (August 1984): 1–40.

79. Gerhart, "The Supreme Court and Antitrust Analysis," 335 and Easterbrook, "The Limits of Antitrust," 7.

80. Lawrence J. White, "The Revolution in Antitrust Analysis of Vertical Relationships: How Did We Get from There to Here?" in this volume.

81. Bork, *The Antitrust Paradox*, and for a somewhat more moderate view from the Chicago school, see Posner, *Antitrust Law*.

82. William S. Comanor, "Vertical Price Fixing, Vertical Market Restric-

tions, and the New Antitrust Policy," *Harvard Law Review* 98 (March 1985) 983–1002.

83. F. M. Scherer, "The Economics of Vertical Restraints," *Antitrust Law Journal* 52 (1983): 687–707.

84. This argument also applies to other kinds of single-firm conduct. See Lawrence J. White, "Resale Price Maintenance and the Problem of Marginal and Inframarginal Customers," *Contemporary Policy Issues* 3 (Spring 1985): 17–21.

85. See the literature cited in Holt and Scheffman, "Strategic Business Behavior and Antitrust," and see Krattenmaker and Salop, "Antitrust Analysis and Anticompetitive Exclusion."

86. See Easterbrook, "The Limits of Antitrust," 17; and William S. Comanor and John B. Kirkwood, "Resale Price Maintenace and Antitrust Policy," *Contemporary Policy Issues* 3 (Spring 1985): 9–16.

87. F. M. Scherer, "The Posnerian Harvest: Separating Wheat from Chaff," *Yale Law Journal* 86 (1977): 974–1002.

88. Easterbrook also makes a similar point. See Easterbrook, "The Limits of Antitrust, 2.

89. See Gerhart, "The Supreme Court and Antitrust Analysis," 334–344; and Campbell, "The Antitrust Record of the First Reagan Administration," 355–358. Of particular interest is their discussion of *Broadcast Music* and Campbell's discussion of *NCAA* v. *Board of Regents*, 104 S. Ct. 2948 (1984).

90. For an application of this reasoning to vertical price restraints, see Robert J. Larner, "Vertical Price Restraints: Per se or Rule of Reason?" in this volume.

91. *Monsanto Co.* v. *Spray-Rite Service Corp.*, 465 U.S. 752 (1984). The Court ruled that a per se violation requires the plaintiff to show a "naked" vertical agreement to fix prices.

92. *Jefferson Parish Hospital District No. 2* v. *Hyde*, 466 U.S. 2 (1984). The Court ruled that tying arrangements are unlawful per se only where the effect on competition is substantial, requiring the plaintiff to demonstrate that the defendant has substantial market power.

93. *Northwest Wholesale Stationers, Inc.* v. *Pacific Stationery & Printing Co.*, 105 S. Ct. 2613. In this decision, the Court held that refusals to deal are per se unlawful only where the plaintiff can demonstrate that the defendant possessed market power or exclusive access to a scarce resource.

94. For a similar view of these decisions, see Campbell, "The Antitrust Record of the First Reagan Administration," 358–359; Easterbrook, "The Limits of Antitrust," 6, n. 13; and Krattenmaker and Salop, "Antitrust Analysis and Anti-Competitive Exclusion," 211–214.

95. U.S. Department of Justice, *Vertical Restraints Guidelines*, January 23, 1985.

96. Franklin M. Fisher and John J. McGowan, "On the Misuse of Accounting Rates of Return to Infer Monopoly Profits," *American Economic Review* (March 1983): 82–97.

97. See Professor Elzinga's discussion of these studies, "Unmasking Monopoly," 34–39.

98. Demsetz, "Barriers to Entry."

99. von Weizsacker, *Barriers to Entry*.

100. For a thorough review of the empirical evidence on resale price maintenance, see Thomas R. Overstreet, Jr., *Resale Price Maintenance: Economic Theories and Empirical Evidence* (Washington, D.C.: Bureau of Economics Staff Report to the Federal Trade Commission, November 1983).

101. Gilligan, "The Competitive Effects of Resale Price Maintenance."

102. For example, see Easterbrook, "The Limits of Antitrust."

103. Ibid., William S. Comanor and John B. Kirkwood, "Resale Price Maintenance and Antitrust Policy," and Paul L. Joskow and Alvin K. Klevorick, "A Framework for Analyzing Predatory Pricing Policy," *Yale Law Journal* 89 (December 1979): 213–270.

104. Joe S. Bain, "The Theory of Monopolistic Competition after Thirty Years: The Impact on Industrial Organization," *American Economic Review* (May 1964): 28–29.

105. Edward H. Chamberlin, *Theory of Monopolistic Competition*, 8th ed. (Cambridge: Harvard University Press, 1962).

106. Ronald H. Coase, "Industrial Organization: A Proposal for Research," in *Policy Issues and Research Opportunities in Industrial Organization*, ed. Victor R. Fuchs (New York National Bureau of Economic Research, 1972), 67.

Postscript:
In Memory of
H. Michael Mann

Robert J. Larner and James W. Meehan, Jr.

H. Michael Mann was born in Camden, New Jersey, on January 30, 1934. He received a bachelor's degree in economics with honors from Haverford College in 1956 and a doctorate in economics from Cornell University in 1962. Mike joined the faculty of the Boston College economics department in 1961 and began a distinguished 23-year career of teaching, scholarly research and writing, and public service in the fields of industrial organization economics and the economics of antitrust and regulation.

Mike's career ended abruptly and tragically when he fell ill in January 1984. He died on March 1, 1985, survived by his wife Nancy and their children Philip and Kay.

We knew Mike as a skilled economist and a cherished friend. Because of his broad interests and the diligence with which he fulfilled each commitment he undertook, it is not surprising that Mike made important contributions in every aspect of his professional life.

Within the economics profession, Mike was best known for his scholarly research and publications. An early paper, "Seller Concentration, Barriers to Entry, and Rates of Return in Thirty Industries, 1950–1960," marked him as a member of the structuralist school within the fields of industrial organization and antitrust policy.[1] In the paper, he found that in the industries within his sample that had an eight-firm concentration ratio of more than 70 percent, the leading firms earned significantly higher average rates of return on net worth than the leading firms in the less concentrated industries. Furthermore, within the group of highly concentrated industries, those industries with very high barriers to entry earned a distinctly higher average profit rate than the industries with substantial or moderate-to-low barriers, indicating that barriers to entry apparently exert an independent influence on profit rate. The paper concluded that "... the 'monopoly problem' appears to exist most noticeably in those industries which are highly concentrated and have high barriers to entry. If public policy seeks to improve resource allocation, industries with these structural characteristics seem to be a good place to start."[2]

Mike soon became a leading exponent of the view that the structure of a market, and in particular the degree of seller concentration and the height of barriers to entry, are the key determinants of the market's performance and of the extent to which it is likely to function in a competitive manner.

Through the early 1980s, the effects, and also the causes, of high seller concentration and barriers to entry were the focus of Mike's research. In this research, he collaborated with John A. Henning and James W. Meehan, Jr. A topic of particular interest was the relationship between advertising and concentration. In a 1967 paper, the three found a positive and statistically significant correlation between advertising intensity (measured by the ratio of advertising expenditures to sales revenue) and concentration.[3] Mike further investigated the causal relationship between the two variables, and in a 1976 paper with Henning concluded that "... advertising intensity is causally prior to concentration."[4]

In addition to being a respected scholar, Mike was a gifted and dedicated teacher at Boston College from 1961 to 1984. He easily transmitted to students the quality of his inquisitive mind and his demand for both sound analysis and careful empirical examination of issues. Although he held strong views on how markets operated, he was always open to opposing ideas and arguments and especially to challenges from students. Always well prepared and articulate in the classroom in explaining the complex aspects of technical or policy issues, he also understood the limits of knowledge and never sought to mask ignorance through obfuscation. If he could not provide an adequate response to a question, he would readily acknowledge it, adding that he would reflect further on the question or seek to learn the pertinent facts before the next meeting of the class. Invariably, he returned to class with a responsive answer.

For Mike, learning was a joint enterprise between teacher and students. He treated each topic as an issue open for debate, and his students were encouraged to find flaws in the theory and empirical analysis. Class discussions usually provoked Mike's students to follow up their questions with additional research, and frequently that effort led to a term paper, a dissertation, or, on occasion, a paper coauthored with Mike. Indeed, the blend of analysis and empirical research that was the hallmark of Mike's writing served as a model for his graduate students in their own research. In the early years of Boston College's graduate program in economics, Mike directed more dissertations than anyone else in the department.

Mike also encouraged his students to get deeply involved in research and learning. As a student of industrial organization, he believed that it was crucial to observe empirically how goods and services are produced, how firms are organized, and how markets work. He integrated his experience as a consultant and government official into the classroom, and he also enlisted his graduate students to work with him on some of his consulting projects. A number of Mike's former students have achieved productive careers in teaching, research, government service, and consulting. Beyond the classroom, Mike played a key role in university governance and local politics, and he urged his students to get involved in these activities as well.

Mike was also a valued member of the Boston College university community for reasons that went beyond his scholarship and teaching. He was active in both department and university governance. He was a major force in the development of a major graduate program in economics at Boston College, and his research and teaching contributed to building a national reputation for the department. In addition, Mike served as chairman of the department of economics during the 1970–1971 academic year and as acting chairman during the second half of the 1974–1975 academic year. At the time of his illness, he had held the position of chairman since July 1982.

In university governance, Mike was instrumental in forming the faculty senate at Boston College, and since 1980 he headed a faculty committee charged with administering a grant from the Mellon Fund Foundation for the development of senior faculty, particularly in fields where research funding was sparse.

A good part of Mike's intense interest in the economics of industrial organization was due to its application to important issues of public policy, particularly antitrust and regulatory policy. Mike's interest in antitrust policy led him to serve a total of three and a half years in top staff positions in the two federal antitrust agencies. He spent the 1968–1969 academic year as the special economic assistant to the assistant attorney general in the Antitrust Division of the Department of Justice, serving under Assistant Attorney General McLaren. Less than two years later, he went to Washington as director of the Bureau of Economics of the Federal Trade Commission, where he served from February 1971 to August 1973. He brought his concern about the effects of high seller concentration to both positions, but he also brought an inquisitive mind and his standards of careful analysis and empirical examination of issues. At the FTC, Mike oversaw a significant expansion in the size of the economics staff and also began an upgrading of its quality. His was a respected voice in the deliberations of the commission; during his tenure, the Bureau of Economics, which had been without a director for a year and a half, grew in stature at the commission and became an equal partner with the two legal bureaus, the Bureau of Competition and the Bureau of Consumer Protection.

With assistance from the Bureau of Economics, the commission undertook policy planning so that it might allocate its enforcement resources more efficiently and effectively. Economists were assigned to investigations at an early stage so that they might work more productively with the attorneys in formulating an analysis of the issues, searching for relevant empirical evidence, recommending to the commission whether a complaint should issue, and preparing an effective case for litigation. Mike's was an important and persuasive voice to the commission in its decision to issue a complaint charging the leading manufacturers of ready-to-eat cereals with shared monopoly. In addition, under Mike's direction, the Bureau of Economics launched a number of studies of the performance of concentrated industries and analyzed the effects on competition of a wide range of trade practices that had previously escaped economic scrutiny at the commission.

As Professor Scherer points out in his contribution to this volume, Mike was not only convinced of the importance of empirical evidence for an adequate understanding and serious evaluation of economic issues and their implications for public policy, but he was also acutely aware of the limitations of publicly available data and the resulting impediments to scholars, analysts, and policymakers. As a consequence, Mike spent a significant part of his time at the FTC directing the development of a line-of-business (LOB) reporting program and working for its approval by the commission. Under the LOB program, the FTC required large corporations to report their sales, profits, advertising outlays, R & D expenditures, and other data at a disaggregated level. The data were used both by researchers at the FTC and by outside scholars in empirically based studies of economic issues with implications for public policy. Although the commission terminated the data collection activities of the LOB program in 1982, data were collected for the years 1973 to 1977, and their analysis has generated a spate of research papers.

Michael Mann's interest in antitrust policy and cases continued after he returned from Washington to the campus of Boston College. He served as a consultant to counsel and expert witness in many of the major antitrust cases of the 1970s and early 1980s. He was an expert witness for complaint counsel in the FTC's *Borden* (ReaLemon) and

General Foods (Maxwell House) cases, and also for the plaintiff in the landmark case *Berkey* v. *Kodak*. Mike was not always on the commission's side, however. He testified as an expert witness on behalf of DuPont in the *Ethyl* case, and also assisted counsel for Flowers Industries in defending several acquisitions that the commission had challenged.

Although Mike was frequently identified as a structuralist during his career, this or any other label seriously oversimplifies his thinking on issues of antitrust policy. For most of his career, Mike did believe firmly that market structure was the key determinant of industry performance, and that structure should be the focus of antitrust policy and a guide to allocating enforcement resources and devising effective relief. But if Mike was a person who explained or debated his views with fervor, he was also a person interested in different points of view and, above all, open to new evidence on old issues. In the last couple of years of his professional life, he began to modify his thinking due to his experience in the antitrust cases in which he consulted and testified and the influence of a number of papers in economics journals. He became increasingly leery of applying generalizations from the structure-conduct-performance paradigm to particular situations and insisted on examining closely the conduct of firms in the industry. His preferred research methodology became the case study, in which market structure was examined, but in which the behavior of the firms in the industry was also analyzed with an eye on whether the effects were to promote efficient production and distribution or to achieve anticompetitive outcomes.

In the 1930s and 1940s, the belief common to the economists who founded the field of industrial organization was that a large number of case studies based on the structure-conduct-performance paradigm would result in the emergence of generalizations about economic issues and implications for antitrust policy that would have wide applicability. While many such studies were done, and a number were done quite well, somewhere along the way conduct was relegated to minor importance. As a consequence, the functioning of markets never became well understood. The more modest goal of Mike's planned future research was to study and analyze conduct within the context of market structure in order to obtain a better understanding of how markets work. From this new knowledge, he hoped, would come more informed antitrust policy.

Michael Mann was a person of many dimensions. His professional achievements as an economist, scholar, educator, and public servant are well documented and speak for themselves. As economists, we were his students, one of us literally and both of us figuratively, and learned much from him. Yet in thinking about him, many of our most cherished memories are of Michael Mann as a person; a man of principle and absolute integrity, devoted to his family, generous and loyal to his friends, and committed to social justice. To his memory we fondly dedicate this book.

NOTES

1. H. Michael Mann, "Seller Concentration, Barriers to Entry, and Rates of Return in Thirty Industries, 1950–1960," *The Review of Economics and Statistics* (August 1966): 296–307. The last section of this volume contains a complete list of Michael Mann's publications, conference papers, congressional testimony, and expert testimony.

2. Ibid., 300.

3. H. Michael Mann, John A. Henning, and James W. Meehan, Jr., "Advertising and Concentration: An Empirical Investigation," *The Journal of Industrial Economics* (November 1967): 24–35.

4. H. Michael Mann and John Henning, "Advertising and Concentration: A Tentative Determination of Cause and Effect," in *Essays on Industrial Organization in Honor of Joe Bain*, ed. Robert T. Masson and P. David Qualls (New York: Ballinger, 1976), 143–154.

Bibliography of the Works of H. Michael Mann

BOOKS

Industrial Concentration: The New Learning (coedited with Harvey J. Goldschmid and J. Fred Weston). Boston: Little, Brown and Co., 1974. Contribution: "Advertising, Concentration and Profitability: The State of
Knowledge and Directions for Public Policy," 137–156.

ARTICLES

"An Appraisal of Model Building in Industrial Organization" (with J. A. Henning), *Research in Law and Economics* 3 (1981): 1–14.

"Concentration of Industry." In *Encyclopedia of Economics*, ed. Douglas Green-
wald, New York: McGraw-Hill Bk. Co., 1981, 178–180.

"Firm Attributes and the Propensity to Influence the Political System" (with
Karen McCormick). In *The Economics of Firm Size, Market Structure
and Social Performance*, ed. John J. Siegfried, Washington, D.C.: U.S.
Government Printing Office 1980, 300–313.

"Comment." In *The Deregulation of the Banking and Securities Industries*, ed.
Lawrence G. Goldberg and Lawrence J. White. Lexington, Mass.: Lexington Bks., 1979, 185–187.

"Market Structure and Excess Capacity: A Look at Theory and Some Evidence"
(with James W. Meehan, Jr., and Glen Ramsay). *Review of Economics
and Statistics*, (February 1979): 156–159.

"Advertising and Oligopoly: Correlations in Search of Understanding" (with
J. A. Henning). In *Issues in Advertising: The Economics of Persuasion*,

ed. D. G. Tuerck. Washington, D.C.: American Enterprise Institute, 1978, 253–266.

"Advertising and Concentration: A Tentative Determination of Cause and Effect" (with J. A. Henning). In *Essays on Industrial Organization in Honor of Joe S. Bain*, ed. Robert T. Masson and P. David Qualls. Cambridge, Mass.: Ballinger, 1976, 143–154.

"Deregulation in the Brokerage Industry: A Look at Origins and Consequences," Subcommittee on Antitrust and Monopoly, U.S. Senate, *The Competition Improvements Act of 1975, 1976.* (Reprinted in *Challenge* [November/December 1976], 48–51).

"Antitrust and the New York Stock Exchange: A Cartel at the End of Its Reign." In *Competition and Regulation*, ed. A. Phillips. Washington, D.C.: Brookings Institution, 1975, 301–327.

"Policy Planning Antitrust Activities: Present Status and Future Prospects" (with James W. Meehan, Jr.). In *The Antitrust Dilemma*, ed. J. A. Dalton and S. L. Levin. Lexington, Mass.: Lexington Books, 1974, 15–25.

"Structural Antitrust Cases: The Benefit-Cost Underpinnings" (with J. W. Meehan, Jr.). *The George Washington Law Review* (August 1974): 921–926.

"Concentration, Barriers to Entry, and Rates of Return Revisited: A Reply." *Journal of Industrial Economics* (April 1973): 203–204.

"Advertising and Concentration: Comment" (with J. A. Henning and J. W. Meehan, Jr.). *Southern Economic Journal* (January 1973): 448–451.

"The Interaction of Barriers and Concentration: A Reply." *Journal of Industrial Economics* (July 1971): 291–293.

"Advertising and Concentration: New Data on an Old Problem" (with J. W. Meehan, Jr.). *The Antitrust Bulletin* (April 1971): 101–104.

"Asymmetry, Barriers to Entry, and Rates of Return in Twenty-Six Concentrated Industries, 1948–1957." *Western Economic Journal* (March 1970): 86–89.

"A Note on Barriers to Entry and Long-Run Profitability." *The Antitrust Bulletin* (Winter 1969): 237–241.

Symposium on Advertising and Concentration. *Journal of Industrial Economics* (November 1969) "Testing Hypotheses in Industrial Economics: A Reply" (with J. A. Henning and J. W. Meehan, Jr.), 81–84; and "Statistical Testing in Industrial Economics: A Reply on Measurement Error and Sampling Procedure" (with J. A. Henning and J. W. Meehan, Jr.), 95–100.

"Concentration and Profitability: An Examination of a Recent Study" (with James W. Meehan, Jr.). *The Antitrust Bulletin* (Summer 1969): 385–395.

"Advertising and Concentration: An Empirical Investigation" (with J. A. Henning and J. W. Meehan, Jr.). *Journal of Industrial Economics* (November 1967): 24–35.

"Seller Concentration, Barriers to Entry, and Rates of Return in Thirty Industries, 1950–1960." *The Review of Economics and Statistics* (August 1966): 296–307.

"Comment: Entry and Oligopoly Theory" (with John Walgreen and Paul Haas). *The Journal of Political Economy* (August 1965): 381–383.

CONFERENCE PAPERS

Commentator on E. Pagoulatis and R. Sorenson, "The Competitive Impact of Advertising in U.S. Food Processing Industries: A Simultaneous Equation Approach," with J. M. Anderson, D. T. Scheffman, and J. T. Whitten. Later published in *Advertising and the Food System*, ed. John Connor and Ronald Ward (Madison: University of Wisconsin, College of Agriculture and Life Sciences, 1985), 275–282.

"Advertising and Quality in Food Products: Some New Evidence on the Nelson Hypothesis." U.S.D.A. Conference on Symposium on Advertising and the Food System, November 6, 1980.

"Firm Attributes and the Propensity to Influence the Political System" (with Karen McCormick). Conference on The Economics of Firm Size, Market Structure and Social Performance. Bureau of Economics, Federal Trade Commission, Washington, D.C., January 18, 1980.

"Advertising and Oligopoly: Correlations in Search of Understanding" (with J. A. Henning). American Enterprise Institute Conference on Issues in Advertising on The Economics of Persuasion, Washington, D.C., June 10–11, 1976.

"True Profitability Measures for Pharmaceutical Firms: Comments." American University Second Seminar on Dynamics of Pharmaceutical Innovation, Washington, D.C., October 16, 1973. Published in *Regulation, Economics, and Pharmaceutical Innovation, 1976*, ed. Joseph D. Cooper.

"Antitrust Policy and Allocative Efficiency: Incompatible?" (with James W. Meehan, Jr.). Conference on Problems of Regulation and Public Utilities, Amos Tuck School of Business Administration at Dartmouth College, August 26–30, 1973.

"Policy Planning Antitrust Activities: Present Status and Future Prospects" (with J.W. Meehan, Jr.). Conference on Industrial Organization: Policy Planning in Antitrust, Southern Illinois University at Edwardsville, April 26–27, 1973.

"Antitrust and the New York Stock Exchange: A Cartel at the End of Its Reign." Brookings Conference on the Role of Competition in Regulated Industries, October 28–29, 1971.

"Product Differentiation and Market-Share Stability." American Marketing Association Conference, September 1, 1970. Abstract published in Conference Proceedings.

OTHER

Presentation before the Securities and Exchange Commissioner Examiner of "A Critique of the New York Stock Exchange's Report on the Economic Effects of Negotiated Commission Rates on the Brokerage Industry, the Market for Corporate Securities, and the Investing Public," October 31, 1968.

Report on "Antitrust and Fisherman's Unions," written for Bureau of Commercial Fisheries, U.S. Department of the Interior, Summer 1966.

CONGRESSIONAL TESTIMONY

Committee on Interior and Insular Affairs, U.S. Senate, *Market Performance and Competition in the Petroleum Industry*, Hearings, Pt. 1, 1974.

Before the Special Committee on Integrated Oil Operations, Committee on Interior and Insular Affairs, U.S. Senate, Washington, D.C., November 29, 1973. Subject: Federal Trade Commission and the Oil Industry. Published in *Special Committee on Integrated Oil Operations*.

Before the Subcommittee on Antitrust and Monopoly of the Committee on the Judiciary, U.S. Senate, Washington, D.C., June 27, 1973. Subject: Concentration in the Energy Sector. Published in Subcommittee on Antitrust and Monopoly, Committee on the Judiciary, U.S. Senate, *The Natural Gas Industry*, Hearings, Pt. 1, 1973.

Before the Monopoly Subcommittee of the Select Committee on Small Business, U.S. Senate, Washington, D.C., March 8, 1973. Subject: Importance of Line of Business Reporting to Federal Trade Commission.

Before the Subcommittee on Antitrust and Monopoly, U.S. Senate, Washington, D.C., April 14, 1972. Subject: Territorial Restrictions. Published in Subcommittee on Antitrust and Monopoly, Committee on the Judiciary, U.S. Senate, *Exclusive Territorial Allocation Legislation*, Hearings, 1972.

Before the Subcommittee on Special Small Business Problems of the Select Committee on Small Business, House of Representatives, Washington, D.C., July 13, 1971. Subject: Oil Company Extensions into Fuels for the Production of Energy. Published in Subcommittee on Special Small Business Problems of the Select Committee on Small Business, House of Representatives, *Concentration by Competing Raw Fuel Industries in the Energy Market and Its Impact on Small Business*, Hearings, 1971.

Before the Subcommittee on Activities of Regulatory Agencies Relating to Small Business of the Select Committee on Small Business, House of Representatives, Washington, D.C., June 25, 1971. Subject: Advertising and Concentration. Published in Subcommittee on Activities of Regulatory Agencies Relating to Small Business of the Select Committee on Small Business, House of Representatives, *Advertising and Small Business*, Hearings, 1971.

Before the Monopoly Subcommittee of the Select Committee on Small Business, U.S. Senate, Washington, D.C., May 26, 1971. Subject: Advertising Intensity, Concentration, and Pricing: Proprietary Drugs. Published in Subcommittee on Monopoly of the Select Committee on Small Business, U.S. Senate, *Advertising of Proprietary Medicines*, Hearings, Pt. 1, 1971.

EXPERT TESTIMONY

Federal Trade Commission: In the Matter of Ethyl Corporation et al., October 1980; testified on behalf of respondent E. I. DuPont de Nemours & Co. in a facilitating practices case.

Federal Trade Commission: In the Matter of the General Foods Corporation, January 1980; testified for complaint counsel in a predatory pricing case.

U.S. District Court, District of Minnesota: *Overhead Door Corporation* v. *Nordpal Corporation*, October 1978; testified on behalf of the plaintiff (a manufacturer) in a vertical restraints case in which the defendant (a distributor) had filed an antitrust counterclaim.

U.S. District Court, Southern District of New York: *Berkey Photo, Inc.* v. *Eastman Kodak Co.*, September 1976; testified on behalf of the plaintiff in a monopolization case. .

Federal Trade Commission: In the Matter of Fruehauf Corporation, May and December 1976; testified on behalf of respondent in a vertical merger case.

Federal Trade Commission: In the Matter of Borden, Inc., May 1975; testified on behalf of complaint counsel in a predatory pricing case.

Ford-Autolite (January 1969) testified on behalf of the Department of Justice regarding product differentiation as a barrier to entry; 315 F. Supp. 372 (1970), affirmed by the Supreme Court in 405 U.S. 562 (1972).

Index

About the Editors and Contributors

DONALD I. BAKER is a partner at Sutherland, Asbill & Brennan, Washington, D.C., and a former Assistant Attorney General for Antitrust at the Department of Justice.

KENNETH G. ELZINGA is Professor of Economics at the University of Virginia and a former Special Economic Advisor to the Assistant Attorney General for Antitrust at the U.S. Department of Justice.

CHARLES A. HOLT is Professor of Economics at the University of Virginia.

ROBERT J. LARNER, former head of the research unit at the Federal Trade Commission's Bureau of Economics, is Vice President of Charles River Associates, Boston.

JAMES W. MEEHAN, JR. is Professor of Economics at Colby College and has spent several years at the Federal Trade Commission as an Economic Advisor and Assistant to the Director of the Bureau of Economics.

DAVID T. SCHEFFMAN is a former Director of the Bureau of Economics at the Federal Trade Commission and has taught economics at several universities.

F. M. SCHERER is Professor of Economics at Swarthmore College and a former Director of the Bureau of Economics at the Federal Trade Commission.

TIMOTHY J. WATERS is a partner at McDermott, Will & Emery, Washington, D.C., and a former Attorney Advisor to the Chairman of the Federal Trade Commission.

LAWRENCE J. WHITE is currently a member of the Federal Home Loan Bank Board, on leave from the economics faculty at New York University. He is a former Director of the Economic Policy Office at the Department of Justice's Antitrust Division.